Dr. Mamuszko:

Thank you for your help in making publication of this book possible.

Best wishes for you and Kathleen for your life's journey

Jane Suh

5/25/02

LIFE'S JOURNEY
Autobiography

Eugene Bak

EAST EUROPEAN MONOGRAPHS, BOULDER
DISTRIBUTED BY COLUMBIA UNIVERSITY PRESS, NEW YORK
2002

EAST EUROPEAN MONOGRAPHS, NO. DCIX

ISBN: 0-88033-497-5

Library of Congress Control Number 2002104961

For more information about the author
or this book, contact:
Polish American Cultural Center JPII
6501 Lansing Ave.
Cleveland, Ohio 44105

Printed in the United States of America

To my grandchildren,
may they carry on the culture
and traditions of their forefathers

CONTENTS

Acknowledgements		vii
Preface		ix
1.	Poland	1
2.	Soviet Union	21
3.	Iran (Persia)	59
4.	Army in Exile	77
5.	Pakistan, Karachi	93
6.	India, Valivade	103
7.	England	119
8.	United States (1952–1970)	133
9.	Franklin, PA (1970–1991)	155
10.	Cleveland, OH (1991–1999)	181
11.	Epilogue	199
Bibliography		203

ACKNOWLEDGEMENTS

I wish to express many thanks to my wife, Barbara, and my children, Mark, Tom and Ewa, who encouraged me to write this autobiography and who made numerous suggestions and corrections to the text.

I also wish to thank the following people who read the manuscript, made invaluable suggestions and improved the readability of the text: Mary Bak, Neal Flinchbaugh, Carolee Mitchner, Dr. Bob Morris and Kate Rein. My thanks to Mike Gergel whose computer skills made much sense out of my feeble attempts to organize the text and the pictures.

Dr. Witold Łukaszewski, professor of Political Science and a fellow Sibirak, shared with me his understanding of history, political insights and first hand knowledge of many historical facts described in the book.

Finally, I would like to extend my special thanks to my friend Jill Mattson who designed the cover. She spent enormous amount of time capturing the essence of my life. In fact, if you look closely, the cover tells the full story, so you can save yourself a lot of time by not reading the book. Jill, I thank you.

PREFACE

This book is an attempt to put on paper the experiences that my family and I endured in pre-war Poland, wartime Poland, the Soviet Union, Iran, Pakistan, India, Britain and the United States. Hopefully, it will serve as a useful reference for my children, grandchildren, and other members of my family so that they may better understand their family history and the events that shaped my life.

The book in no measure is to be construed as portraying me as a hero or a person who has done anything extraordinary although I did have some extraordinary experiences. If anyone shall be labeled heroes it should be my parents, Piotr and Helena Bąk, for they were the ones who performed truly heroic acts. I was merely present during many of these events.

At the end of the book, I have enclosed a bibliography of the sources that I used for historical background. I felt that this background is essential to set the stage for the events that took place during my journeys. It is important to capture the atmosphere of the times and to understand the circumstances that shaped these times. This autobiography is not meant to be a historical study, as many historical books are available that describe this time period. The main sources for this book are my own recollections as well as those of my parents, family members, and friends. I have tried to check these recollections for historical accuracy in the references cited. To the best of my knowledge, these events are factual as stated.

Finally, this book was not written to be a work of literary merit, but simply to provide a recollection of the events that shaped my life. I hope you may find the book and its tale interesting.

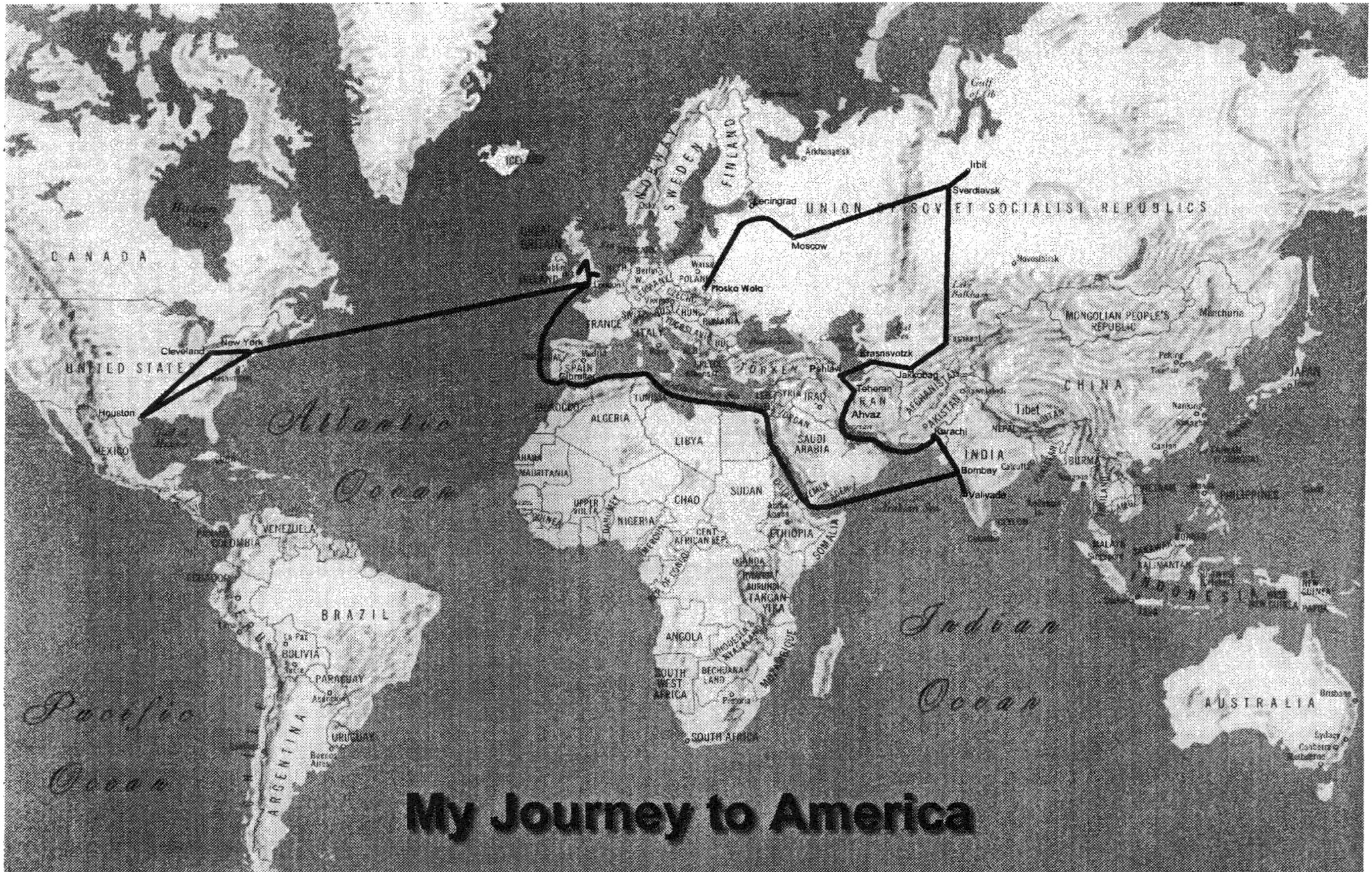
My Journey to America
Irbit
Sverdlovsk
Leningrad
Moscow
Ploska Wola
Krasnovotzk
Pahlavi
Teheran
Jakkobag
Ahvaz
Karachi
Bombay
Valivade
Cleveland
New York
Houston
UNION OF SOVIET SOCIALIST REPUBLICS
CANADA
UNITED STATES
MEXICO
BRAZIL
BOLIVIA
PARAGUAY
URUGUAY
ARGENTINA
VENEZUELA
COLOMBIA
FINLAND
SWEDEN
POLAND
FRANCE
SPAIN
ITALY
TURKEY
IRAQ
IRAN
AFGHANISTAN
PAKISTAN
INDIA
CHINA
MONGOLIAN PEOPLE'S REPUBLIC
Manchuria
Tibet
JAPAN
BURMA
PHILIPPINES
INDONESIA
AUSTRALIA
ALGERIA
LIBYA
SUDAN
CHAD
NIGERIA
ETHIOPIA
SOMALIA
SAUDI ARABIA
ANGOLA
SOUTH AFRICA
Atlantic Ocean
Indian Ocean
Pacific Ocean

POLAND

I was born in Polska Wola, a small village located about 20 kilometers east of the county (*powiat*) town of Podhajce and about 25 kilometers south of the province (*województwo*) city of Tarnopol in the southeastern part of Poland. The village was located on the banks of the river Strypa a tributary of the river Dniestr. Formerly known as Rudka, the village was renamed Polska Wola in the 1930s to reflect a large Polish population that immigrated to the area after the Polish–Bolshevik war of 1920.

The village had about 50 homes and about 300 inhabitants. Ukrainians and Poles that were native to the area lived in two nearby villages of Hajworonka and Zarwanica. These villages go back to medieval times and are mentioned in a number of history books dealing with the area. The villages rested along the trails used by the Tartars and Cossacks to crisscross the region through the centuries.

My parents moved to Polska Wola in 1923. A Catholic priest named Rev. Rysz, from my mother's native village of Haczów, was assigned to a parish in Wiśniowczyk, a village about two kilometers from Polska Wola. It was Rev. Rysz who persuaded a number of people in Haczów and the surrounding area to move to Podole, as that region of Poland was known. He told people that the soil in Podole was fertile and the land inexpensive. These villagers were farmers, and since the arguments of Rev. Rysz were so compelling, many of them sold their homes and land in their villages and moved to the new frontier. My maternal grandfather, Stanisław Wulw, who was an adventurous fellow, decided to sell his house and small farm and move with his wife and four children (a son, Władysław, and three daughters: Felicia, Karolina, and my mother, Helena) to Podole where he purchased 17 acres of land and built a very modest house.

My adventurous grandfather journeyed to the United States three times before World War I, during the time when many Poles immigrated to the United States from the Austrian sector of Poland known as *Galicja*. Several people from the Haczów area including our relatives in the Wulw, Ziemiański and Papciak families immigrated to the United States at this time. They settled in the Ford City, Pennsylvania area and also in the vicinity of Wheeling, West Virginia. My grandfather worked in the coal mines of West Virginia and western Pennsylvania and earned additional income as a bass player in the local band. Although adventurous, he unfortunately was not a very shrewd businessman. Each time he returned to Poland, he invested his hard earned money in Polish war bonds or lent some of it to locals. At the time, there was rampant inflation in Poland, and soon the bonds and loans became worthless. My paternal grandparents, on the other hand, had much better financial acumen. They invested their money in real estate buying a four-family home in Rzeszów, a city in southeastern Poland, and also buying land in Podole.

My maternal grandparents were well-established in their native village. My grandfather was a farmer and my grandmother Anna Ziemiańska (nee Rosenbaiger) was a seamstress who had several apprentices working for her. She died in 1923 soon after arriving in Podole, when my mother was only eight years old. They lived in Haczów, a village near the provincial town of Brzozów. The village dates back to the mid-14th century and in fact a wooden church still stands there that dates back to medieval times. Today it is the largest wooden church in Europe. The village has a well-documented history and the church is famous for a Polish Pieta, *Matka Boska Bolesna*.

My paternal grandparents, Antoni and Anna (nee Dereń) Bąk, were from the village of Humniska, also in the Province of Brzozów. Humniska is also an old village dating back to the 14th century. It too has preserved an original church dating back to those times. My father's parents were well-to-do farmers. They sold their house and land and moved to Podole at about the same time as my mother's parents. They purchased about 140 acres of land some of which they gave away to their married children as was the custom at the time. My father's parents gave him 14 acres of land, and my mother received three acres from her parents. Usually, the parents gave some land to their children as a marriage gift and kept part of the property for themselves while they were still alive. The reason for this was to avoid problems later in life, for often after giving up all of their land to children, parents suffered from poverty and humiliation. Keeping some land provided them with some sense of security and independence.

Moving to Podole was not a simple matter since it was like moving to a new frontier. After World War I and the War with the Bolsheviks in 1920, Podole was devastated by many battle fronts which moved back and forth through that area. As a result of these wars, the land had not been farmed for many years and thus was overgrown with weeds and brush. It also was necessary to remove mines and artillery shells and fill in the trenches to make the land safe for farming. The soil, however, was fertile and the landscape hilly and beautiful with an abundance of trees and green pastures. The climate in this area tended to be severe—very cold in winter and very hot in summer. The land was inexpensive as a result of the break-up of large estates, which were acquired by the Polish government after the war of 1920 and sold to settlers at affordable prices. And so, the area quickly became populated with Polish nationals from the western part of Poland. Before long, the landscape turned into fields of wheat, rye, potatoes, beets and many forms of wildflowers which transformed the war stricken landscape into a picturesque setting.

My parents met at my uncle Józek and Aunt Karolina's wedding. My father was the brother of the groom and my mother was the sister of the bride. My parents were married in 1932, resulting in two brothers being married to two sisters. Consequently, our family bonds were (and still are) even stronger than usual. Soon after marrying my parents built a temporary home in Polska Wola which was to be used as a barn after a permanent house was constructed. The home consisted of a single room with an entrance area, a storage space for household items, and a wood-burning stove for cooking and baking. There was no electricity, no running water and no indoor plumbing. The outhouse was in the stable. The potable water was drawn with a hand ratchet and bucket from a deep well a few yards from the house. My parents had plans to build a brick house and had hired local workers to make the bricks. Unfortunately, the process of making bricks back then was long and tedious because the bricks had to be made by hand. My parents did not expect to have the new house constructed for at least two or three years.

At the new homestead my parents owned two horses, two cows, chickens, a few turkeys, and a dog—your typical farm menagerie. The farming produced a variety of products such as wheat, oats, barley, rye, potatoes and various vegetables. On one point, Rev. Rysz was right—the soil in Podole was indeed very fertile, despite the occasional artillery shell.

Since my father was not much of a farmer, he hired local Ukrainians to do the farming and work around the house. He spent most of his time devoted to his business as a middleman between farmers and wholesalers in Podhajce and other surrounding towns like Buczacz and Tarnopol. The business involved buying farm products such, as eggs, and sorting, packing and delivering them to wholesalers in the cities. He also collected other farm products, like potatoes, vegetables and grains, during the season and delivered them to the wholesalers. The delivery was done by horse and wagon for most of the year, except in winter when a sleigh replaced the wagon. On return trips, he brought back supplies to the local grocery store. The business kept him away from home most of the time, leaving my mother to manage the housework as best she could. In addition to the normal house chores, which included cooking, baking, washing, and raising two small children, she also had to feed and milk the cows, feed the farm animals, and maintain a vegetable garden. It's hard to imagine that she was able to manage all this without modern conveniences like washing machines, stoves and other electrical appliances that we are so accustomed to today.

I was born July 18, 1933 in our temporary house. A midwife helped with the delivery because there was no doctor available in the village. I had a younger brother, Janek, who died six months after he was born. My sister, Alina, was born on October 28, 1937.

Day-to-day life was harsh in Polska Wola. Farming with primitive equipment and no machinery was difficult. The farms were usually small and often could not support a family. However, people were generally happy and enjoyed life. My aunts and uncles from Rzeszów liked our peaceful life in the country and visited us every summer and on holidays. We have always been a very close family. My godmother was Aunt Karolina. Godmother in Polish is a tongue-twister, *chrzestna matka*, and as a young child, I could not pronounce it. Therefore, I renamed my godmother, *Macia* (Macha). The name stuck, and from that day on, everyone in our family called Aunt Karolina, Macia. My childhood was very simple. There were few toys, no playgrounds and no other children close by. My daily routine was to walk across the meadow to Aunt Macia's, get my bottle refilled with milk, and return home. Sometimes I went with my mother into the fields to take lunch to the people working there. Anytime I ventured outside the house alone I had to dodge the turkeys in our yard, which, for some reason, were fond of attacking me. When I was older, one of my chores was to tend the cows grazing in the field. Indeed, life was very simple for me in those days.

Holidays were special occasions when we would celebrate with our families and neighbors. The biggest celebration, of course, was Christmas; it always had a special meaning for us. The preparations for Christmas started early. Cleaning the house, decorating, cooking and baking were done days ahead. The Christmas tree was put up the day before Christmas, never earlier. It was a live tree with handmade paper decorations. Items such as apples, candy, cookies and candles completed the ornaments. At the appearance of the first star, we sat down for Christmas Eve dinner, called *wigilia* (Vee-ghee-lia). Wigilia was the main event of the Christmas season. For wigilia we usually got together with my uncle and aunt's family. The supper started with the sharing of *opłatek* (opwateck), which is an unconsecrated bread wafer similar to the type used during Holy Communion. The wafer is embossed with religious scenes and religious figures. Each person received a wafer blessed by a priest and then broke off a piece of the wafer to share with everyone at the table individually. While sharing the wafer we would express wishes of goodwill, good health and good fortune for the coming year. Sharing of *opłatek* was and still is the essence of Polish Christmas Eve celebration. Christmas Eve supper consisted of eleven meatless dishes. A typical meal included various dishes of fish (usually carp and herring), borsch with mushroom dumplings, sauerkraut with mushrooms, *pierogi* with several kinds of fillings, *kutia* or noodles with poppy seed and honey, and an assortment of baked goods. The Christmas tradition also required leaving an empty seat and a separate place setting at the table for an unexpected visitor. Any visitor was welcome at the dinner table regardless of his religious beliefs or social status. After supper, we sang Christmas carols, and at midnight, we went to a mass at our parish church in Wiśniowczyk, about two kilometers from our home. We walked to church together, children particularly enjoying the walk since there was an occasional snow fight, usually on the way back home. It was customary to exchange small gifts at Christmastime. However, children received gifts mainly on St. Nicolas Day, December 6th. On that day children gathered at the community center. St. Nicolas, who did not resemble the bearded jolly fellow as we know him today, dressed in bishop's robes, appeared on stage and distributed gifts.

A particularly festive Christmas tradition was caroling, *Po Kolędzie*. Young people dressed up as various characters such as devils, angels and various animals. The group walked from house to house singing Christmas carols. As a reward, they were given money, baked goods or candy that they shared with each other afterward.

The new year was celebrated with a dance on New Year's Eve, called *Sylwester*, which lasted until the wee hours of the morning. A band of local residents played for the event. The next day was a day for visiting friends and relatives. A local tradition for children was to visit relatives very early in the morning, grab a handful of grain (wheat or rye), and pelt the relatives still in bed with the grain, while singing wishes of good health and good luck for the coming year. After a long night many did not welcome these visits. Another New Year's tradition in our area was to play pranks on friends and neighbors. It was not unusual, for example, to find someone's disassembled wagon reassembled on the roof of a barn. Windows and doorknobs were tarred, and items of everyday use were hidden. Early risers on New Year's Day were destined to be early risers for the rest of the year. After the new year, the pastor of our church visited our houses and blessed them. He inscribed *K+M+B* markings above the doors with white chalk. These markings, representing the initials of the three kings, Kaspar, Melchior, and Balthasar were preserved until the following year.

Other holidays that were particularly joyous were *Karnawał* (Carnival) and Easter. *Karnawał* was the time between Christmas holidays and the beginning of Lent. It was a time of celebration, dances and get-togethers that came to a culmination on the last Tuesday before Lent, called Fat Tuesday. On Fat Tuesday we indulged in a great variety of foods, especially cakes and pastries. The favorites were *faworki*, sometimes called *chrusty* (hroostee) and *pączki* (ponchki), jelly-filled doughnuts. Carnival came to an end on Ash Wednesday when delicious food was forsaken for *żurek* (sour soup made from white borsch) and herring.

Young and old alike eagerly awaited Easter—especially after forty days of Lent when, in addition to fasting, we also abstained from all festive celebrations such as dances and weddings. Easter meant the beginning of a happier season. Easter really began with the Holy Week when all preparations for the holiday started. The women got together to bake and prepare food. They also made *pisanki,* brilliantly colored Easter eggs, particularly exquisite among the Ukrainian women. On Holy Thursday and Holy Friday, we went to church for the Christ Passion and to visit "Christ's grave." We fasted the whole week—eating no meat and having only one full meal a day. On Good Friday, we ate only a small meal or no meal at all. On Holy Saturday, the priest blessed beautifully decorated baskets filled with samplings of food, such as *kiełbasa*, *babka*, ham, boiled eggs, butter, salt, and cakes made in the form of an Easter lamb. The blessing usually was done in one of our neighbors' houses or in the church in Wiśniowczyk. With the fasting and other activities throughout the week, expectations for the arrival of Easter Sunday were quite high. Finally, Sunday arrived and we all went to the sunrise mass, *Rezurekcja*, in our best Easter outfits. After the mass, we had Easter breakfast, the most festive meal of Easter. The meal consisted of boiled eggs, kiełbasa, ham, babka, freshly made butter and an assortment of baked goods. Dessert was usually *pączki*, poppy seed rolls, and the specialties of that particular house. Before the meal, we would share pieces of the blessed egg with each other while expressing best wishes. This tradition is practiced in our family to this day. Another tradition for the children was an egg fight. Children would hold a hard boiled egg in their hand and tap an egg in another child's hand to see which egg cracked first. The child who had the last unbroken egg was the winner. The day after Easter was a church holiday but was best known by the name *Śmigus Dyngus*, or Wet Monday. It was traditional to throw water on friends and family members, especially while they were still in bed. The young men usually sprinkled perfume on the young ladies.

Boże Ciało, or Corpus Christi, was celebrated on Thursday 60 days after Easter, usually in early June. This holiday required constructing four altars outside the church in recognition of the four evangelists. The service consisted of a procession that went from altar to altar while singing religious songs. Upon reaching the altar, the priest recited the epistle from one of the evangelists. The priest, dressed in elaborate robes and carrying the Blessed Sacrament, led the procession. Young girls, dressed in national costumes, preceded the priest and tossed fresh flowers in the direction of the Blessed Sacrament.

Another notable holiday celebrated in Poland was the Constitution Day of May Third, or *Trzeciego Maja*. It commemorated the day the Polish Constitution of 1791 was ratified. The constitution established a truly democratically elected government in Poland and was the first of its kind in Europe, and second in the world after the United States. *Trzeciego Maja* was celebrated with a military parade and a dance in the local community center. The Polish Independence Day was celebrated on November 11. Poland gained independence on November 11, 1918, at the end of World War I, after 123 years of enslavement by Austria, Prussia and Russia. The day was celebrated with military parades and other festivities. Another important day in Polish history was the *Dzień Żołnierza* (Soldier's Day) celebrated on Assumption Day, August 15, in memory of the Polish Army's victory over the Bolsheviks at Vistula in 1920.

Noc Świętojańska, also called *Sobótka* was celebrated on June 23, the Eve of St. John's Day. This holiday had its origin in the pagan days, dating back to the 10th century. It celebrated the year's shortest night and also was associated with the worship of fire, water and love. The holiday was so popular in the pagan days, before Christianity was introduced in Poland, that over the years, the Church adopted the holiday, modifying its intent rather than fighting the pagan custom. On the eve of St. John's Day, tradition called for the people to lit bonfires to repel evil spirits. Girls dressed in white danced and sang love songs by the bonfires, and boys showed off their agility by leaping over the fire. The young ladies prepared wreaths of fresh flowers, lit candles in the middle of the wreaths, and floated the wreaths down the river. The boys retrieved the wreaths downstream. Tradition said that the boy and girl with the same wreath were destined to marry each other. Occasionally, the tradition averted an undesirable prearranged marriage. People made wishes that night, that they hoped would come true in the coming year. For the young ladies, the wish was usually to get married. Another tradition claimed that on the eve of Saint John, fern plants flowered and anyone finding the blooming fern would become rich. Young people ventured into the woods looking for the flowering fern. To the best of my knowledge, no one has ever found one....yet.

Another holiday celebrated in our village was *Dożynki*. *Dożynki*, or a day of thanksgiving for the recently completed harvest, was similar to Thanksgiving in the United States. A harvest wreath symbolizing *Dożynki* was woven by hired help on the farms and ceremoniously presented to the owner of the farm. The wreath symbolized the crops and fruits of the earth that had just been harvested. In our area, the wreath was handed to the *sołtys* (the equivalent of the mayor) at a ceremony at the community center.

A very festive day was the *Zaduszki*, or All Souls Day, celebrated on November 2. The whole community marched in procession that evening from the church to the cemetery, sang religious songs, lit candles, and placed flowers on the graves of loved ones. The illuminated cemetery was an impressive sight. This holiday is similar to Memorial Day in the United States.

This peaceful existence in our village was shattered on September 1, 1939, when Hitler's Germany invaded Poland. Initially, our family did not feel any direct effect of the invasion; however, many members of the families in our village were called into active duty and army reserves. We were, of course, very concerned about the developments on the German front. We listened very attentively to my uncle's battery powered radio, the only radio in our area. We were always happy to hear *Hejnał*, the trumpet call from the tower of the *Mariacki* Church in Kraków, played over the radio at noon, before the news was read. We figured that as long as *Hejnał* was being played, Poland had not perished. We also expected that England and France would enter the war. Together with Poland, the allies would quickly defeat the Germans.

Seventeen days later, on September 17, 1939, the Soviet Union invaded Poland from the East. The invasion was the result of an agreement signed in Moscow by the German foreign minister Ribbentrop and the Soviet foreign minister Molotov. The agreement divided Poland between Germany and the Soviet Union. This was a treacherous act since Poland and the Soviet Union had a non-aggression pact that was signed in 1932 and renewed only a few months before. Stalin, however, stated that since Germany invaded Poland, Poland ceased to exist, and he was not bound by any previously signed pacts. His excuse to invade Poland was to protect the minority Ukrainians and Byelorussians. After the invasion the Russians openly supported the Ukrainian and Byelorussian anti-Polish groups and encouraged them to take hostile action against the Poles in their areas.

Soon after the invasion we could see the consequences of the war. The Russian cavalry moved through our area, which was only 100 kilometers from the Russian border. They bivouacked along the small stream running between our property and the property of my uncle Józek. The Russian soldiers were poorly clothed and poorly equipped but reasonably well disciplined. They caused no troublesome incidents of which we were aware. However, the Ukrainian nationalists living in our area were another story. The Ukrainians applauded as the Russians entered Poland. They saw an opportunity to gain independence for the Ukraine. They also wanted to get even with the Poles for the injustice and persecution to which they claimed they had been subjected under Polish rule. Bands of these nationalists were roaming our area, robbing, looting and burning the houses of Polish farmers. Some of the stories told to us by eyewitness friends were gruesome. One lady from a neighboring village told us that she witnessed one group of these nationalists setting a house on fire and tossing the escaping occupants back into the burning house. In the nearby village of Michałpole, Ukrainian nationalists from the neighboring village of Pętlikowce Nowe raided the Michałpole farmers and ordered them out of their homes. The Ukrainian nationalists took all farmers' possessions and then destroyed their homes. The farmers had to seek shelter in neighboring villages. People in the villages were so afraid that they slept in the fields for fear of being attacked in their homes at night. The Archbishop of our diocese ordered all priests in small parishes to find shelter with local farmers because there were threats that these bands of Ukrainians would attack the parishes. The pastor of our church, Rev. Jan Pipusz, left Wiśniowczyk at the urging of some of our parishioners. The Russians caught him and confiscated all his belongings, but allowed him to return to Wiśniowczyk. These were not isolated cases, and history books document these incidents in great detail. The Russians initially tolerated, and in some cases encouraged, these acts of violence by the nationalists against the Poles. It was in the Soviets' interest to stir up fear among the general Polish population. The Soviets believed that people in fear were unlikely to organize and defend their country. Later, however, the Soviets started to arrest these Ukrainian nationalists as well. In our village, as a precaution, men formed a vigilante group armed with axes, scythes and picks and patrolled the village at night. To the best of my knowledge, outside of some isolated threats, there were no clashes with Ukrainians.

After the Russian invasion, the Polish army was in disarray with no chance to fight on both fronts. Many Polish soldiers were taken prisoner by the invading Russian army, my uncle Romek among them. Many others were trying to make their way to Romania, a neutral country at the time. From Romania, they were hoping to reach France to join Polish armed forces being formed there by the new Polish Government-in-Exile under General Władysław Sikorski.

One incident that occurred in our area illustrates the plight of the Polish soldiers. A plane landed in our fields, and its two pilots came to our house asking for shelter and civilian clothes. They changed into civilian clothes, burnt their uniforms, stayed overnight in the stable, and left the next morning. Unfortunately, they were caught and arrested the next day, and most likely were deported to Siberia with the rest of their comrades. This was a fairly common occurrence in the southeastern part of Poland; soldiers arrived individually or in small groups at the homes of local farmers, changed to civilian clothes and tried to return to their homes or cross the border to Romania to escape the Russians. Some were successful, but most were caught, imprisoned and later sent to Siberia.

Stalin had every intention to permanently incorporate the eastern part of Poland into the Soviet Union. In late October 1939, the Soviets organized elections in the occupied territories of Poland. All candidates for office were either Russians or people sympathetic to the Soviet Union. Every eligible person was required to vote. The elections were organized in great detail. There was a great amount of effort on the part of the Soviets to educate and indoctrinate the voting population. The so-called instructors explained in great detail how to vote. There was no question in anybody's mind as to the consequences of deviating from those instructions. The result, of course, was an overwhelming victory for the communist candidates. The newly-elected officials then petitioned the Soviet Union to absorb the occupied territories into the Soviet Union. On November 1, 1939, the Supreme Soviet of the Soviet Union formally incorporated the eastern part of Poland into the Soviet Union, and our area became part of the Ukrainian Soviet Republic.

Stalin was not satisfied with just incorporating the eastern part of Poland into the Soviet Union; he wanted to completely Sovietize the area. To reach his goal, Stalin planned to eliminate all elements of the Polish society that could potentially organize opposition and maintain Polish historical and cultural continuity. The main targets of these persecutions were individuals considered elite: government officials, teachers, intellectuals and people identified as most patriotic.

The NKVD, a predecessor of the KGB, the Soviet political service, moved to Poland on the heels of the Russian army. The NKVD started arresting army officers, non-commissioned officers, and policemen that avoided imprisonment during the initial stages of the war. Later, the NKVD began to arrest owners of large factories, commercial firms, and politically active farmers that settled in the area after World War I. Theoretically, according to the Soviet Penal Code, every Polish citizen who was suspected of planning to overthrow the Soviet system or to undermine or weaken the communist authorities or the newly-formed farm councils was subject to arrest. Those arrested were deprived of all their personal belongings. They were then thrown in jail to *soften them up*. The interrogations followed, accompanied by frequent beatings, deprivation of sleep, and loneliness. After such treatment, the prisoners usually were ready to sign any confession presented to them. The usual sentence of five to ten years of hard labor was soon followed by deportation to Siberia.

The Soviets also put in place the machinery to create fear and terror among the Polish population. They recruited informants, in many cases blackmailing these individuals into service with threats against their families. These informants were to report to the Russians everything that was going on in the areas where they lived. They were expected to make reports on suspicious incidents on a regular basis. Therefore, in some cases, these individuals created fictitious stories just to protect their dear ones. The arrests resulting from information provided by these informants instilled fear among the general population, fear of being arrested and fear of being sent to Siberia. This fear was the means by which the Soviets gained and maintained control over the population. As a result, everyone became suspicious of each other, and no one dared to speak openly.

Another target of the Soviet persecution was the church. Soviet authorities ordered some churches closed. Others were levied such high taxes that they could not afford to stay open. Some sources estimate that the Russians closed close to 4,000 Catholic, Greek Catholic and Russian Orthodox churches in less than two years.

The Russians also adjusted school curriculum. History was modified, and special indoctrination courses on communism were introduced. Religious education was banned, and all crosses were removed from classrooms.

The well-to-do farmers, called *kulaks* by the Russians, were forced to give up their land as the Soviets started to nationalize the farms into collective farms. These new farms, called *kilhozes,* were modeled on the system used in the Soviet Union. Major businesses also were nationalized and the owners, often declared exploiters, were arrested and imprisoned.

Another immediate consequence of this Sovietization was the introduction of the Soviet currency, the *ruble*, at the exchange rate equal to the Polish *złoty*. This, in effect, devalued the *złoty* enabling the Russians to buy everything in sight for practically a song. At first, the Russians could not believe that the goods in Polish store windows were authentic. They figured the displays were fake, like those in the stores in the Soviet Union. Once they determined that the goods were indeed real the Russians went on buying binges, and stores became empty almost overnight, especially in the cities. Long lines stretched in front of stores as people rushed to buy whatever happened to be left, not necessarily what they needed. The loss of the purchasing power of the *złoty* created undue hardship on older people who depended on savings for their livelihood, since their savings had become practically worthless overnight. The Russians, meanwhile, cultivated their taste for watches. In fact, anything that ticked they bought. However, when questioned about the Soviet Union, they stoutly replied *vsio yest*, they had everything. Some of their comments bordered on ridiculous, as they even claimed to have factories that made oranges.

The news of many arrests, interrogations and imprisonments of the Polish population by the Soviets reached our village as well. One night, we met Michał Mazur, a Ukrainian who had previously worked for us, but quit when the war broke out because it was politically dangerous to work for Polish people. He came to warn us of impending arrests and deportations in our area as well. He suggested that my father and Uncle Staszek, a seminarian studying for the priesthood who was visiting us at the time, leave the area and move to Lwów, or even to German occupied Rzeszów where my grandmother lived. My father, of course, did not seriously consider leaving, but as a precaution, he built a passage between our house and the stable so he could escape if the Russians came to arrest him. The passage could also serve as an escape route for the whole family in case the Ukrainian nationalists attacked us. We never suspected that the Russians would deport entire families.

Early in February of 1940, my father and Uncle Staszek decided it was too dangerous for Uncle Staszek to stay in the area. They went to Lwów where they stayed for a few days at a friend's house. They again heard many more stories of arrests, interrogations and imprisonment usually involving the educated, government officials and army personnel. My father decided to return home. The trip took him longer than usual because the trains were not running regularly and it was impossible to get other forms of transportation. Little did he know what lay ahead.

At approximately 4 a.m. on February 10, 1940, there was a knock at our door and a NKVD officer accompanied by four Russian soldiers armed with rifles stormed our house. The NKVD officer announced that we had to leave our house and that we were being resettled to another part of Poland. As I mentioned before, my father was not home. My mother was in a state of shock. I believe only a mother with small children can fully understand my mother's predicament. The soldiers searched the house looking for arms, propaganda literature, or anything that would connect us with some kind of anti-Soviet activity. All Poles were suspected as potential counterrevolutionaries. The NKVD officer questioned my mother where was my father, and she truthfully replied that he went to Lwów with my uncle. Apparently the response satisfied him and since nothing suspicious was found in the house, the NKVD officer departed leaving one soldier to oversee the preparation for our deportation. We had my five-year-old cousin, Krysia, and a young boy who did odd jobs for us staying at our house for the night. The Russian ordered the Ukrainian driver of a horse-drawn sleigh, which was waiting outside to take them home. When my cousin arrived at her house, only a quarter of a mile from our home, her parents were still asleep. They had no idea what was going on, but the Ukrainian alerted them to the situation and they immediately started making preparations to leave.

My mother, who was 24 years old at the time, exhibited a tremendous presence of mind. After the initial shock had dissipated, she got us dressed and randomly started gathering things, stuffing them into potato sacks, blankets, sheets and whatever else she could find. We obviously were not prepared to travel; we had no suitcases or other travel accessories. We were given only one hour to get ready. My mother placed a down bed cover, called *pierzyna*, on the sleigh and then put my sister and me on top of the cover and covered us with another *pierzyna*. The temperature outside was well below zero Fahrenheit, and with the wind blowing it seemed a lot colder (the winter of 1940 was one of the harshest in memory). My mother continued to gather clothing, food and other household articles and load them on the sleigh. We had wine in large glass jugs which she transferred into milk containers because the Russian would not allow her to take the jugs. That wine became a very important part of our sustenance in the journey ahead. She even took a wide leather belt used to drive farm machinery, thinking it could be sold or used for soling shoes. She also took a large box of tobacco that my father kept in the house and for which he was very grateful. The Russian soldier was a kind soul for he not only permitted my mother to take everything she wanted, but at times, even helped her pack. He particularly encouraged her to take a lot of warm clothing.

The same procedure was being repeated across our village. All people who originally came to Podole from the central part of Poland and the native Poles who were not related to the local Ukrainian population were being deported. All were awakened at approximately 4 o'clock in the morning, ordered to pack their belongings onto a single sleigh, and transported to the congregation point, which was the community center. Most people were less fortunate than we were. They were given very little time to pack and were not allowed to take much with them. My uncle Józek's family was one of the less fortunate. They were allowed only half an hour to get ready. Fortunately, the Ukrainian horseman who brought their daughter home had provided them with some additional warning. The NKVD officer told my uncle not to pack too much for they were going to a place where there was plenty of everything. My grandfather, his wife, and my mother's brother Władek and his family lived across the river from us. They also were awakened at 4 o'clock in the morning and ordered to pack and leave. We met them at the community center. My grandfather offered to help us and wanted to move our sleigh closer to theirs to keep us together, for he knew my father was away and my mother was alone. However, my mother preferred to stay close to her sister and brother-in-law.

By daybreak, all sleighs were assembled at the community center. Russian soldiers armed with rifles and bayonets guarded the sleighs and the entire perimeter of the community center. A general chaos ruled the area, complete with confusion, commotion, crying and shouting. The horses, sleighs and the drivers were all recruited from the local Ukrainian farmers. Michał Mazur, the fellow who had worked for us, came over to our sleigh and helped my mother secure our belongings to the sleigh. He also gave her a few rubles before he left. Later we learned that he was arrested and imprisoned by the NKVD for helping us.

We rode from the community center to the railway station in Podhajce, some 20 kilometers away, in one long convoy. We had left our village and our homes, never to return again.

We arrived at the railroad station in Podhajce at mid-morning. Already, hundreds of people were there and it was sheer bedlam. People, horses and sleighs all moved in different directions. My uncle Józek held the reins of our horses with his so we would not be separated. Shortly after our arrival at the station, we started boarding a train of either freight cars or boarded-up cattle cars. Inside we found two levels of wood decking, a coal stove in the middle of the car, and an open hole in the floor to be used as a toilet. Thirty-five or forty people were put in our car. Some were from our village and others were from nearby villages. In all, about 2,000 people who were present at the station were being deported. We stayed at the station, locked in rail cars, for two days. Some of the relatives and neighbors who were not being deported tried to bring food to us. Some were successful in their attempts, but many were not, mostly depending on the whim of the Russian soldiers guarding the train.

In the meantime, the news of our deportation reached my father who was already on his way home. He arrived at the station that evening and asked the Russians for permission to join his family. The Russians refused, stating that all cars were locked and that no one goes in or out. That night, he walked along the tracks calling my mother and uncle's names. We heard him, and my uncle pried two boards from the car's wall to let him in. My father always joked that he was the only person in our village that volunteered to be deported. We all knew that he never considered doing otherwise.

We finally left Podhajce on the third day, and a few hours later, we reached the railway station Podwołoszczyk on the border between Poland and Russia. We had to change trains at the border because Polish rail cars could not be used on Russian tracks due to a difference in the width of Russian railroads. The Russian boxcars were no more "luxuriously" equipped than the Polish cars: two levels of decking, small barred windows on either side of the boxcar; a coal stove in the middle; and an open hole in the floor. The transfer took about half a day. The train was constantly guarded by Russian troops. The troops had their quarters on the train in separate rail cars, spaced between the cars that carried the deportees. That evening, as the train was leaving Poland, all the locomotives at the station on the Polish side of the border gave out a wailing whistle as if saying farewell to us, farewell forever. It was the saddest moment in our lives and there wasn't a single person in the car who did not cry. Somehow, we all knew at that moment that we were not coming back. This event was not, however, unique in Polish history. Throughout the ages, there were many deportations of Polish people, and this was simply history repeating itself. In our minds, we knew we undoubtedly were bound for that one dreaded place—*Siberia.*

My maternal great grandmother
Rosenbaiger (seated) and her two daughters.

My maternal grandmother Ziemiańska (seated)
with her sisters in the native Haczów costumes.
In the background is a 14th century church.

My mother, Helena, sitting on the lap of Aunt Felka. Aunt Macia is to their right. Haczów, Poland, 1917.

Aunt Maria Bąk in front of Uncle Józek's house in Polska Wola, Poland, 1935.

Uncle Władek Wulw and his family,
Poland, 1946.

My mother with her parents and Aunt Macia,
Haczów, 1922.

My grandfather Antoni Bąk (in background) on his farm in Podole.

Medieval church in my father's village of Humniska.

My father (second from the left) with his mother and brothers, Staszek, Romek and Józek, 1938.

My paternal grandmother, Aunt Jania (nun) and Aunt Marysia with family, Rzeszów, 1956.

Cousin Anulka and I in Poland, 1935.

My sister, Alina, and I in Poland, 1938.

Soviet Union

This journey of ours was being duplicated all across eastern Poland. It is estimated that in February of 1940 alone, the Russians deported 220,000 people from Poland. The deportees were mostly farmers who had settled in the eastern part of Poland after World War I, like us. The majority of this group was taken to Siberia and settled in camps, called *specposioleks*, located in large forests.

There were three other deportations from Poland to the Soviet Union. The second deportation in April of 1940 included more farmers and other groups of Polish citizens: Army personnel who avoided capture during the September campaign, families of captured officers who were already in prison, police, civil servants, and owners of factories and commercial establishments. These citizens were deported mainly to the Kazakh Soviet Socialist Republic (Kazakhstan). The third deportation took place in June of 1940. This time, the Russians deported mainly Polish citizens who had escaped from German-occupied Poland. The last massive deportation took place in June 1941 and included farmers who avoided the earlier deportations and people suspected of low loyalty to the new system. These citizens were deported to Siberia as well as Kazakhstan. In total, the Russians deported over 1.5 million people from Poland including over 380,000 children.

These deportations were well-planned, well-organized, and efficiently executed operations. There was nothing about them that suggested haste or lack of authority from the highest levels of the Soviet hierarchy. Later, we found out that the decision to deport Polish citizens to the Soviet Union was made as early as December 1939, and a list of potential deportees was prepared at that time.

Deportees were scattered across the Soviet Union as far as the Arctic Sea, the Siberian tundra, coal mines in Kamchatka, gold mines in Kolyma, and the steppes in Kazakhstan. In fact historians estimate that Poles ended up in about 2800 different places in 56 different Soviet *Oblasts* (states). The map showing the location of the Polish labor camps is very similar to the map of the destructive labor camps presented in Alexander Solzhenitsyn's *The Gulag Archipelago.* In many cases the Polish camps were the forerunners of the camps shown in Solzhenitsyn's book. The Soviets expanded these camps after the war to accommodate an even larger number of prisoners. Besides Poles, this form of ethnic cleansing also affected many other nationalities in the Soviet Union. Sometimes entire ethnic groups were eliminated, like the Crimean Tartars. However, Polish people were considered a particularly threatening element to the Soviet system. Consequently, Polish deportees and prisoners were sent to places where the climate was harshest and often unbearable to persons used to Poland's relatively milder climate. They were sent to places where there were labor shortages and where work was the hardest.

Siberia, to us Poles, is much more than just a geographical area. It is synonymous with the suffering and death to which Polish people have been subjected over the centuries at the hands of the Russians. Therefore, Siberia is not only the area that lies east of the Ural Mountains, but all places in the entire territory of Russia where Polish people were deported, where they suffered and where they died. To all Poles, these parts of the Soviet Union became known as *Nieludzka Ziemia* (The Inhumane Land), the Cursed Land, or Polish *Golgotha.* Of course, native Siberians object to these terms. To them, Siberia is an unspoiled land, beautiful in nature and rich in minerals. But to us Poles, who suffered, who were subjected to great pain and often death, Siberia always will remain the *Nieludzka Ziemia.*

Adam Dobroński in his book *Losy Sybiraków* (The Fate of the Sibiraks), describes seven plagues that the Polish deportees endured in Siberia: Hunger, harsh climate, hard labor, repression, disease, loneliness and death. Not everyone suffered all seven plagues and some plagues varied in degree for different individuals in different places. One common denominator, however, was death, the final crowning of all suffering.

Hunger affected all of us. Hunger also had a tremendous psychological effect on us and caused the total erosion of our humanity. In the Soviet Union, hunger was used as a political tool. The Soviets wanted to make sure that we always felt it, never got accustomed to it, and devoted all of our thoughts and energy to satisfy it. They believed that hungry people were easier to govern. Hunger combined with hard labor and devouring sickness also accelerated death.

The primitive surroundings and harsh climate were unbearable for us. Even the severe weather in Poland paled in comparison to the harshness of Siberia. As I previously stated, the winter of 1940 was one of the harshest in history. We were unaccustomed to such conditions and were, therefore, totally unprepared for them. Those being deported were not always allowed to take warm clothing with them. In summertime the mosquitoes and gnats were unbearable. The bed bugs, roaches and lice crawling at night deprived us of much needed sleep.

Hard labor was another universal plague that Polish deportees had to face in Siberia. Poles were sent to the Soviet Union during times of war, when there was a great need for labor. The Soviets were not concerned with the survivability of these people; they were expendable. The authorities of each camp, usually the NKVD, were responsible for the total output of the camp. They were required to fulfill the plan, no costs spared. The NKVD's approach was to exploit the prisoners as much as possible in the first three months of imprisonment, when the prisoners and the deportees were strongest. Later, as people became weaker, they were of little use and became expendable. The hunger and harsh conditions would accelerate their end.

The way the system worked, prisoners performed the hardest work first, then lighter work, and then went to *slaboseelki*, or halfway houses, until they died. Their final trip was to the cemetery. New prisoners-slaves arrived systematically, so the weak were replaced and the process was repeated. In the Soviet Union, perceived enemies of the Soviet system were always available; if shortages developed, new paragraphs were written in the law books, and another category of people became guilty.

The Soviets did not need crematoriums to get rid of people. They used different methods that were equally effective in achieving the same results—the elimination of anyone opposed to their totalitarian system. The Soviet methods consisted of hard work and more hard work until a person could endure life no longer, gave up and died. The end result of the Soviet method was just as final. However, the Soviets gained additional benefit from these prisoners and deportees before they died, free labor. The Soviets rationalized all this by stating that they did not kill people, people just died from natural causes.

Repression was another form of plague that affected the deportees. We lived in constant fear of being arrested, imprisoned and separated from our loved ones. In the Soviet Union, the communist system was supreme; it was above everything. The system demanded the unconditional loyalty and anyone who deviated from it was considered the enemy of the people. The Soviets ruled by fear and thus eliminated all hope of a better future. For the Soviet leaders, everything was done for the good of society, the good of the state, and the good of communism. To Russians, gulags were a natural part of their lives. The Russians used to have a saying that best illustrated this point, "*Kto nie byl, tot budiet, kto byl nie zabudiet*," or "Who was not there will get there; who was there will never forget."

No one was safe from repression. New excuses were constantly being invented to create additional convicts; all it took was a new paragraph in the law books. The Soviets used to say, "Give us a person and we shall find a paragraph." Polish citizens also were subjected to ridicule about their religion, their patriotism, and their cultural upbringing.

The major causes of disease among the deportees were hunger, cold climate, hard labor, horrible living and working conditions, hopelessness and constant fear of punishment. People with previous health problems did not have a chance. There was no way they could survive the horrendous conditions they were exposed to in Siberia. The deportees were exposed to such diseases as pneumonia, pellagra, scurvy, dysentery, night blindness, kidney and urinary tract infections and frostbite. Additionally, new deportees were exposed to such epidemic diseases as typhoid, fever and malaria. Children were particularly susceptible to these diseases, in addition to scarlet fever and measles. There were few, if any, medications. People relied on old remedies using various extracts from herbs, plants and roots. Many people died from diseases that were never diagnosed. There were many cases of psychological disorders; among them schizophrenia and depression. The hospitals, if available, were poorly equipped and lacked medicine. All a hospital provided was a temporary rest from hard labor, some piece of mind, a bug free bed, and a relatively decent meal.

Loneliness affected particularly single people, older people and orphans. People who were deported without families worried about their relatives, wondering if they were still alive and where they were located. Lack of information about their loved ones had a depressing effect on them. There were no books to read. Russian newspapers, if available, were laced with propaganda, half-truths, or outright lies. No writing paper or envelopes were available for those who wished to write letters; in many cases there was no mail. In spring, when nature came to life, nostalgia set in. People longed for the things that once were: Home, peaceful life, social and cultural outlets, and a sense of freedom. The survivors never took these things for granted again. Old people felt equally lonely, but above all, they were scared they would die without the benefit of sacraments. They wished that they could be buried in their church cemetery with a marker on their grave, and not in a faraway land where no one knew or cared if they ever existed.

Orphans presented a particularly sad situation. There was no one to look after them once their parents died. Often these children were no more than 10 or 11 years old, fending for themselves, begging or even stealing to survive. Many wandered around dressed in rags, with scabs and lice all over their bodies, looking like they had just emerged out of a sewer. These orphans had no future unless someone took pity on them and took them under their wing or sent them to an orphanage. Many were destined to grow up to be criminals.

Death was the final stage of suffering for many Poles in Siberia. For some, death came quickly. For others it took time. In all, about one-third of the deported population or about half a million people, died in Siberia. Most died in the first two years after the deportation, some as early as the first stages of the deportation during the trip to Siberia in the cattle cars. The dying deportees were physically exhausted, emotionally drained, without the benefit of sacraments, and in many cases, without the benefit of saying goodbye to loved ones. They left knowing that no one would ever hear about their death, that they would not rest in their family cemetery, and that their graves would not even be marked. They died like animals not leaving any trace of their existence.

I feel it is important that the reader understands the Polish perspective of Siberia to better appreciate the hardships that Polish people were subjected to at the hands of the Soviets. Our family was one of thousands of families that went through the Siberian experience. Our saga adds additional credence to the stories of those who emerged from that experience.

It took over a month to reach our destination town of Irbit in Western Siberia. In total, we traveled about 2,000 miles by train. The journey was a memorable one. It was dark, cold and extremely crowded in that railroad car with 35 to 40 people in a relatively small space. We were constantly hungry and thirsty. We slept on the wooden platforms with only blanket, if anything, between the platform and us. We were packed next to one another like sardines. The first few days the Russians did not even open the doors to the rail cars when the train stopped. The doors were locked from the outside. Apparently they wanted to keep us in the dark regarding our final destination. Sometimes the train was shunted to a siding and we stayed in one place for hours before the train moved on again. These were particularly anxious moments for us, as we did not know if it was the end of our journey or what would happen to us next. We traveled mostly at night, and when we did travel during the day we never went through large cities. Apparently the Soviets did not want the Russians to know about the magnitude of these deportations either. Later, when we were deeper into Soviet territory, the Russians opened the doors to our cars when the train stopped. Russian soldiers stood guard on both sides of the tracks and allowed only designated persons from each car to go and get food. At these stops, we were given some soup, bread, water and a bucket of coal. Sometimes we were able to get hot water from the steam locomotive; we used that water to make hot tea. The amount of food and water were inadequate to satisfy our hunger and thirst, and we did not have enough water to wash ourselves. We tried to reach out through the small windows of the car and collect snow and icicles from the roof to melt for water, but the amount was far too small to use for anything but drinking.

A number of our fellow deportees became ill, and some experienced frostbite on their hands or feet. The amount of coal that was issued at the stops was too small to keep the stove burning all the time. It was especially uncomfortable for people located near the walls of the car, for those spots were extremely cold. There were many cracks in the walls of the car and cold air constantly penetrated through them. To keep warm, we kept our winter clothing on day and night. Later, hygiene became a problem due to lack of washing facilities. We were initially bashful about using the hole in the floor for a toilet with everyone watching. Eventually someone put a blanket around the hole. Soon we all got used to it and it became second nature. It was almost impossible to keep the area clean around the hole, and the stench inside the boxcar became unbearable.

We all became covered with lice and were easily irritated. At times, arguments developed even among relatives and friends. Children were particularly restless. They could not understand why they couldn't get more food, why it was so cold, why the trip was taking so long, and why they couldn't play. Infants presented another acute problem. There was no milk to feed them and they had to eat what the grown-ups were given. The soup issued by the

Russians was not the most nutritious food for infants and small children, and the rations taken from Poland were quickly running out. Those who were fortunate to take some supplies from Poland shared them with others, but it became apparent that these supplies would not last long. There was also no place to bathe the children or even wash diapers. We were all so exhausted and at times didn't care where we were headed as long as we got there quickly. Prayers helped to keep our sanity during those dark days. Together we recited the rosary and sang religious songs.

Some died on the train during the journey. These were mainly the very old or the very young; they just could not cope with the horrible conditions they were exposed to during the trip. Russian guards told the families of the ones who died to leave the bodies by the railroad tracks, that someone would be by to take care of them.

Our train started heading north shortly after we crossed the Polish border. We traveled along the Baltic republics toward Finland, at first, but changed direction because the Finnish forces were repulsing the Russians and there was a danger that we could run into the war zone.

We reached a large mountain range about three weeks after we left Poland. Most of us had never seen the mountains before. At any other time, these mountains might have been beautiful, but to us it was just a matter of crossing another threshold to a place of no return. Since we were traveling mostly east, we assumed the mountains to be the Ural Mountains and Siberia to be just ahead of us.

Our destination was a camp about 40 kilometers from a town called Irbit, which lies about 250 kilometers northeast of Sverdlovsk, east of the Ural Mountains in Western Siberia. We arrived in Irbit on March 17, 1940. The Russians uncoupled about half a dozen cars and left us waiting at the station for several hours in temperatures of minus 40 degrees before being picked up by horse drawn sleighs and transported to a camp. The trip from the railway station to the camp deep in the Siberian forest took two days. Only children and luggage were able to ride in the sleigh; adults had to walk. Many people were unprepared to walk in such harsh conditions and ended up with frostbitten feet. The combination of sweat from the long march and subfreezing temperatures caused some to catch pneumonia. We stayed overnight in a huge barrack that seemed to serve no other purpose since it was situated in the thick of the woods all by itself. The camp that we finally reached was a timber logging camp and we were brought in to harvest trees and collect their sap in summers.

Our first impression of the camp was very depressing. It looked to us as if no human being had ever set foot on this ground before. The camp was located in the thick forest with snow several feet deep and hardly any daylight. There were four long log barracks with a separate barrack for the NKVD commandant. There was also the Russian *bania* or steam room and a kitchen with a mess hall. When we arrived, we were ordered to go to the *bania* to wash ourselves and get rid of the lice. Our clothes also were steamed to kill the lice. All this was only effective for a short period of time; lice always returned and eventually became a permanent fixture in our lives. Throughout our stay in the Soviet Union, lice and bed bugs were our constant companions. We soon learned the Russian approach to dealing with this problem; we just learned to live with them. Another problem was the rats that roamed in the barracks at night frightening everyone with strange noises, especially the children. Also at night, one could hear wolves howling outside, roaming, and seeking food.

Men, women, and children 15 years and older had to work in the woods logging the trees. The trees were first felled by sawing them with a large handsaw operated by two men. Women and children trimmed the branches with axes, and the trees were then cut into predetermined lengths and stacked in piles to be loaded later onto huge sleighs. The snow on the ground was two to three feet deep and made the work much more difficult. The trees had to be shoveled out of the deep snow after they were cut down and cut into logs. The logs then were dragged through the snow to the areas where they were piled. The work was demanding and the workdays were 10 to 12 hours long. It was easy to get sick because one moment people perspired and the next they were chilled by the subfreezing temperatures. Those who worked were entitled to purchase the full amount of food rations. Those who were sick and couldn't work were allotted a reduced amount of food. It was almost impossible to be excused from work except in extreme cases of sickness. People who became ill could not work. If they could not work, they could not get adequate food. Without adequate food, they could not get well and eventually died either from sickness or starvation.

Our first Easter in Siberia was one week after we arrived at the camp. There was no mass, no *święconka*, no blessing of the food baskets, no Easter eggs, and no singing of the joyous Easter songs. We just huddled together and prayed, asking God, "Why us?" and, "What's next?" There was no *Śmigus Dyngus* on Easter Monday.

About two months after we arrived in Irbit, the NKVD commandant from Kutyr, a camp located between Irbit and Sverdlovsk, came to our camp to take 10 families with him to his camp. My uncle and his family were selected, but our family was not. We asked and begged the commandant not to separate us and he finally acquiesced and took both families. As we were leaving, our friends in the camp gave us letters for their loved ones and begged us not to forget about them. They assumed we were going to a better place and would be more likely to survive. Most of the people in the camp did not expect to leave that place alive. We left about 200 people in that camp and we did not hear from them or about them until after the war. Few of them, very few, returned to Poland. We learned later that death continued to take its toll after we left Irbit. People died from starvation and diseases that were undiagnosed but mostly related to malnutrition.

The saddest story was that of the orphaned children who were left to their own resources after their parents died, often forced to steal to survive. In 1944, a Polish communist organization called the Polish Patriots established an orphanage in Monetoy near Sverdlovsk. A number of children from the Irbit area were admitted to that orphanage and returned to Poland in 1946. Two of the survivors, Kazik Omachel and his sister, Władzia, were relatives of my grandfather's second wife. They managed to reach the orphanage in 1944 and returned to Poland in 1946. Their mother had died from starvation and they had lost an older sister from tuberculosis. Their father was forcibly drafted to the army and was killed in the battle of Lenino. Before joining the orphanage, they stayed for two years with my mother's stepmother and my grandfather. Unfortunately, in the orphanage, these children also were subjected to intense propaganda and indoctrination to communism and many of them became hardened communists. The Omachels were among the fortunate, however, because not too many others survived the *Nieludzka Ziemia.*

For us, it was back on the horse drawn sleigh, a two-day journey to Irbit, another day on the train and on to a new unknown gulag. Our new location was *specposiolek* or a forced labor camp, called Kutyr, about 10 kilometers from the town of Malinovka, which lies between Irbit and Sverdlovsk in Western Siberia. People living in Kutyr were mostly from the Wołyn region of Poland. There were a few Russian families who inhabited this camp as well. This was in contrast to Irbit, where most people were from our region of Poland, with few Russians, other than the commandant, his assistant and the people who supervised the logging.

My father became ill just before we left Irbit. When we reached Irbit, after two days on a sleigh, we were taken to a railway station. My father laid down in the waiting room trying to stay warm, but the stationmaster told us to remove "that trash" from his waiting room. My mother, with the help of Uncle Józek, moved my father to the platform. It was very cold outside and mother tried to bundle us under as many covers as she could find. She tried to be calm and appear strong but we could see the tears running down her face in two continuous streams, the tears that just would not stop flowing. I can still see her suffering face in front of me, even to this day, whenever I think of those days in the Soviet Union. We were forced to stay outside in the cold on the platform for several hours until the train arrived. My father developed a severe case of pneumonia and was immediately hospitalized when we arrived in Malinovka. The rest of us went by sleigh to Kutyr, our home for the next two years.

Kutyr was a camp very similar in appearance to the camp in Irbit, but it was located in an area less remote, closer to a more populated area of Siberia. This camp was also in the forest. We were housed in log barracks 100 feet long and 30 feet wide, made from pine tree logs with moss stuffed between them to seal the gaps. There was a corridor in the middle and a wood burning stove in the center of the corridor to heat the whole barrack. Each family had to take turns keeping the stove burning day and night, and acting as a watchman against fire. The rooms were on either side of the corridor, one room per family and 10 to 15 families to each barrack. Each family was assigned a room that was about 12 feet long and 10 feet wide with a single window and a small stove for cooking. The rooms had wooden platforms that served as a bed for the entire family. Unfortunately, these platforms were always infested with bed bugs and it was difficult to get any sleep. There were three such barracks in our camp. As in Irbit, there was a kitchen with a mess hall, commandant quarters, a one-room school, and stables for horses. The toilets were latrines on the outskirts of the camp. These latrines were nothing more than large ditches dug in the ground with a single wall separating them from the barracks.

About 200 people were in the camp. The Russians, mostly ex-prisoners or so-called *zaklucheni*, who had already served their sentences, lived separately in small log cabins. The *zaklucheni*, even though they had already served their sentences had no place to go, for if they returned to their previous homes they would be shunned by people who were afraid of being associated with political undesirables. Even members of their own families did not want to acknowledge them, so these ex-prisoners usually stayed in the areas where they were imprisoned after serving their sentences. They were used as supervisors of the prisoners or were given more desirable jobs inside and outside of the camp.

One fixture in the labor camps, including ours, were the steam baths, called *banias*. These were big steam rooms where people went once a week to take steam baths, not only to get clean, but also to kill the lice. Clothes were also steamed out in adjacent rooms. These steam rooms were called *vshoboyka*, or lice killers, and appropriately so. These *vshoboykas* were very common throughout the Soviet gulags and the Russians were very fond of them and liked to brag about them. One of my father's Russian co-workers asked if we had *vshoboykas* in Poland, and when my father responded negatively, the Russian was astonished and said, "Poland must be a very poor country if they cannot afford the *vshoboykas*." My father just laughed. The steaming helped eradicate the lice for a couple of days or so, before a new herd moved in. To control the lice in the barracks, we tried to wash the wood platforms and walls with boiling water, but this procedure was not very effective. Women and girls had a difficult time keeping the lice out of their hair. Some even tried kerosene to eradicate the lice.

Upon arrival in Kutyr, my mother was assigned to carry buckets of water from a nearby stream to the tanks in the steam baths. Carrying two buckets up a long hill is hard work, especially when weak and malnourished. It was early May and still very cold in Siberia. She often got wet when splashed by cold water, further worsening her condition. She soon developed pneumonia and was taken to the same hospital as my father in Malinovka. She was transported to the hospital in a horse drawn wagon. They had to cross a flooded stream and my mother was totally soaked by the gushing waters. She arrived at the hospital chilled to the bone which certainly aggravated her condition. During my parents' stay in the hospital, my sister and I stayed with my aunt and uncle. The hospital released both my father and mother after a few days even though both were still not fully recovered. The hospital claimed that my parents had stayed in the hospital long enough and the hospital needed space for other people who were more seriously ill. My father, on his return, was immediately assigned to work in the stables, cleaning them and attending to the horses. This was considered a prime assignment since the work was relatively light and one could keep warm being out of the elements most of the time. My mother, on the other hand, was too sick to work and her condition was not getting any better. We were very concerned that she would die. A pharmacist from Poland, a Polish Jew, offered to help. He had brought some medicine from Poland and made a mixture of different ingredients that he gave my mother. On the warm days we carried her outside so she could get some sun and fresh air. She started to get better in a few weeks and eventually recovered fully. That pharmacist saved my mother's life and she was always grateful to him, even though now she does not remember his name or what eventually happened to him.

Kutyr was a timber logging camp. Russians called timber-logging *lesopovaly*. Forced labor was used to cut down trees and transport the logs for such uses as building materials, railroad ties, paper, and fuel to generate electricity. All men, women, and children over 15 years of age were required to work. The work in the forest consisted of clearing snow from area around the trees, then cutting the trees about ten inches from the ground. Fallen trees usually were buried in snow and had to be shoveled out. Some enterprising people made fires around the fallen trees, to try to melt the snow rather than shovel it. The fallen trees then were trimmed and cut to specified lengths and stacked in big piles before being loaded on sleighs for transport. The timber was transported to its destination by huge sleighs pulled by tractors. These sleighs looked like the flat bed of a train or a tractor-trailer. The sleighs had one huge runner in the middle and smaller runners on each side of the sleigh. The runner in the middle slid on a racetrack or an ice channel and the runners on the sides served as outriggers and stabilizers, sliding on smaller channels on each side. Those who were too sick to work at logging swept these channels every day. One tractor pulled several sleighs loaded with logs.

I loved to take joy rides on these sleighs when they were passing our camp. I stood in the back of the empty sleighs holding on to the cross beam or rode on top of the logs when the sleighs were loaded. One day, when I was having a good time riding in the back of the sleigh, it tilted on the curve shifting loose beams to one side. The sliding beams smashed all fingers in my left hand. My hand was a mess, blood everywhere. I ran to Aunt Macia's barrack, as I was afraid to go to ours for the fear of being punished. Aunt Macia washed my hand and wrapped it in clean rags and let me stay at their place until I calmed down before returning to my family barrack. My father scolded me and told me that he would not punish me unless I cried. I crawled under the covers on the bed and sobbed quietly so no one could hear me. To this day, I have a scar on my left middle finger as a reminder of that incident.

Each day, men and women marched to the forest as a group. The trip to the work area in the forest, sometimes several kilometers away, took a good chunk of energy out of the workers. They spent up to 12 hours cutting, trimming and stacking the trees in piles. A Russian inspector counted the number of logs each brigade stacked, marked the logs, and credited the brigade for the work done. People got paid meager wages in rubles, barely enough to buy the allotted portions of bread and soup. If they had any extra money, they could buy items from the camp store; however, the store shelves were usually empty. The group marched back to the camp at night. It was a sorry sight to watch these workers returning from the day's work. They were tired, hungry, cold, and could hardly drag their feet back to the camp.

In the spring and summer some women cut grass around the riverbed for hay for the cattle in the nearby kilhoz. In the wintertime, the women worked around the camp clearing snow from the campsite or sweeping snow off the sleigh tracks in the forest. Aunt Macia worked in the forest as a cook for the Russian laborers from another camp. In the morning, she prepared *keepiatok* (tea) for the workers before they started their work. The camp was several kilometers away and she had to get up at four o'clock in the morning and walk through the woods by herself to the area where the Russians worked to have tea ready by six o'clock. Half the time, she was scared out of her wits since the woods were dark and spooky with the sounds of different animals and the occasional howling of wolves. She said the only things that kept her going were prayers and the thought of her children back in the camp. She prepared meals for the workers during the day and returned to the barracks in the camp at night. My uncle worked as a logger in the forest with the other Polish workers from the camp. When the laborers returned to the camp at night, we all went to the mess hall to get our meal. The food consisted of soup, made mostly from fish heads, occasionally with some turnip, cabbage or potato in it, and a slice of dark bread. That was it. People who worked and achieved a prescribed amount of work were credited with full rations that they could purchase at the kitchen; those who did not achieve the norm were allotted reduced portions of food. The norm was usually established by the amount of work performed by healthy, strong men. Most of the work, however, was done by the weak and undernourished people. Also many were never adequately rested due to sleep interrupted by crawling bugs or by gnats and mosquitoes. Therefore, it was not possible to perform the work at high levels of exertion for any length of time and few people were able to receive maximum food rations. Anytime we complained to the commandant about the unrealistic norms his standard answer would be, "You will get used to it. If not, you will die."

All able-bodied people were required to work. It was difficult to obtain permission to stay in the barracks; one had to be seriously ill. The penalty for not reporting to work was up to four months in jail. One day, the commandant caught Aunt Macia staying away from work without permission. She was jailed for a few days as punishment. The commandant said he was very lenient because it was her first infraction. Of course, her food rations were immediately reduced for missing work. There was a saying in the gulags: "*Kto nie robotayet, ten nie kushayet,*" or loosely translated, "He who doesn't work, doesn't eat." Children and women who did not work in the forest but did chores around the camp also were given reduced food portions. A typical full portion was about 400 grams of heavy dark bread (about two to three slices) and a quart of soup.

Bread became the most precious possession for all of us in the camp. It acquired some mystical meaning. It was more than just food; it was a symbol that represented our longing to satisfy hunger. We always ate the bread over a piece of cloth as not to lose a single crumb; it was a treasure not to be shared with others.

Food rations were totally inadequate not only because of the low calorie content, but because of low nutritional content. Consequently, people became sick at epidemic levels with typhoid, dysentery, pneumonia or tuberculosis. Many developed ulcers all over their bodies and some started losing their hair and teeth. Lack of any kind of medication made death even more likely. One of those who became ill was Krysia, my six-year-old cousin, who stayed with us the night we were deported from Poland. Her stomach became very enlarged, apparently from typhoid, and she died a few days after becoming ill. Her last wish before she died was to have a potato for a meal. Unfortunately, it was not possible to make her wish come true. She was put in a simple pine box and buried in an area cemetery. Only her mother, father and sister were allowed to attend the burial rites.

The death rate was high not only in our camp but also in other similar camps throughout the Soviet Union. Another victim of the Soviet gulag was my grandfather, my mother's father. He died from starvation in a camp near Irbit. How ironic! He was the fellow who traveled to America three different times, where he made a good living, only to return to Poland to be deported to Siberia and die of starvation.

The lack of any training for the workers combined with their weak physical condition often resulted in a number of unfortunate accidents. A falling tree killed one young man, and we all watched in sadness as the men brought his body back to the camp that evening. There were other accidents less tragic but still resulting in injuries that prevented a person from working and earning full food rations.

The winters in our area were extremely harsh. Temperatures often reached 40 degrees below zero. Frostbite was very common. People could not dress warmly enough. Typical clothes were Russian *kufayka,* or quilted overcoats, quilted pants, shoes made from pressed felt called *valonki,* and *onuce* or layers of rags wrapped around the feet in place of socks. Another layer of rags was then wrapped over *valonki.* and soaked in water, which froze to form an additional layer of insulation.

Another problem people experienced in our camp was night blindness, what we called *kurza ślepota.* This blindness resulted from lack of vitamins. People afflicted with *kurza ślepota* lost their vision as soon as darkness descended. Since all work started and ended in the dark, they usually had to be accompanied by someone at all times. Occasionally, someone afflicted with night blindness got lost and had to be searched for by friends and relatives.

Young children were required to attend kindergarten or school. I started in the first grade, and my sister, who was four years old at the time, went to *dziet sad* or pre-school, a kind of day care. School was not just an educational institution but an indoctrination place as well. The Russian teacher told us that there was no God and only Stalin could make things better for us. He was our *batko*, or grandfather, and he loved us, and if we were good he would send us presents. We were told we should be grateful to him for all the good things that happened in our lives. We were told the communist system was the greatest political system in the world, where everybody was free and equal, and we were fortunate to live under such a system. All of this, according to our teachers, was achieved due to the great genius of Stalin, Lenin, Marx and Engels. We children, of course, did not understand what they were talking about. The teachers also encouraged us to report what our parents were saying at home. Young children could easily be swayed, especially when they were hungry and someone offered them an extra slice of bread. However, even a young child could see the difference between the life we had in Poland and the life we had in the camp. Given enough time, though the communists would have succeeded in warping the minds of these unsuspecting children as they had done to so many others in the Soviet Union and communist dominated Poland.

On school days we would get two buns of bread at school. My mother has told me that sometimes I ate only one bun and brought the other to share with her when she was sick. I had to do this discreetly, always afraid of being caught and punished. The point here is not what I have done or what I did not do, but how much we were afraid to do anything deemed unacceptable by the Soviets, even such a small and innocent infraction as sharing the bread with my mother. Fear terrorized us all, adults and children alike. During the two years of schooling, I learned to speak Russian fluently. In fact, I became so fluent, that my mother was concerned that I would forget my Polish.

Our parents tried to counteract this propaganda barrage by telling us stories about Poland. We were told about Poland's past glories, taught Polish history, poetry, songs and fairy tales, and reminded of all the things about Poland that we loved. In many instances, these tales were exaggerated, but to us children, Poland became a land of fairy tales, a land of milk and honey. National figures became our heroes and idols. Attempts were made to teach the children the Latin alphabet, Polish letters, verses and songs. Some parents were not able to teach their children because they themselves were uneducated; others were just too exhausted from hard work and relied on relatives or friends to do the teaching. My uncle Józek was a good teacher. We liked to gather around him at every opportunity and listen to him tell stories. To this day, I remember a little poem he taught us, "*Kto ty jesteś, Polak mały...*" ("Who are you, I am a little Polish boy..."). He hated communism with such a passion that when his daughter Anulka attached a red ribbon to her hair, he became extremely angry and impulsively ripped the ribbon along with some hair from the surprised girl.

The indoctrination of adults took a slightly different angle. All Poles were called rich capitalists who sucked the blood from the poor. We were told Poland did not exist anymore and we would never return home. Our commandant used to say, "You will see hair grow on the palm of your hand before you will ever see Poland again." We were told we must accept the new system and work hard because in the Soviet Union "He who doesn't work, doesn't eat." The Soviets tried to convince the Poles to accept Russian citizenship; we were entitled to the citizenship because we were born in what was now the Ukraine, one of the Soviet Republics. The Soviets claimed that those who accepted Russian citizenship would be able to travel someday to visit their relatives. On the other hand, those who did not would rot in the gulags. They also promised better conditions for those who became Russian citizens. When the persuasion did not work, the Soviets used threats and blackmail, such as reducing food rations or assigning harder work for those who refused to cooperate. For us Poles, to accept Russian citizenship amounted to an admission that we would never return to Poland. In our minds, it would also amount to an act of high treason.

Escape from Siberia was nearly impossible. The harsh climate, the NKVD guards, lack of transportation, and inability to stash away supplies all were factors working against anyone contemplating an escape. All residents in the Soviet Union were obligated to report any suspicious individuals or strangers to the authorities. No one was permitted to travel without proper documents. A few brave souls who tried to escape were caught, arrested and imprisoned. Most were sent to the most horrible labor camps in Kolyma, Kamchatka or Nova Zemlia from where return was unlikely.

There were few forms of opposition in the camps. Opposition usually consisted of a demonstration of religious beliefs or patriotism. There were many jokes directed at the Russians. For example, we purposely mispronounced the names of the Soviet leaders; thus Stalin became *Sralin* ("shithead" in Polish) and Voroshilov became *Vshilov* ("lice"). The jokes and mispronounced names provided us with some sense of defiance if nothing else. Some considered fudging the numbers on the output of their work as a form of defiance, but in all likelihood that was more an economic rather than political act. In any case, any form of opposition was extremely dangerous, and we always had to be on the lookout for the stooges who were eager to report these infractions to the commandant in exchange for a better work assignment or extra food ration.

We prayed a lot, mostly at night in the barracks, and our faith gave us hope that things would get better eventually. For example, we gathered in small groups in May for devotions to the Blessed Mary when we would say the rosary and sing songs devoted to Her. One night, the NKVD commandant walked into my uncle's room, unannounced, while we were praying. He demanded to know what we were doing. My uncle told him we were praying.

The commandant said that there was no God and we were wasting our time, but my uncle's response was, "My grandmother taught my mother how to pray; my mother taught me how to pray; and I will teach my children how to pray." The commandant left slamming the door without saying another word. My uncle was not trying to be a hero, but his faith, as the faith of all of us, was stronger than the fear of the consequences of disobeying the communists.

At Christmastime, we sang Christmas carols. The next day the commandant summoned my father and my uncle to his office and warned them that they would face jail if the practice continued. Christmas was a particularly difficult time for us. Our thoughts were about other Christmases, the ones in Poland. We missed not being able to attend the midnight mass and we missed other Christmas festivities. When we broke bread with each other on Christmas Eve, our wishes were for good health, to be able to survive, and maybe some day to return to Poland. Our faith and deep love for Poland were the main source of our strength. We dreamed that someday we would be able to go to church, receive sacraments and celebrate religious and national holidays in freedom. This faith and love of Poland became stronger as time went on and sustained us, not only in the Soviet Union, but also in the travels and difficulties we faced later.

One of the few Russians in our camp was a fellow named Shurmin, who was in charge of all workers logging the trees. He was the so-called *zakluchony,* or ex-convict (political). He was a kind fellow who often overlooked smaller infractions by the workers, took it easy on the people who were sick, or gave credit for additional work when the day's work was below the norm. Occasionally, some of the workers sawed off the ends of the logs in the piles that were already marked by Shurmin and moved them to new piles to be stamped and counted again. The piles were moved frequently so no one noticed the difference. Shurmin, in all likelihood, knew about the practice but chose not to say anything. He knew the score; he was in our shoes not that long before. Occasionally, someone met a Russian among the *zakluchonys* who spoke a few words of Polish. They turned out to be the descendants of Poles deported to Siberia in the late 19th century after the 1863 Polish uprisings were crushed and insurrectionists were deported to Siberia.

Another Russian in our camp was a fellow named Zhiranov, who was in charge of the store in the camp. He was in the camp with his wife and two sons. The boys were my age and we became friends and played together a lot. Zhiranov's wife gave me food on occasion, so there was an additional incentive for me to spend more time in their barrack.

The summers arrived late in Siberia. The ice melted in May and the days did not get warm until much later. The summer also created another problem for the population: swarms of mosquitoes and gnats appeared and they caused painful bites that were difficult to heal. However, life in the summer became a little easier. Not only was the weather warmer, but we also could go into the woods to pick berries and mushrooms to provide additional food. It also was possible to sell the berries to the store that collected them to be sent to factories for the production of juice and jam. One day, the Soviet authorities arrested Zhiranov, the Russian storekeeper, because berries were missing from the wooden barrel in which they were stored. The authorities accused Zhiranov of stealing the berries. The storekeeper claimed the barrel was leaking. My father who was called as a witness at the trial confirmed that, in fact, he saw the barrel was leaking. Zhiranov was released from jail, and my father gained a friend. Later, when we went to the Zhiranov barrack, his wife showed us holy icons that she kept locked in a trunk. It was their way to show us that they really trusted us.

As I mentioned before, my father's job was cleaning the stables, tending to the horses, taking the officials to Malinovka, and bringing supplies from town. This assignment turned out to be a blessing for our family. He often took clothing or other articles to town and traded them for food. My mother should be given a lot of credit for having the presence of mind to pack all these articles when we were leaving Poland. These articles were our means of survival throughout our stay in the Soviet Union. The trading, of course, was illegal and my father could be punished if he were caught. However, he was always careful to hide the articles under the carriage of the wagon or inside other items that he was transporting. He was never caught, and all in our family considered him smarter than the NKVD. Occasionally, he brought oats from the stables and we ground them and had oatmeal. Oh! What a treat that was! He also brought vodka for the officials who, in turn, did favors for my father. Our survival, in a great measure, was the result of my father's ingenuity and his ability to outmaneuver the Soviet system.

Stealing from the state in the Soviet Union was not looked upon as a crime by the deportees but as an acceptable way to help us survive. People differentiated between stealing from the State and stealing from individuals. Stealing from the state was easier to justify. When you had an opportunity to steal from the state, whether the object was food or other articles, you had to weigh the benefits and the consequences of the act and the probability of being caught. When the odds were in your favor, you committed the act. Moral and religious considerations were usually not a part of that decision. The penalties for stealing when caught were severe even for minor infractions, but in spite of the fear of punishment, stealing was commonly practiced. One day, the assistant commandant of our camp approached my father with a proposition. He pointed out that there was a new shipment of cattle being delivered to a kilhoz a few kilometers from our camp. He suggested my father steal a cow from that shipment, slaughter the cow, and share the meat with him. He, of course, would wash his hands of the whole affair. My father would be on his own, but there would be no repercussions from the camp authorities. And so, with the help of Uncle Józek, my father expertly executed the plan at night. Our families were able to have meat for the next few weeks.

Sometimes, my mother and Uncle Józek would venture by foot to a distant kilhoz where it was possible to trade clothing or other articles for potatoes and vegetables. One had to obtain permission from the commandant to leave the camp, so these excursions were not very frequent. One time during winter, they did not return for two days and we thought we would never see them again, that they froze to death somewhere in the woods. In reality, they were lost and almost did freeze. Fortunately, they stumbled across a cabin in the woods and the Russian family that lived there took them in, gave them food, and let them stay overnight. They returned with potatoes that, although frozen, made wonderful potato pancakes and potato soup.

As I mentioned before, our survival depended in great measure on my father's ingenuity, guts and some measure of luck. Others in our camp were less fortunate. The malnutrition, severe weather, and hard work took their toll. The death rate was high, and hardly a month went by without someone dying. One of the residents of our camp was a fellow named Kisilewicz. He was the father of a large family and he constantly talked about how he wished his children would die quickly. He could not bear watching them suffer any longer. His children had pellagra, a disease caused by a deficiency of vitamins. Pellagra causes bleeding of the gums, followed by rotting of the teeth until they eventually fall out completely. Ulcers appear on the body, and small chunks of flesh begin to fall off until the body begins to smell like a corpse. The legs usually get bloated and are so weak that it is impossible to walk. On top of that, diarrhea usually sets in. The swelling progresses from the feet and legs to the upper body, compressing the circulation and putting pressure on the heart and lungs. The body gets weaker by the day and eventually shuts down. This man watched his children die one at a time. His prayers for a quick death for his children were very understandable.

There did not seem to be an end in sight to our hardship. Even though we maintained our faith and hoped that some day we would be free again, it did not look like we could survive to see that day. We were able to endure the hardships because we firmly believed God had not abandoned us, and we would be able to get out of that *Nieludzka Ziemia*. Our only dreams were that someday we would return to Poland and someday have enough food to satisfy our hunger.

We tried to get some news about what was happening in Europe, but the information was sketchy and its accuracy questionable. Newspapers were more suitable as paper for rolling tobacco into cigarettes than getting the news. The Russians were telling us that the great alliance between Hitler and Stalin was conquering Europe, and Poland did not exist any longer. They continued to urge us to change our citizenship to Russian, claiming it was a privilege to be a citizen of the Soviet Union. We continued to resist them, believing that someday we would be able to return to Poland.

The news of the German invasion of the Soviet Union on June 22, 1941, arrived in our camp a few days late, but it spread through the camp like a wildfire. We did not know how this would affect us but we knew things couldn't get any worse. Sure enough, on July 30, 1941, the Polish Prime Minister, General Sikorski, and the Russian ambassador to England, I. M. Majski, signed the Polish–Russian pact in London. The pact established diplomatic relations between Poland and the Soviet Union. The pact also declared the agreements between the Soviet Union and Germany signed in 1939 null and void. It did not address the issue of the future borders between Poland and the Soviet Union or the status of the eastern part of Poland absorbed by the Soviet Union in 1939. To us, this was an important issue since it would decide whether our homeland and, consequently, our citizenship would be Polish or Russian.

The Sikorski–Majski agreement stipulated that the Soviet Union would grant amnesty to all Polish citizens on Russian soil, be they deportees, prisoners of war or political prisoners. The agreement also stipulated the establishment of the Polish army on the territory of the Soviet Union. This army was to be formed from the Polish prisoners of war and volunteers from the deportees. On August 12, 1941, M. Kalinin, Chairman of the Soviet Presidium, signed a decree officially granting amnesty to the Polish people in the Soviet Union.

The news of the Russian–German war, the Sikorski–Majski agreement and the amnesty filtered to the Polish settlements slowly due to poor communication, lack of knowledge of the exact location of the camps and in many cases, by design from the Soviet authorities. However, once the news reached the camps, it raised hopes and created a lot of excitement, even euphoria, among the prisoners and deportees.

A few months after we heard the news about the amnesty, my uncle Romek came to our camp. He had been a prisoner of war after being imprisoned in Rowne, Poland, during the September campaign. When the Germans advanced on Russia in 1941, the Russians moved Polish prisoners deeper into Russia. There was no transport available and the prisoners were forced to march hundreds of kilometers on foot. Those who could not keep up the pace were shot and their bodies left behind. Fortunately, my uncle kept up with the march and wound up in a prison in Western Siberia. He was released after the amnesty and came to our camp to tell us about the army being formed in the Kazakhstan and Uzbekistan regions of Russia. He told us to stay put and that he would return with more information and necessary travel documents. Several men from our camp did not want to wait and left the camp secretly with Uncle Romek to join the army, among them Uncle Józek. We never saw him again. He died from typhoid and dysentery in a Polish army camp in Guzar, Uzbekistan. He was buried there among the thousands of other soldiers and deportees who met similar fate.

Another visitor to our camp after the amnesty was a Polish Catholic priest. It was a joyous moment for us. We were able to go to confession, to attend mass and thank God for the recent developments. It was the first time in over two years we were allowed to worship God openly. The priests who were deported to Siberia and released after the amnesty visited various gulags to attend to the religious needs of the population, as well as to provide moral support and inform the Polish population about the status of the new army.

Several weeks later, Uncle Romek returned to the camp and told us that we could leave with him as soon as we received official permission from the local NKVD commandant. My father knew the commandant well. He had taken him to town on many occasions and even brought him vodka a few times. My father asked the commandant for release papers, the so-called *roschot*, but the commandant refused, stating that he was not authorized to release any deportees. But, he said he would be able to help for the right price. He wanted to give his wife a gift, and he liked a coat my mother brought from Poland. We gave him the coat and he told us, "Go and even the devil will not be able to catch you." We did not, however, receive the *roschot*, the official release papers.

Our family, along with my aunt Macia, her daughter, Anulka, and Uncle Romek left the camp the next morning when it was still dark. The Russian who worked with my father in the stables let us take a horse and wagon to the rail station in town. I knew we were leaving that morning, so I decided to walk to town with a group of men who were going to work there. I did not tell my parents I was going with these men. It was about 10 kilometers to town and the men walked briskly. I tried to keep up with the men, but it was a difficult task. When we reached town, I had severe cramps in my muscles and could barely walk. In the meantime my parents were frantically looking for me at the camp. Finally, someone told them that they saw me walking with a group of men toward town. Needless to say, my reunion with my parents was not a very pleasant one, for me anyway.

We boarded the train from Malinovka to Berezovsk; Uncle Romek already had the train tickets, which were very difficult to get because the trains were overcrowded with travelers who were trying to move away from the war zone. We had to change trains in Berezovsk, a small town near the city of Sverdlovsk. The train was not due until the following day and we stayed overnight in the house of a Russian widow. The next day at the train station before we departed, Aunt Macia realized she had forgotten a package at the widow's house. She went back to the house where we stayed but found it empty and locked. A neighbor told her that the NKVD had arrested the woman for housing the labor camp escapees. Apparently, someone had already reported our departure to the NKVD. To the best of my knowledge, our family was the only family who left our camp.

The train we boarded in Berezovsk was a passenger train. It was extremely crowded with Russian army personnel, Russian civilians and other Polish deportees from different camps. Russians seemed to be on the move at the time because of the war. Everyone was trying to avoid German bombings. The journey to Uzbekistan took several days. Sverdlovsk was the first major city where we stopped. Again the station was very crowded. We saw a number of Polish refugees at the station and we were shocked by their appearance. They were dressed in tattered clothes. Some were without shoes, with their feet wrapped only in rags. Most looked like walking skeletons. Also, for the first time, we saw Polish army personnel. The Polish authorities set up informational centers, the so-called *delegatura*, throughout the Soviet Union to assist prisoners in getting to army recruiting posts. The army personnel we saw in Sverdlovsk were part of these centers. From Sverdlovsk we went to Chelyabinsk, then to Orenburg and to Tashkent. As we moved farther south, it became extremely hot, with temperatures reaching over 100 degrees during the day. The nights brought some relief from the heat, but the train was too crowded and noisy to have any chance to get some sleep. The train moved very slowly and stopped frequently, often in deserted areas. One never knew how long the train would remain at the stop and if it was safe to venture away from the train to buy some food or water. On one occasion, my mother left the train to get some water. No sooner was she a few yards away than the train started to move again. It took a great effort on her part to catch up with the departing the train. Fortunately, Uncle Romek was waiting for her at the steps of the rail car and was able to pull her back on. In some respects, this part of the journey was not much better than the journey during the deportation to the Soviet Union. We were all exhausted, weak and hungry. Fortunately, my uncle brought some money with him and we still had a few belongings to trade, so we were able to purchase some food from the Russian peasants who seemed to appear from nowhere whenever the train stopped.

Our next stop was Tashkent where we changed trains. The station again was extremely crowded. There was a constant bustle of people with large groups sitting on their belongings and waiting for trains. It was a very unsafe environment. Thieves were everywhere and many people were robbed. The thieves were mostly young boys, the so-called *urchins* who were known throughout Russia in the days of Stalin's terror and during the war. These urchins were orphaned juveniles, whose parents were either imprisoned and sent to gulags or killed in the war. The Soviet government put these young children in orphanages where they usually got in trouble. In order to avoid punishment they escaped. These urchins roamed the streets of the cities terrorizing citizens. Many were arrested and put back in the camps only to escape again. Their illicit activities included stealing, threatening people, and occasionally, murder. Our family stayed close together, trying to wait for our train in safety. The train was scheduled to leave the next day. Unfortunately, train schedules were meaningless, and trains arrived and departed without any regularity and without prior notice. The night spent on the platform at the train station seemed like a lifetime and we were very glad to see daylight. We were finally able to leave Tashkent around noon that day.

Our final destination on this leg of our journey was the city of Jakkobag, in the Uzbek Socialist Republic near the border of Afghanistan. The Polish army was being formed in several nearby cities of Dzhal-Abad, Guzar, and Yangi-Yul as well as Jakkobag, with the headquarters in Yangi-Yul. My father joined the Polish army in July 1942, and he was assigned to the 6th Lwów Infantry Division, stationed in Jakkobag, the same unit as Uncle Romek.

Upon arrival in Jakkobag, we rented an Uzbek's hut, rather a portion of an Uzbek's hut, since we had to share the hut with his family. We stayed in Uzbekistan for a few weeks. During that time, Aunt Macia spent days searching for Uncle Józek, but to no avail. No one had seen him or heard from him. Later, in Iran, she ran across a fellow from our village in Poland, who said he had visited my uncle in the hospital in Guzar. When he went back to the hospital the next day, someone else occupied Uncle Józek's bed. He assumed my uncle had died that night.

Uzbekistan was extremely hot in the summertime; the only relief was to be found in the shade. That was a problem, since there were no trees in the area and the only shaded area was inside the crowded, uncomfortable hut. The hut was made of thin strips of wood covered inside and outside with mud mixed with straw. Here, as in Siberia, lice were a big problem. In addition, there were hordes of flies during the day and mosquitoes at night. We slept on straw placed on the ground. Once a day, my cousin Anulka and I went to the army camp to get food, which the soldiers shared with us. The Russians provided rations only for army personnel, not for civilians. The meals given to us by the army were meager. They usually consisted of a small piece of bread, some soup, and occasionally some meat, potato or a vegetable. At least we knew where our next meal was coming from. When we brought the food to our hut, the food was already cold. There was no kitchen, not even a stove in the Uzbek's hut. However, we were able to heat the food outside on an open fire. There was no wood available for burning, so we used dried animal droppings for fuel. These droppings were collected in the fields, dried in the sun, and stacked by the hut for future use. The droppings were also a precious commodity since there weren't many animals in the area either.

The problems and difficulties we experienced in the southern republics of the Soviet Union were very different and, in many cases, more severe than the problems we faced in Siberia. We were subjected to extreme heat, lack of adequate food, poor sanitary facilities, and diseases of epidemic proportions. An enormous number of people, well over 70,000, were in a relatively small area, and the authorities were totally unprepared to handle such a large influx of people. New arrivals came daily, joining other recruits and their families. Many of them were children who had lost their parents. Many were in very poor physical condition from over two years in the labor camps and from undertaking the long journey to reach the army. Some people journeyed from forced labor camps as far away as northern Siberia, Kolyma, Krasnoyarsk, Novosibirsk and Workuta. Many recruits came from various prisoner of war camps, Uncle Romek among them. Still others came from the political prisons, places like the infamous Lubianka, where General Władysław Anders, the commanding general of the Polish armed forces in Russia, had been imprisoned.

Many did not make it to the newly forming army. For that matter, many did not even survive the Soviet gulags, prisons, gold mines, kilhozes, and other forced labor camps. It is estimated that about two-thirds of the 1.6 million people deported from Poland to the Soviet Union remained in Russia and about one-third of those deported either died or were executed between 1940 and 1942.

The most notorious of the NKVD's crimes was the Katyn Massacre. In the Katyn forest near Smolensk, in Kharkov, Ukraine, and in Mednoye, northwest of Moscow, the NKVD murdered 21,000 Polish prisoners from the three prisoner of war camps of Kozielsk, Starobelsk and Ostashkow. The prisoners were shot in the back of the head and buried in mass graves. The murdered prisoners were the cream of the crop of the Polish intelligentsia: Army officers, lawyers, doctors and university professors. In the eyes of the Soviets they were too dangerous to the communist system to be allowed to survive. Initially, the Soviets denied responsibility for these crimes, blaming the Germans for the atrocities. However, documents released in 1992 by the KGB and delivered by Boris Yeltsin to then Polish president Lech Wałęsa, clearly showed that L. Beria, then chief of the NKVD, recommended these prisoners be executed. The NKVD stated that these prisoners proved beyond any doubt that they could not be converted to the communist ideology and posed a threat to the Soviet Union. Stalin personally initialed the execution decree.

It is estimated that an additional 10,000 Polish prisoners died in slave labor in the Kolyma mines, giving credence to the notion among the native Russians that a return from Kolyma was not possible. Less than 600 Polish prisoners reported to the newly-formed Polish army from Kolyma. The stories told by them about the conditions in the areas where they were imprisoned painted horrifying pictures that Polish citizens were subjected to in the Soviet Union.

The conditions in Jakkobag and other camps that sprang up around Polish army camps began to deteriorate as time went on. The Russians began to reduce the amount of food allotted to the Polish army and, as a result, the army had less food to share with civilians. The population that experienced malnutrition over such a long period of time now became prey to such diseases as typhoid, dysentery, malaria and other tropical diseases. The biggest problem was the lack of potable water. Contaminated water was the main cause of disease, especially dysentery. There were no adequate facilities to treat the water to make it suitable for human consumption. In addition, there was no easy way to boil water. Lack of medicine added to the difficulties. Heat seemed to accelerate the spread of these diseases. Polish authorities tried their best to help the situation, but a lack of medical supplies and hospital facilities made it a losing battle. People were dying at a very alarming rate. New cemeteries sprang up around the Polish settlements. There was hardly a family untouched by death either in the labor camps or at the recruiting centers. It is estimated that about 10 percent of all the people who arrived at the army camps in Uzbekistan died there in less than a year's time.

The result of the high death rate among reporting refugees was that many children became orphans without anyone looking after them. There were over 300 such orphans in our area alone, over 3,000 around the army enlistment posts, plus an additional 50,000 scattered all over the Soviet Union. The Polish Government-in-Exile and General Anders made these children a high priority for receiving assistance. Anders created a special cadet corps of both teenage girls and boys, the so-called *Junaki* and *Junaczki*, and made them part of the army contingent. These boys and girls were attached to the army when it was being evacuated to Iran, and they followed the army to Iraq and Palestine. Another group of orphans was evacuated from Russia with the relief group from India that delivered food, clothing and medicine to orphanages in Russia. The Polish ambassador to India, who organized this relief, received permission from the Indian government to bring about 600 Polish orphans to Balachadi near Jamnagar in northwest

India. The Indian government offered them hospitality for the duration of the war. The trucks returning from Russia after dropping off relief supplies were able to bring these orphans first to Meshed in Iran and later to Balachadi in India. Other orphaned children were sent to orphanages in Esfahan in Iran, to Santa Rosa in Mexico, to Pahiatan in New Zealand, and to South Africa, Northern Rhodesia (Zambia) and Tanganyika (Tanzania) on the African continent.

We stayed in Uzbekistan for a few weeks, and in August of 1942, we were told that the army and the families were being evacuated to Persia (Iran). This was welcome news to us, since there was a possibility the Soviets would keep the Polish army in the Soviet Union and use it on the Russian–German front. It would have been a sure death sentence for the soldiers. General Sikorski, who wanted the Poles rather than the Russians to liberate Poland, favored such an approach. However, both General Anders, who distrusted the Soviets, and the British, who wanted the Polish army in the Near East to defend the oil fields there, opposed the plan. Finally, General Anders convinced General Sikorski that the Soviets could not be trusted and the Polish army should be evacuated from the Soviet Union as soon as possible. The Soviets were not sure they could trust the Polish army either after all to which they had subjected the Polish citizens. When food shortages worsened as a result of German advances deeper into Russia, the Soviets agreed to the evacuation of the Polish troops to Iran.

Another area of disagreement between the Soviets and General Anders was the definition of who was considered Polish and who was not. To Soviets, only the ethnic Poles were allowed to join the army and leave the Soviet Union. Anders wanted this group to include all Polish citizens regardless of race or religion. This would include Jews and Orthodox Christians. Anders prevailed and all Polish citizens who joined the army, and their families, were allowed to leave. One noteworthy individual who benefited from Anders' victory was Menachem Begin, the future Prime Minister of Israel. Begin joined the Polish army but later deserted, along with several hundred Jewish nationals, when the army reached Palestine. The British, who had the administrative jurisdiction over Palestine at that time, were not too thrilled with these departures. However, the Polish army authorities did not pursue or try to recapture these "deserters," sympathizing with their desire to remain in Palestine. My father told me they even had a farewell party for a few of their Jewish friends before they left the camp. In fairness, it must be said not all Polish Jews left the army in Palestine. Many remained and fought gallantly on many fronts. The Star of David marks many graves at Polish military cemeteries giving proof that many Polish Jews fought and died for Poland.

The orders finally arrived for us to get ready to leave Jakkobag. We gathered our few possessions and walked several kilometers to the area where we boarded a train bound for the port city of Krasnovodsk in Turkmenistan on the Caspian Sea. This time, we were without Father, who had traveled earlier with the army. It was only my mother, my sister and I, and my aunt Macia with her daughter, Anulka. The train was very crowded with army personnel and civilians. People were sitting on benches, on the floor, and on their belongings. During the day it was unbearably hot. The roof of the railcar became like a solar panel absorbing the heat from the sun. There was no ventilation. People standing in front of the windows blocked any fresh air from coming into the compartment. On top of that, we had very little water or food, and there were no working bathrooms on the train. On the way to the port, we were told that no ships were available to transport us to Iran. We were unloaded several kilometers from the city and were left outdoors for two days. Finally, the ships arrived and, again, we boarded the train and resumed our journey to Krasnovodsk. We reached the port the next afternoon. We were to walk from the rail station to the port, which was some distance away. My mother and Aunt Macia decided to leave us children at the station square and take our belongings to the port, then return to pick us up. There were a lot of people at the station square, so they felt it was safe to leave us there. The night arrived quickly. Most of the people left, and there we were—three children, ages eleven, nine and four, all alone on the square, not knowing what had happened to our mothers. It was dark, and we were scared, crying our eyes out, not knowing what was going to happen to us. We were overjoyed when our mothers finally arrived.

For the next two days, we stayed on the beach in the open air waiting for our ship. Normally, a beach would mean white sand, sun, and swimming in the sea. Let me assure you, this was no ordinary beach. The heat was unbearable with no shelter available except for a blanket suspended on a few sticks. There were no bathroom facilities and there was a terrible stench coming from the filthy water. The Caspian Sea was one huge cesspool, fed by oil discharged from a nearby refinery and ships emptying their bilge water and human waste. No one dared to swim in the water and, besides, there was nowhere to wash off the salt and filth even if one did venture to take the swim. The shortage of fresh water was very acute, exasperated by the extreme heat. The beach was overcrowded with thousands of people and it was very difficult to move around.

While we were waiting for the ship, my sister, Alina, became very ill. The army doctor who came to see her told us she had a high fever and should be hospitalized. However, he advised we should do everything in our power to keep her with us. The Soviets would not allow anyone sick to leave the Soviet Union. He said that if we put her in the hospital it was unlikely we would ever see her again. The doctor did not have any medicine to give Alina. Alina was only four years old but somehow, she understood the situation. She bravely walked under her own power to board the ship and did not attract attention to the fact that she was ill.

We left Krasnovodsk on August 13, 1942, leaving that horrible phase of our lives behind us. Before we boarded the ship, the NKVD ordered everyone to surrender all Russian currency. The penalty for being caught carrying any rubles was detention in the Soviet Union. The NKVD provided big boxes into which we dropped the money. I wonder whose pockets that money ended up in and if it were the NKVD's last effort of reprisal against the Poles. We found out in Iran that we could have exchanged the rubles for Iranian currency in Iran.

The journey across the Caspian Sea took two days. It was a very traumatic trip. We were overjoyed to finally be able to leave the ungodly conditions we experienced in the Soviet Union. This, however, was our first sea voyage and we were very apprehensive about it. The ship was a Russian freighter. There was no food, no drinking water and no sanitary facilities on the ship. People made makeshift areas for toilets by blanketing sections of the deck for that purpose. Many people were sick with dysentery and the lines were very long to get to the cordoned off areas. Many had to go right back to the end of the line as soon as they relieved themselves. There were a few people who died during the crossing. They were wrapped in blankets and tossed overboard.

There were about 5,000 soldiers and civilians on the freighter crammed everywhere. The ship could not possibly hold any more people, though there were many people left on the beach hoping to get on board. We were very fortunate to be able to board the ship since it was to be one of the last ships permitted to leave the Soviet Union. Almost every person on our ship was sick. My sister had a high fever and needed water since she was badly dehydrated. We went around the ship begging people for a few drops of water. Finally, some soldiers took pity on us and gave us some water from their canteens. My mother moistened a piece of cloth with water and applied the moistened cloth to Alina's face to keep down the fever. After seeing corpses tossed overboard, we prayed not so much for my sister's recovery but that she would die on land so we could bury her rather than toss her into the sea.

We arrived in Pahlavi, today's Rasht, the Iranian port city on the Caspian Sea. The seas were rough and the ship could not dock at the port, so we had to be transferred to a smaller ship and brought to shore. A plank was laid down between the two ships and we were asked to walk across it. Walking a narrow plank in rough seas was no easy feat, especially for a young child. It was a traumatic and scary experience. We reached the shore on the small ship and were transported to a camp that was set up on the beach. The small ship made several trips to the freighter to pick up passengers, civilians first, but had to stop transporting people when it became dark. Many people, mostly soldiers, my father among them, remained on the ship until the next day. We were concerned with the ship's safety because the seas appeared to become even rougher as the night approached. At dawn, we were relieved to see the freighter still afloat and anchored. The transfer of the balance of passengers was completed that day.

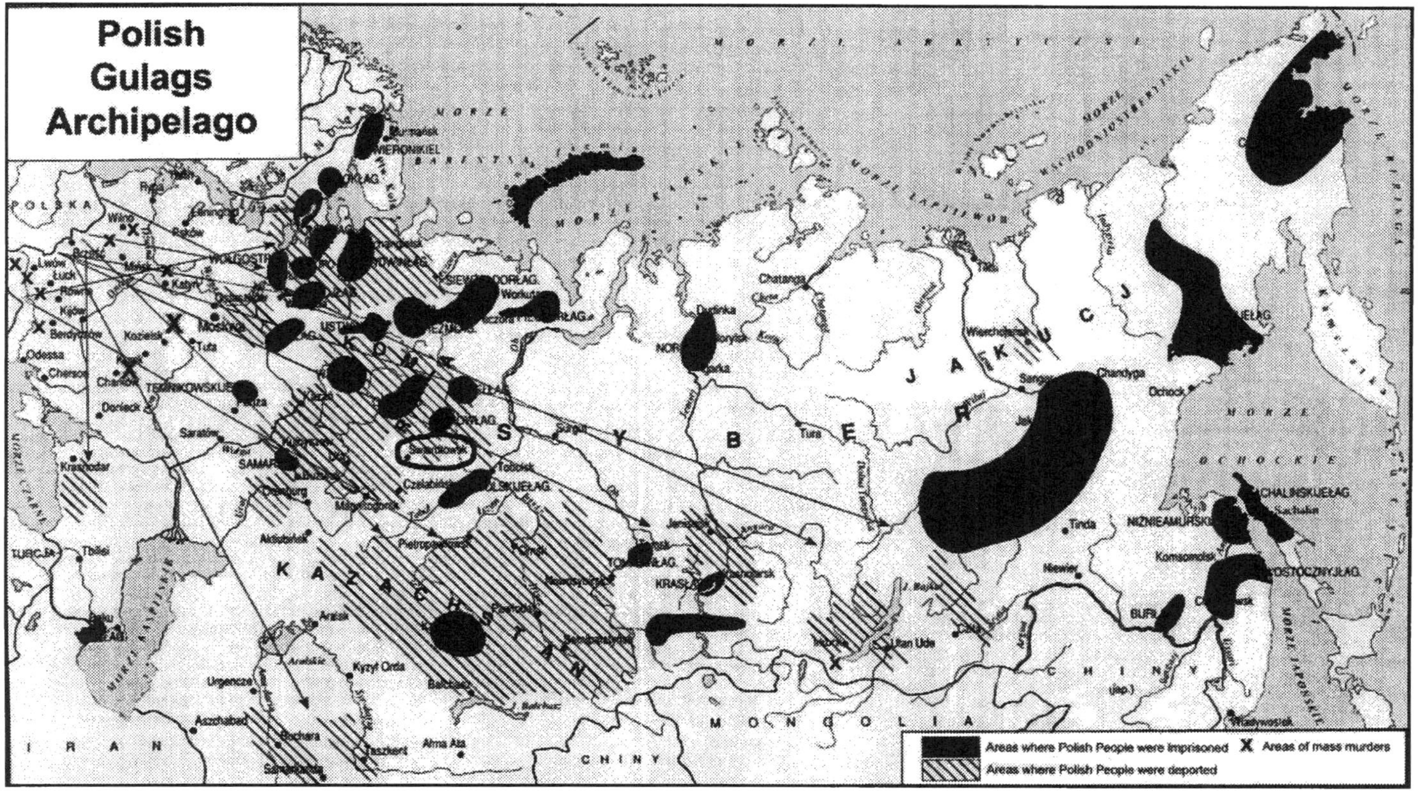

Polish Gulags Archipelago in the Soviet Union. Our camp was NE of Svierdlvsk (circled). (Ref. 5, Losy Sybraków)

Polish deportees from Podole at work in Siberian Forest, 1941. (Ref. 1, Kronikarskie Zapisy)

Typical Siberian work detail (brigade) in Soviet gulag. A group of Polish deportees from Wołyn, Poland, 1941. (Ref. 8, Z Kresów)

Typical *Vshoboyka*, or steam room, in Siberia.
(Ref. 17, Piłsudski Inst.)

Hut in Uzbekistan, Soviet Union, 1941. (Ref. 16, PAVA)

General Sikorski and Russian Ambassador Majski sign Polish-Russian Agreement granting amnesty to Poles.
Churchill and Eden witness the ceremony, July 30, 1941.
(Ref. 16, PAVA)

Polish recruits on the way to the newly formed army, 1941.
(Ref. 10, Szmagier)

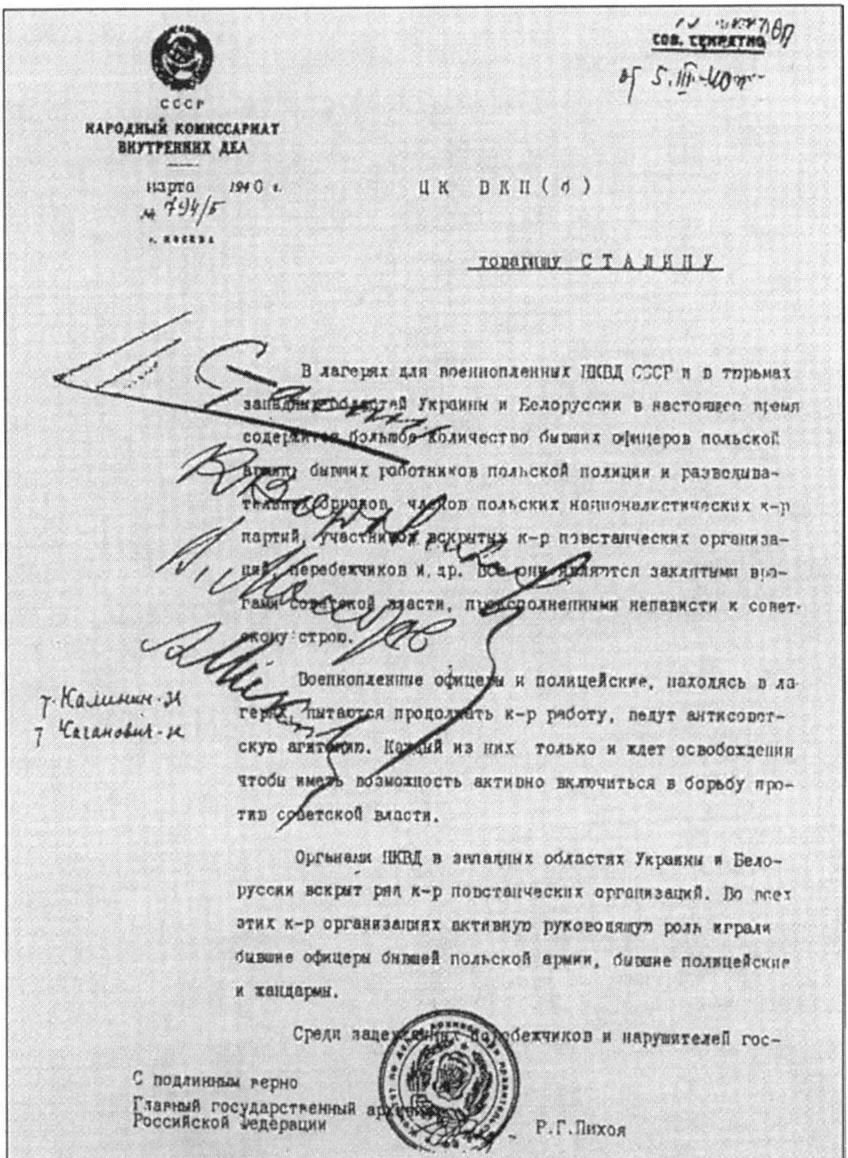

СССР
НАРОДНЫЙ КОМИССАРИАТ
ВНУТРЕННИХ ДЕЛ

марта 1940 г.
№ 794/Б
г. Москва

СОВ. СЕКРЕТНО

ЦК ВКП(б)

товарищу СТАЛИНУ

В лагерях для военнопленных НКВД СССР и в тюрьмах западных областей Украины и Белоруссии в настоящее время содержится большое количество бывших офицеров польской армии, бывших работников польской полиции и разведывательных органов, членов польских националистических к-р партий, участников вскрытых к-р повстанческих организаций, перебежчиков и др. Все они являются заклятыми врагами советской власти, преисполненными ненависти к советскому строю.

Военнопленные офицеры и полицейские, находясь в лагерях, пытаются продолжать к-р работу, ведут антисоветскую агитацию. Каждый из них только и ждет освобождения, чтобы иметь возможность активно включиться в борьбу против советской власти.

Органами НКВД в западных областях Украины и Белоруссии вскрыт ряд к-р повстанческих организаций. Во всех этих к-р организациях активную руководящую роль играли бывшие офицеры бывшей польской армии, бывшие полицейские и жандармы.

Среди задержанных перебежчиков и нарушителей гос-

С подлинным верно
Главный государственный архивист
Российской Федерации
Р.Г.Пихоя

First page of a memorandum from NKVD chief V. Beria to Stalin recommending Polish officers be executed. Stalin and other Soviet Politburo members initial their OK.

Polish deportees on the way to army camps after the amnesty. (Ref. 16, PAVA)

Polish children after amnesty, 1942. (Ref. 19, Exiled Children)

Children at the army camps after amnesty, 1942.
(Ref. 17, Piłsudski Inst.)

Children at the orphanage after amnesty, 1942.
(Ref. 16, PAVA)

Evacuation of Polish refugees from the Soviet Union, August 1942. Those on the ship were the fortunate ones who escaped to Iran. The rest were left behind. (Ref. 10, Szmagier)

Ship with Polish refugees arriving in Pahlavi, Iran, August 1942. (Ref. 16, PAVA)

IRAN (PERSIA)

In all, about 116,000 people, 75,000 soldiers and 41,000 civilians including 18,000 children, were evacuated from the Soviet Union in two separate evacuations. The first evacuation took place in March of 1942. About 44,000 people, mostly soldiers, were evacuated at that time. The second evacuation took place in August and September 1942 and involved 72,000 people. The logistics of moving, housing, setting up sanitary facilities, and feeding that many people were enormous. The Polish authorities had help from the British and Iranian governments. However the Russians who occupied the northern part of Iran at that time were not making things any easier for the Poles. They were still a stark reminder of the things that we left behind.

The Polish authorities with the help of the British and the Iranians, set up temporary camps on the beach of Pahlavi. There were two camps for the civilians and three for army personnel. The first, the so-called dirty camp, was set up as a cleansing area. All arriving refugees had to pass through the cleansing area first. The cleansing process started with our hair being shaved. We were then required to discard all clothing and take a shower. For many refugees, it was the first time in a long while that they were able to wash themselves with soap. Our old clothes had to be burned because they were infested with lice and bugs. We were given clean clothes provided by the Polish authorities. It was a true day of cleansing. We felt like we finally had left the *Nieludzka Ziemia* behind us. It was a great relief and joy for all of us.

Pahlavi was designated as a quarantine for all incoming Poles from the Soviet Union. After going through the cleansing area, most people were required to stay in Pahlavi at least two to three weeks, to make certain they did not bring any contagious diseases with them.

After going through the cleansing area we were moved to the civilian clean camp. The only shelter in the clean camp was a tarp over our heads. Sticks planted in the sand on the beach held up the tarp. It was the rainy season, and heavy rains accompanied by howling winds greeted us the first few days. The tarp cover was inadequate to keep the rain out, so we lay on the ground covered with army issued rubber coats trying to keep dry. There were about 3,000 people who did not have any cover at all. There were not enough sheds, tents or even tarps for all the people during the peak arrival dates, when three or even four ships from the Soviet Union arrived in Pahlavi on the same day. The authorities were not prepared for such a large influx of people in such a short time.

Unlike Krasnovodsk, the water in the Caspian Sea in Pahlavi was clean, especially when the tide was coming in. On sunny days, we could swim in the sea. Also, my sister miraculously got better when we reached Pahlavi. It must have been the result of all the prayers offered on her behalf by so many people.

Our camp was visited by a number of Polish and British dignitaries to assess the situation and the condition of the evacuees. One of the visitors was Bishop Józef Gawlina, the spiritual leader of Poles in exile. Another was General Władysław Anders, the Commander of the newly formed Polish Armed Forces. To us, General Anders was the liberator, our Moses, who led us from the *Nieludzka Ziemia* to Iran across the Caspian Sea. A large crowd, many of them orphaned children, met him on the shores of the Caspian Sea. How poetic, this hero, our Moses, meeting his liberated people at the shores of the sea. The only thing missing was the parting of the sea, the rest of the Poles in the Soviet Union crossing over, and the subsequent drowning of the pursuing Russians.

The army provided food and clothing for the civilians. The change in diet was too drastic for the malnourished masses. The meals often included soups rich in fats and meats, mainly lamb. Most people's systems were not accustomed to such a rich diet. One had to be very disciplined not to gorge on the available food, but to slowly rebalance the digestive system. Also, the industrious Iranians set up stands just outside the camp, selling meat, baked goods, eggs and fresh fruit, thus providing additional temptations for the starved population. Here, as in the Soviet Union, there were many incidences of typhoid and dysentery and the death rate was astronomically high, at least during the early days of our stay in Pahlavi. It is estimated that over 500 people died in those first few days. A big difference between the camps in Pahlavi and the camps in the Soviet Union was that, in Pahlavi we had access to medical facilities, hospitals, doctors and medicine.

I became one of the victims of dysentery. The biggest problem for me was reaching the latrines in time. They were located on the outskirts of the camp some distance away. One night, I went to the latrines but got lost on the way back. I was very weak and had no strength to search for our place for very long, so I just lay down next to some family and fell asleep. The next morning, my mother began frantically looking for me. She spotted me sound asleep some distance away. She took me to the doctor who immediately put me in the field hospital. The next morning, the hospital was evacuated to Tehran. When my mother visited the hospital the following day, she was told that all patients had been transferred to Tehran. She was shocked; to her, Tehran could have been at the other end of the world. She had no idea what she was going to do next to find me, her nine-year-old son.

Our journey to Tehran was an odyssey in itself. We were put on an old bus with an Iranian driver who must have been drunk based on the way he drove. All children on that bus were sick with dysentery. We stopped many times as we traveled through the Elburz Mountains to Tehran. The road was carved into the edge of the mountains, a single narrow lane without any barriers on the edges. Smashed vehicles of all types rested in the ravines. Below us, we could see streams flowing rapidly down mountains and emptying into meadows that looked like pastures and farmlands. It was all very beautiful, but not for us children who were sick, scared and exhausted. We reached the beautiful city of Qazvin by nightfall, the same city that was devastated by a major earthquake some 30 years later. We stayed overnight in a large government building allocated for our use by the Iranian government. We slept on blankets laid on a tiled floor. The chill seemed to permeate from the floor, making sleeping very uncomfortable. That did not matter though. Because we were sick and exhausted from the day's trip, any rest and easy access to toilet facilities was a welcome relief. We arrived at a hospital just outside Tehran the next day.

The hospital was organized specifically for the Polish evacuees from the Soviet Union. It was a large field hospital consisting of a number of huge tents. My tent housed the patients with intestinal problems. I was prescribed a strict diet. As time went on, I was not getting any better and I felt incredibly hungry all the time. After several days, I couldn't take it any longer. I didn't care if I died as long as I got plenty to eat first. My hospital neighbor felt the same way. We decided to take some action. We wandered into the kitchen area late in the evening, stole some potatoes and baked them in the coals still hot after the evening meal preparation. After eating the potatoes, we felt severe cramps in our stomachs, but it didn't matter because we weren't hungry anymore and our stomachs were full. After a few similar excursions to the kitchen, we started to feel better and stronger. Apparently, our malnutrition was more severe than the dysentery. Once we started getting better, we were given more substantial food and were well on our way to recovery.

The hospital had about 800 beds, but at times there were over 1,000 patients in the hospital so temporary accommodations had to be provided. The entire population was in poor physical condition, and resistance to diseases was almost nonexistent. Many suffered from malnutrition and lack of vitamins demonstrated by loss of hair, missing teeth, bleeding gums, and ulcers all over their bodies. Most people had some degree of dysentery, and some had typhoid and malaria. Initially, the death rate of the new arrivals to Iran was alarmingly high. Documents from that time indicate that about 2,100, or about six percent of the total Polish population in Iran, died in the first two years after their arrival (1942–1943). As time passed, people became healthier, stronger, and started to build some resistance to diseases. By 1944, the number of beds in the field hospital was reduced to about 200. These statistics show the enormous health problems that existed at the time of our arrival in Iran.

I stayed in the hospital for about a month. When I was being discharged, the hospital officials asked me where I wanted to go. I was nine years old and I had not heard from my mother during the month I was in the hospital. I didn't have any knowledge of where she was and I had absolutely no idea where to go. There were four camps around Tehran, housing Polish refugees. I chose to go to camp No. 5 where there was an orphanage. There were about 360 orphans in the camp. The orphans were children whose parents both had died in the Soviet Union during the formative days of the Polish army or in Iran, or whose mothers died and whose fathers had joined the army. This camp was one of three orphanages on Iranian territory. The other orphanages were in camp No. 4 in Esfahan, several hundred kilometers south of Tehran, where there were about 2,000 orphans, and in Meshed, northeast of Tehran on the Afghanistan border, where there were about 380 orphans. The funds to pay for the care of the Polish orphans were provided by Pope Pius XII, the Mission of the Anglican Church, the French Convent of Sisters, the Swiss Order of Priest and Brothers, various agencies of the Iranian government, and by the well-to-do Iranian population.

I could have chosen to go either to camp No. 5 or to the camp in Esfahan. I selected camp No. 5 because it was located closest to Tehran and I hoped it would be easier for my mother to find me there. Camp No. 5 consisted of army tents that served as our housing. We slept on blankets placed on bare ground. Meals were served in a mess hall. Sanitary facilities were latrines at the edge of the camp. I spent days wandering about the camp, asking people if they knew my mother or had heard of her whereabouts. This was to no avail.

In the meantime, my mother, my sister, Aunt Macia and her daughter, Anulka, were transferred from Pahlavi to a another camp outside Tehran. As soon as they arrived in the camp, my mother went to the hospital to inquire about me. The hospital authorities told her that I was alive and that they had discharged me a few weeks earlier but had no record of where I went. My mother found out that there were four camps in the vicinity of Tehran and two more camps further away. She decided to start searching for me in the camps closest to Tehran. She went from camp to camp, checking the records but could not find my name in any of them. Not trusting the records, she proceeded to walk around each camp inquiring about a nine-year-old boy who matched my description. Sometimes people directed her to other children with similar but not identical names, like *Genek Pak.* When she arrived at camp No. 5, the authorities told her that they had no record or knowledge of anyone by my name. A young girl, however, overheard my mother asking me and told her she knew a boy who fit the description. The girl brought my mother to the area near our tent. As they approached the tent, I recognized my mother immediately. She was wearing a dress from Poland that I remembered. I ran to meet her, but she backed off saying, "You are not my son." Apparently, I looked so different that she could not even recognize me. I was skin and bones, except for a huge belly, and still had not fully recovered from my stay in the hospital. She thought I was an orphan who wanted to find a family, any family, who would take him in. This was not an uncommon practice among the orphaned children. But once I started asking questions about the other members of our family, especially Aunt Macia, she realized it was me. After all, how many Aunt Macias were there in this world? The joy experienced by both of us was beyond anybody's imagination, and even to this day, when we reminisce about that moment, tears come to our eyes.

At this point, it was late in the day and my mother felt it would be safer for me to stay in the camp overnight. She said she would return the next day to pick me up. However, there was no way I was going to spend another night in that place. Deep down, I also was afraid I would be abandoned again. I convinced Mother to take me with her. We were able to catch a ride to downtown Tehran on a military truck. It was dark by the time we reached the city. The driver dropped us off in the downtown area and we had to walk to another part of the city, toward my mother's camp. It's hard to describe the walk through the streets of Tehran—a young European mother, walking at night with a little boy, in a strange city crowded with Iranians. Needless to say, we stuck out like a sore thumb and my mother was extremely worried. However, I was overjoyed to be finally with her and didn't seem to notice any danger. Eventually, a Polish army truck picked us up and dropped us off in Polish camp No. 1, which was about two kilometers from the camp where our family stayed. We walked the rest of the way on a deserted road, but at least we were not being stared at by a bunch of Iranians. When we arrived at our camp, the joy experienced by our family was unbelievable. At last, we were all together again after being separated for three months.

Our camp in Tehran, camp No. 2, was located about eight kilometers southeast of Tehran in a place called Doshan Tappeh. The landscape was fairly flat with desert-like terrain and not much natural vegetation. The Elburz Mountains were in the background to the northeast with the dominant Mt. Demavand on the horizon. Many orchards and vegetable fields surrounded the camp, irrigated by the numerous water wells scattered around the area. The main crops cultivated by the local farmers were figs and pomegranates.

High stone walls surrounded the camp. The camp had been an Iranian military base before the war and the walls kept the area secure from strangers. It was located near the military airport, which was heavily guarded by British and Iranian troops. The camp had about 100 barracks and was inhabited by as many as 8,000 refugees. It also was necessary to set up temporary tents to house the excess refugees during the peak immigration period, when there were over 22,000 Polish refugees in all camps around Tehran. Later, as the refugees departed for India and Africa, the tents were removed. We, along with the majority of refugees, were housed in old army barracks built by the Germans for the Iranian army. Some families were housed in the nearby unfinished army munitions factory or in tents. Several families lived in each barrack, normally about 80 people per barrack. We slept on plywood platforms with mattresses made from straw. The partitions between families were made of blankets hang on ropes. It was extremely crowded and noisy. The sanitary facilities were located at the outskirts of the camp, some 300 yards away from the barracks. The baths were in large rooms with many showerheads. When showering, we had no privacy and no warm water.

The British government provided funds for food and support for the refugees. The British lent the Poles about 10 British pounds per person per month, the loans to be repaid by the Polish government after the war. Supplies were purchased locally with the cooperation of the Iranian authorities. The funds were adequate for our basic needs but sometimes the logistics to deliver supplies to a camp were difficult. The breadbasket of Iran was in the northern part of the country, which was occupied at that time by the Russians, who sometimes made it difficult for grain to be delivered to camps on time.

Food was prepared in the communal kitchen, army style. The women in the camp helped with kitchen chores, duties assigned on a rotating basis. They served meals, washed pots and pans, and cleaned the kitchen. We went to the kitchen with pots and buckets, and the kitchen staff issued a meal for the whole family. We brought the food back to the barracks and served it on aluminum plates. The meals were quite adequate: Tea, bread and porridge for breakfast; soup, bread, potatoes, sometimes corned beef from the army C rations, and occasionally vegetables for the main meal served at noon. In the evening, we received tea, bread, margarine and yellow cheese. Compared to the food we had in Russia, these meals seemed like feasts and most people considered the extreme hunger experienced in the Soviet Union a bad dream.

One of the most acute problems among the refugees was the shortage of clothing and shoes. Most of us brought very little with us during our long journey. Contaminated clothes were confiscated and burned in Pahlavi during the cleansing phase. The British issued only the bare necessities. The Americans provided some help through the so-called Lend-Lease agreement by which we received clothing, shoes and other goods. The Polish government was expected to reimburse the Americans after the war for these items. We were also issued clothing provided by the Red Cross, the Polish American Congress, and a number of relief agencies in the United States, Great Britain and Iran. The clothes did not fit very well in most cases, but they were clean and kept us warm. As time went by, the Polish women put their sewing skills to work and modified the clothes to the point that one could display them in a

Versace showroom—well, maybe as rags in a Versace showroom. Later, authorities purchased cotton fabric, and Polish tailors and seamstresses made some clothes in the camps. The problem with shoes was more difficult. Most shoes did not fit and were difficult to modify. We got used to wearing shoes one or two sizes too big, but again bigger shoes were better than no shoes at all. Slowly we began to resemble human beings again as opposed to the skeletons in rags we were when we left the Soviet Union.

Polish authorities began to put together an education system for the children. For the first time since we left Poland, we were able to attend Polish schools. As a nine-year-old boy, I was only in the first grade. Our first classes were held outdoors under the shade of some trees because the buildings designated for classrooms were filthy and poorly lit. We sat on stones and listened to the teachers' lectures. We again learned the Polish alphabet and grammar. Books, notebooks, paper and pencils were not available. At first, we used little hand-held blackboards and chalk to practice writing. Later, we were able to get notebooks and pencils. Textbooks were not available for a long time. There were no facilities in the camps to print textbooks and the printing presses in Iran had no Polish characters. Not only children, but also the entire Polish population in the camps suffered from the lack of printed material. The need for academic books for students is self-evident. However, you cannot appreciate the full value of literary works, the classics, newspapers, magazines, and other printed matter until you are deprived of it. This was a big void in our lives, at least initially. Polish authorities in London finally were able to get textbooks printed by Polish printers in England, and the camp personnel published a *samizdat* type of newspaper, printed in Tehran. Eventually we were able to get Polish newspapers from England. Later, new barracks were converted specifically into classrooms that were cleaner and better lit. The new classrooms had blackboards and tables and benches for the students. There were as many as six to eight students to each table. No one complained, though, because we were all attending a real Polish school with Polish teachers.

The Polish community in Iran eventually put together a cultural infrastructure in the camp with plays, concerts and cultural events for adults and children. The Boy Scouts and Girl Scouts were formed, and about 50 percent of the children joined them. They provided an opportunity for the children to participate in sports, recreation and visits to Tehran and other Iranian points of interest. They also provided moral and psychological support to the youngsters who had been exposed to so much suffering.

The Polish population was psychologically drained and in a very difficult situation. It was true that technically we were free. However, there was hardly a family that had not lost someone in the Soviet Union or in the camps after leaving the Soviet Union. Many of us had relatives who remained in the Soviet Union; my uncle Władek and his family still were there. Many had relatives in Poland under German occupation. Our grandmother, my father's mother, two aunts and an uncle were still living in German-occupied Rzeszów and we had not heard from them since leaving Poland. Fathers and husbands were off fighting the Germans, and concern for their safety was on everybody's mind. There was tremendous uncertainty in our daily lives. Our future was in question. Most likely we would be sent to Africa or India, which to us seemed like going in the opposite direction from where we wanted to go, back to our homes in free Poland. Physically, we were healing well, but psychologically, the progress was slow. It was going to take a long time for us to feel secure and comfortable again.

We attended church on Sundays and holidays at the camp chapel. The chapel was a simple altar constructed under a cover with the congregation standing outside. We were all very happy to bring to life our religious beliefs and to be able to express our feelings openly without the fear of the NKVD or other spies watching our every step. A few milestones occurred while we were in Tehran. My cousin Leszek was born in December 1942 in a Tehran hospital. He would never see his father, who was left behind in an unmarked grave in Russia. Also in December of 1942, my mother became seriously ill with typhoid and was hospitalized. Our first Christmas in freedom was not a joyous one since our mother and aunt were both in the hospital. During their stay in the hospital, my father's cousin, Aniela Dereń, cared for us. She stayed with us and became an adopted member of our family after my mother returned. When we visited my mother in the hospital, we were horrified by her appearance—skin and bones. She had lost all of her hair and appeared to be on her deathbed. Many others were in the same predicament. Fortunately, my mother recovered, but many did not. The Polish cemetery in Iran was located outside camp No. 1 and was getting larger by the day. As I mentioned before, over 2,100 people died in the camps in Pahlavi and Tehran in less than two years. My mother returned to the camp after she got well, but shortly afterward, returned to the hospital for an emergency appendectomy. No Polish-speaking surgeons were at the hospital, and a Jewish surgeon, who was originally from Poland and had moved to Iran before the war, performed the surgery. In 1943, my cousin Anulka and I went to our First Communion. It was a festive and memorable moment for us, although the celebration was very modest by today's standards.

We had opportunities, on many occasions, to come in contact with the local Iranian population in Tehran as well as in areas surrounding the camps. We found the Iranians to be very friendly and charming with sharp minds and a fantastic talent for languages. Not only could they converse in English, French and of course Farsi or Arabic, but upon our arrival, they learned Polish very quickly. When we visited downtown Tehran on a few occasions, one could see signs in the windows of stores proclaiming "*Mówimy po Polsku*" or "We speak Polish here." Over all, Tehran made a very positive impression on us. It was a large city, full of life. Streets were wide and tree lined. The main boulevard was Shah Reza, and the main commercial street was Lelazar. A big bazaar was at the end of Naser Street. Cars along with horses, camels, oxen and other animals were on the streets. The stores were well stocked with food, clothing, and such items as carpets, leather goods, suitcases, jewelry, bronze articles, and a variety of articles made of wood. All this was very strange to us accustomed to the Russian drabness and shortage of basic goods. The Iranians were very friendly in contrast to the British, who were rather aloof. The British treated the Iranians with little respect and were very boorish toward them. Colonialism was at its peak at that time, and the British were trying to demonstrate their perceived superiority over the dominated nations. In all fairness, I must say the British treated us Poles with great respect. I assume the glorious performance of the Polish airmen in the Battle of Britain had a lot to do with it.

On July 5,1943, shocking news reached our camp. General Sikorski, the Commander in Chief of the Polish Armed Forces and the Premier of the Polish Government-in-Exile, was killed in an airplane crash off the coast of Gibraltar. To the refugees, he was our savior, the one who had negotiated the release of the Polish deportees and prisoners from the *Nieludzka Ziemia* and enabled the Polish people to escape Soviet bondage. The camp was in shock; people were crying and hugging each other for moral support. I don't believe there was a dry eye in the entire Polish community. We knew we had lost not only a great leader but also a spokesman for Poland and the Polish cause in the international arena. General Sikorski was a well-known and respected statesman. He dealt as an equal with Stalin, Churchill, Roosevelt, and other leaders of the Western Coalition. All leaders respected his opinions and consulted with him. He, after all, represented the fourth largest army fighting the Nazis. There was no one in the Polish political arena who could possibly replace him. We had lost a great leader and we all knew it. The Polish community held a memorial parade on one of the main avenues of Tehran on July 9, 1943, the day of General Sikorski's funeral in London. The street was lined with Polish, Iranian, British and American spectators who wanted to pay their respects to the memory of General Sikorski. All Polish political and religious organizations, Polish and Iranian scouts, and contingents of army units from Poland, Iran, Britain and the United States marched in the parade. Many people were crying, and many non-Poles expressed their respects and condolences.

We were transferred from Tehran to Ahvaz in late 1943. Ahvaz was an interim camp situated in southwestern Iran. Through this camp passed all transports of Polish refugees going on to Africa and India. We were selected to go to Africa, but my aunt Macia and cousin Aniela were not. They were to remain in Tehran for the time being. My mother and aunt did not want to be separated so they went to the camp office and stated that either we all go, or no one goes. I don't believe the camp official ever saw such determination on anyone's face, and he relented and put us all on the same transport to Ahvaz.

The journey to Ahvaz took two days by train. It was a picturesque trip through the Iranian countryside and mountains. We went through dozens of tunnels of various lengths—some that took the train several minutes to traverse. Well-armed Hindu military personnel guarded each tunnel. There were sand bags and machine guns set up at the entrances and exits of the tunnels. It was a time of war, and the Germans were just across the Caucus Mountains—and very much interested in Iranian oil.

Ahvaz is located in the desert at the southwestern part of Iran, close to the Persian Gulf. Ahvaz had to be one of the hottest spots on earth with temperatures regularly exceeding 120 degrees in the middle of the day. We were required to stay indoors during the noon hours and wear protective headgear whenever we ventured outside. It was also miserably hot inside the barracks. We hung wet towels or blankets inside the barracks. The evaporating water made the barracks cooler and slightly increased the humidity of the air making breathing a little easier. There were very few trees or vegetation, only sand. We also were subjected to a number of severe sandstorms. At first, they scared the daylights out of us. These storms came without warning and the strong wind blew sand into the air making it so thick that it was hard to breathe or see. Sand penetrated everything outside and inside the barracks, and the cleanup after each storm was long and tedious.

The camp in Ahvaz was initially constructed to house about 2,000 occupants, but at its peak, as many as 5,000 refugees lived in the camp. The camp gave the impression of a small city. We were housed in Iranian army horse stables that were cleaned and converted for our use. There were no separate rooms for individual families, no furniture, just wooden platforms to sleep on. Here again, as in Tehran, we made our own quarters by making partitions with blankets strung by rope.

The schools in Ahvaz were already well organized with a grade school and high school by the time we arrived in the camp. The school also was located in the stables, having been cleaned and converted into classrooms. Notebooks, pencils and textbooks now were available. I was somewhat embarrassed being only in the second grade and ten years old, although I was not the only one in that situation. Most of the children were in poor physical and psychological condition and were not able to keep up with their studies because they were in and out of hospitals and moving from one camp to another. The teachers did a marvelous job teaching us not only the academic subjects but also helping us adjust to yet another new life and providing psychological guidance. Here, as in Pahlavi and Tehran, our health continued to be a big problem. In addition to the carryover problems from Russia, dysentery, typhoid and vitamin deficiency, malaria became the main concern. Our weakened bodies did not have the resistance to fight malaria and many of us were infected with it. The heat and the primitive living conditions made matters worse. The hospital was always overflowing with patients.

American and British military bases were not far from our camp. On occasion, the Americans and British invited children to their bases and showered them with gifts of chocolate, chewing gum and other goodies. We looked forward to these visits on weekends and holidays as they were a real treat. The Americans were particularly hospitable and generous. A few of the soldiers spoke Polish, which made communication easier. Hardly anyone in our camp spoke English.

We spent Christmas of 1943 in Ahvaz. Oh, how different Christmas it was. We found a branch of a dead tree, without leaves, and used it as a Christmas tree. We made our own decorations and used small candles for lights. It seemed to me like it was the most beautiful tree I have ever had in my life. The *wigilia* was simple but solemn. We shared *opłatek* and our wishes were for everyone to spend the next Christmas in free Poland. We attended the midnight mass and sang beautiful Polish carols. At the end of the mass we sang the hymn *Boże Coś Polskę*, which loosely translated means "God you have protected Poland from peril in the past; return free Poland back to us." It became a tradition among the refugees to end all events with the singing of that hymn. Again, it was a good feeling to be able to express our faith so freely and openly. I don't believe it is possible to appreciate the full meaning of freedom until you have experienced the loss of it as we had.

Our Christmas spirit was dampened, however, by most disturbing news about the discussions held in Tehran by Roosevelt, Churchill, and Stalin. Rumors were that the three powers considered exchanging conquered German territory to the west and north of Poland for the Polish territory behind the so-called Curzon Line. Curzon Line was a suggested cease fire line between Poland and the Soviet Union during the 1920 war. The line was suggested by the British foreign minister Lord Curzon but was totally unacceptable to the Poles at that time. That line would now become the new border between Poland and the Soviet Union. In other words, this would allow the USSR to annex the eastern part of Poland. This meant that our homes would be located outside of Poland and that we would not be able to return to them unless we were willing to live in the Soviet Union. It was ironic that the agreement was reached in Tehran, the city where we were first able to breathe freedom after having left the Soviet hell.

As I mentioned before, Ahvaz, as all other locations in Iran, was never intended to be a permanent location for Polish refugees for the entire duration of the war. First, the Russian army occupied northern Iran, and having Poles at such a close proximity to the Russians posed a diplomatic dilemma for the British government, which at that time was trying to appease the Russians. Of course, the Russian presence had an unsettling effect on the refugees. Also, the Germans were making quick advances on the Russian front, and in the summer of 1942, they had already reached the Caucus Mountains across from Iran. The proximity of Germans to Tehran posed the danger to Polish civilians of possible bombings by the Luftwaffe. The British and Polish governments made a decision to relocate Polish refugees to British Commonwealth countries. First, the authorities wanted to give the refugees a chance to recover from their Soviet experience and improve their physical condition before sending them on another long voyage. There were logistical difficulties in relocating such a large number of people as well. A relocation of this magnitude required a large number of trucks, ships and railroad cars to transport over 40,000 refugees. Many of these resources were required for the war effort, so only a limited number of transports could be allocated for the purpose of relocating refugees. Therefore, the relocation was slow-paced and proceeded over several years. Most of the Polish refugees left Iran in 1943 and early 1944. They were relocated either to Africa or India. Those who remained in Iran (about 4,000) were transferred to Lebanon in 1945.

We left Ahvaz in early 1944 with a group of refugees headed for Africa. We left the camp in army trucks and were transported to the railroad station in Ahvaz. From there, we went by train to the port city of Khorramshahr on the Persian Gulf. The train ride took almost a day. It was extremely hot, and even though we were somewhat accustomed to the desert heat, it was still unbearable during the long hours it took us to get to the port. To our surprise, we were to travel on a freighter that was converted to a troop carrier rather than on a passenger ship. We were informed that we would be transferred to a passenger ship once we reached Karachi, our first stop on the way to Africa.

We boarded the ship and left port the same day with about 800 other passengers. It took several hours to reach the Persian Gulf and another two days to cross the Gulf and reach the Straits of Hormuz. During the crossing, we held several drills on how to put on life jackets and board lifeboats. These drills lasted up to an hour and were very tiring because of the extreme heat. After we reached the Straits of Hormuz at the Gulf of Oman, we had to wait for a navy convoy to escort us and other military transport ships across the Arabian Sea to Karachi. We needed an escort because there were reports that German and Japanese submarines were prowling those waters trying to torpedo military transports. The submarines had already sunk over 40 ships in that area during the past two years. We waited for two days for all the ships to assemble. These were the most hellish days of our trip to Karachi. The extreme heat, the lack of fresh water and decent food were some of the hardships we faced. The ship needed to stay completely dark at night, and we were forced to spend nights under the deck in large halls in unbearable heat because the captain of the ship was afraid people would smoke and the light from the cigarettes would attract attention to our position. The convoy of several military transports and navy vessels finally assembled and we were able to continue the trip. The navy ships circled the convoy during the entire crossing, forming a protective shield. Our ship also was lightly armed; it had a cannon mounted on the bow and several machine guns on its sides. Fortunately, no submarines were detected during our trip.

Once we reached the Arabian Sea, the heat eased considerably. It took four days to cross this body of water. The most welcome sign after eight days of travel were sea gulls and an increase in the number of ships around us, indicating that land must not be far away. We passed Manora Island before we entered Karachi. Manora Island had been a well-known tourist spot before the war but now was a fortress guarding the port of Karachi. We docked next to a well-lit, beautiful passenger ship. We were told the ship would take us to Africa. However, we never boarded the passenger ship because my cousin Leszek became seriously ill during the trip. Macia took him to a doctor and he immediately ordered Leszek to the hospital in Karachi. Naturally, Aunt Macia could not continue the trip to Africa. My mother went to the authorities asking permission to stay in Karachi because we wanted to stay together as a family. After a lengthy discussion and explanations, the authorities agreed to let the entire family stay in Karachi. We were transferred to the Polish refugee camp some 20 kilometers from Karachi.

The cleansing camp in Pahlavi, Iran, 1942.
(Ref. 16, PAVA)

Temporary camp in Pahlavi for Polish refugees evacuated from Russia. Pahlavi, 1942. (Ref 19, Exiled Children)

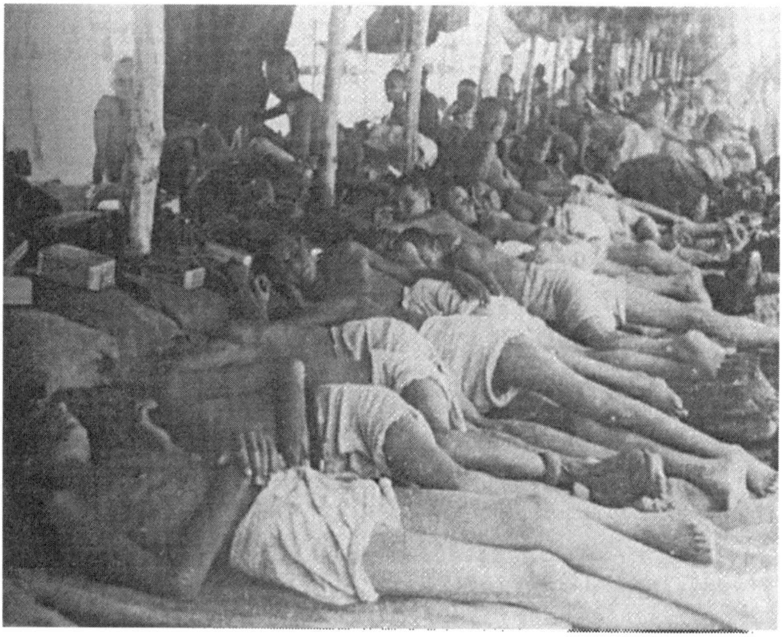

Polish children in Pahlavi, Iran, after evacuation from Russia, 1942. (Ref. 7, Stolen Childhood)

"Junaczki" Girls Cadet Corps after arrival in Pahlavi, 1942. (Ref. 7, Stolen Childhood)

Orphanage camp in Tehran where I lived, 1942.
(Ref. 19, Exiled Children)

The mess hall in the orphanage in Tehran, 1942.
(Ref 17, Piłsudski Institute)

Polish refugee camp outside of Tehran, Iran, 1943.

Soup kitchen in refugee camp, 1943.
(Ref. 10, Szmagier)

Trucks transporting Polish refugees from Pahlavi to Tehran, 1942.
(Ref. 16 PAVA)

Typical classroom in school in Ahvaz, Iran, 1943.
(Ref. 19, Exiled Children)

Alina, Anulka and I with Uncle Romek
when he visited us in Tehran, 1943.

Visiting my mother in the hospital in Tehran
with Alina and Anulka, 1942.

ARMY IN EXILE

It is difficult if not impossible to write about the Polish refugees from the Soviet Union and their escape from the *Nieludzka Ziemia* without mentioning the Polish Army in Exile. Every single family in the refugee camps had a husband, father, brother or someone close to them enlisted in the army. The two were intertwined so much that they were inseparable.

The Polish Army in Exile actually took form on Soviet soil. An agreement negotiated between General Sikorski and I. M. Majski, the Russian ambassador to Britain, was signed in London on July 30, 1941, at the urging of Great Britain. Mr. W. Churchill and Mr. A. Eden, the British Foreign Minister, witnessed the signing ceremony. The Soviet government officially granted amnesty to all Polish citizens on Soviet territory on August 12, 1941, and two days later, on August 14, 1941, the Polish–Russian Military Agreement was signed. The agreement stipulated that a Polish army would be organized as soon as possible and that the army would be accountable to the Polish government and subject to Polish military laws and regulations. General Władysław Anders, who at the time was a prisoner in the infamous Lubianka prison in Moscow, was named the Commander-in-Chief of Polish Forces in Russia. Soon after, the Soviet government started releasing Polish prisoners of war held in Soviet prisons and gulags.

It is estimated that the Soviets took about 300,000 prisoners of war during the September 1939 campaign. These prisoners now were flooding to the areas designated as future army camps in Buzuluk, Tatistchuo, and Totskoie near Kuybyshev in the southeastern European part of the Soviet Union.

It soon became evident that the number of officers reporting to the new army was unusually low and none were from the three prisoner of war camps of Starobielsk, Kozielsk and Ostashkov. About 21,000 prisoners had been located there, including the cream of the Polish officers corps. The Soviet authorities either ignored all the inquiries on the fate of these prisoners or their replies were very evasive. It was not until later that we learned about the fate of these prisoners. They were brutally shot by the NKVD and buried in mass graves in Katyn Forest, near the city of Smolensk; in Kharkov in the Ukraine; and in Mednoye, south of Moscow.

The physical condition of the arriving future soldiers was deplorable. Many of them were malnourished, sick and exhausted from the two years in prison plus the long journey from the prisons and gulags to the new army camps. Most of them had no boots and were clad in rags. Some were still dressed in tattered relics of old Polish military uniforms. Some of the arrivals were missing limbs or eyes, many were covered with ulcers, and all looked like walking skeletons from horror stories. However, once they arrived at the gathering camps and saw the Polish flag fluttering over them, their spirits perked up and their backs strengthened. They became soldiers in spirit, if not in appearance.

One wonders how these prisoners could survive such horrible conditions. In every case, the answer to that question is faith and patriotism. The story of the creation of the icon of *Our Lady of Kozielsk* is a perfect illustration of the depth of that faith. Sculptor Tadeusz A. Zieliński, under the most difficult circumstances, in secrecy, carved the image of the Blessed Virgin Mary on a piece of board using self-made tools. The prisoners in the camp used this carved image of the Virgin Mary for secret venerations. Later it was smuggled in a suitcase with a fake bottom to another camp in Griazioviec. After the amnesty, the icon was used at the first mass for the Polish army. The icon was later named *Our Lady of Kozielsk* and adopted by the Polish Army in Exile as their official religious symbol.

The situation at the army camps was very difficult due to the extreme weather conditions with temperatures often reaching minus 50 degrees, and icy winds adding to the chill. Most soldiers were housed in tents since there was no housing available. They were sick, exhausted, and in rags, so death took its toll. Many froze to death in their tents, and many more died of pneumonia, typhus and other diseases caused by parasites present due to poor sanitary conditions. The inadequate food rations supplied by the Russians made matters even worse. The army had no uniforms, arms, ammunition or other military equipment. It was only after they moved to the southern Soviet Republics that the British supplied some uniforms, but not nearly enough.

The decision was made to move the army to the southern part of Russia in early 1942. New headquarters were established at Yangi-Yul near the city of Tashkent in Uzbekistan. From the outset, the number of refugees reaching the camps had increased dramatically even though Soviet authorities had put many obstacles in their way. The Soviets wanted to keep the healthiest and strongest people in the camps to continue the forced labor. The NKVD in some camps did not believe (or simply ignored) that the Poles were given amnesty. This sort of amnesty had never happened before in the entire history of the Soviet gulags. The Russians often forced trains with refugees on the way to army camps to be stranded in steppes without supplies. They also diverted some of the trains to places in Turkmenistan, along the river Amu-Daria, where they forced the refugees to work in kilhozes or dig water channels for irrigation of farmlands. Therefore many of the released prisoners and deportees did not make it to the army recruiting centers and remained in the Soviet Union until the end of the war. It was a shocking disappointment to them knowing that there was an opportunity to leave the Soviet Union and they were unable to do so.

General Anders made a decision during the early stages of the army's formation to include civilians as part of the evacuation process even though Russians objected. Anders saw that it was the only way to save Polish civilians from certain death by starvation. That is why we are so indebted to General Anders and consider him one of Poland's greatest heroes. Anders also insisted that all Polish citizens, regardless of religion or national origin, were to be included in the new army. This was of utmost importance to the many national minorities who were deported from Poland, including Jews, White Russians, Ruthenians and Ukrainians. The

Russians objected to this view, their point being that the amnesty applied only to ethnic Polish people. Anders prevailed on this point. Thus he was able to save 4,000 Jews from certain starvation. The Russians could, of course, limit the number of civilians at the camps by limiting the amount of food they provided, which they did. However, Anders issued instructions to the army that they were to share food provisions with the civilian population. One can imagine the difficulty this caused. The number of food rations the Russians provided for the army was initially for only 44,000 soldiers, later reduced to 30,000. This was totally inadequate for the about 70,000 troops and an additional 30,000 civilians. The situation was getting more desperate with each passing day.

The army was transferred from Buzuluk to Uzbekistan in early 1942. There were several camps scattered in the southern portion of Uzbekistan. We arrived in the Uzbek Republic in July 1942, and by that time, the army already was well organized. My father and my uncle Romek were assigned to the 6th Lwów Infantry Division at Jakkobag, and we found lodging in the nearby Uzbek village. When we arrived, the food shortages were acute and the disease epidemic was at its peak. The army shared its food rations with the civilians at great sacrifices to themselves, and it was obvious that this situation could not last much longer.

At first the Soviet government wanted to form and arm only one Polish division at a time and send that division to the front under Russian command. However, General Anders insisted that the whole Polish army must fight as a unit and if the Russians could not feed and arm the whole army, then the army should be evacuated to the Middle East. General Sikorski initially wanted to keep the Polish armed forces in the Soviet Union so the Poles could liberate Poland and, at the same time, preserve the Polish–Russian pre-war borders. To us civilians, this was a struggle of fundamental importance, for if the army stayed, we would not be able to get out of the Soviet Union. Anders eventually prevailed, helped by the fact that the British wanted the Polish army in the Middle East to protect the oil fields from the Germans. The issue of the evacuation of the civilian population became a sticky point not only with the Russians but the British as well. The British did not want to have the additional burden to care for civilians. Here again, General Anders was able to argue successfully that leaving the soldiers' families in the Soviet Union, to an unknown fate, would create undue stress on the soldiers constantly worrying about the condition of their loved ones left behind. Finally, all sides agreed that all soldiers, as well as the civilians gathered around the army camps, would be evacuated.

After the evacuation of the Polish army in August of 1942, the Soviets again began to subject the remaining Poles in the Soviet Union to massive persecution. Poles were under a constant suspicion as a potential fifth column for the Germans. Many were forced to change citizenship, which Poles considered equivalent to treason. There were massive resettlements from Siberia to Kazakhstan; in fact, there is a very large Polish ethnic population in Kazakhstan to this day. The persecution eased somewhat in 1943 after a new Polish army was formed under the auspices of the Polish communists, the so-called Union of Polish Patriots. The new army was under the command of renegade Colonel Zygmunt Berling, who had deserted the Polish army in Krasnovodsk. Stalin himself later promoted Berling to general. It was ironic that the division was named after Tadeusz Kościuszko who led an insurrection against the Russians in 1792. The Kościuszko Division fought alongside the Russian army on the German front. My uncle Władek was recruited in 1943 to this newly formed Polish army and was wounded in the battle of Lenino. He returned to his family in Siberia after he was discharged from the army. He and his family returned to Poland in 1946. However, many Poles stayed permanently in the Soviet Union since Poland was not free of communism and their homesteads were part of the Soviet Union anyway.

The exact number of Polish citizens left behind in the Soviet Union will never be known. More information is being uncovered as thousands of documents are being declassified and made available to the public and more and more eyewitnesses are speaking out. After we left the Soviet Union, the Documentation Office, established by General Anders, was charged with gathering information about the plight of the prisoners and deportees. That office obtained statements from Poles, who had been through the Soviet prisons and camps. After the fall of the Soviet Union, there were a number of disclosures by the Russian government about the Soviet atrocities against Polish citizens during World War II, including the admission that the Soviets were responsible for the Katyn massacre. There were several organizations formed after Poland had its first independent elections after the overthrow of the communists in 1989, which began documenting the Siberian experience. *Karta* in Warsaw was one such organization, and *Związek Sybiraków*, with chapters in all major Polish cities, was another. A clearer picture is being developed about the Soviet experience from these documents. However, the complete story may never be known.

The army, together with civilians, was evacuated from the port city of Krasnovodsk on the Caspian Sea to Pahlavi in Iran. The Russians provided 25 ships for the evacuation, all freight vessels or oil tankers, some which made several crossings. It should be noted that at that time, Pahlavi was in the Russian occupation zone after the British and Russians had invaded and occupied Iran in August 1941. Iran was sympathetic toward Germans before the war, and the British and Russians invaded Iran to prevent the Germans from getting access to Iranian oil. The British deposed the Shah and replaced him with his son, Reza Pahlavi. The Russian soldiers were conspicuous in many areas of Pahlavi, and we were a little apprehensive about their presence, though not enough to dampen our joy of being out of the Soviet Union.

My father and Uncle Romek were evacuated from the Soviet Union on the same ship as we were at the end of August 1942.

Temporary camps were set up for the army and civilians on the beaches of Pahlavi. There were two camps for civilians and three for the army personnel. The army personnel were processed through the quarantine, just like the civilians. The soldiers first went through the same dirty camp where they were subject to a complete cleansing, leaving behind their old uniforms or civilian clothes. The soldiers who were suspected of having contagious diseases were sent immediately to hospitals specially designated for that purpose. The biggest problem among the soldiers, as well as among the civilians, was poor physical condition. My father became a victim of dysentery when he arrived in Iran. Partly it was his own doing, as he gorged on the food that was readily available in Pahlavi. As he explained, "Kiełbasa and sweets don't mix." Our dietary system accustomed to diets bordering on starvation could not tolerate drastic changes. These abrupt changes often led to bouts of dysentery. My father was hospitalized and we did not see him again until the end of the war, when we joined him in England in September of 1947. This spanned a period of over five years.

The army was transferred from Pahlavi to Gedera in Palestine and to two areas in Iraq near the cities of Khanaqin and Qizil Ribat, northeast of Baghdad. The camps consisted of a city of tents pitched on the sands of the desert. The Polish army was incorporated into the British army in the Middle East under the command of British General Maitland Wilson and was given the task of defending the Iraqi–Iranian frontier against the Germans. The British supplied food, uniforms, equipment, arms and munitions to the Polish army. As soon as the Polish soldiers arrived in Iraq, they began intensive training even though their physical condition was still very poor. However, they never complained but prepared themselves with enthusiasm for their new life as soldiers and, hopefully, as defenders of their beloved Poland. My father was too weak to remain in the infantry so he was assigned to the 8th Heavy Anti-Aircraft Artillery. It was a very fortuitous assignment that possibly saved his life later during the battle of Monte Cassino.

The Polish soldiers had to be trained with new weapons, mechanization, handling of armored equipment, and general modern warfare. Many of them were farmers, laborers, storekeepers, students, etc., and soldiering was new to them. The army had to train over 20,000 drivers alone for the mechanized equipment. The task was monumental. Slowly, however, these one-time skeletons in rags began to look and act like real soldiers. They even had time for some recreation and sightseeing. They organized concerts, theater shows, and excursions to Palestine to visit holy places in Bethlehem, Jerusalem and other biblical cities. My father took advantage of these excursions and visited many sites in Bethlehem and Jerusalem. He was very impressed with the beauty and richness of the churches and basilicas. He even had the opportunity to swim in the Dead Sea, which was an interesting experience since the water is so dense with salt that one can float on it for hours.

Anders and the Polish government continued to press the Soviet government and the Allies about the missing Polish officers. The Soviets again ignored the inquiries and the Allies, not wanting to offend Stalin, told Poles to wait for an appropriate opportunity to make further inquiries. On April 13, 1943, the Germans reported discovering the corpses of thousands of Polish officers in the mass graves at Katyn. When the Polish government asked the International Red Cross to look into the matter, the Soviets accused the Poles of cooperation with Hitler and broke off relations with the Polish government. The Red Cross sent an International Commission to investigate the Katyn massacre and confirmed that the officers were murdered in 1940, or long before the Germans occupied the area. The prisoners were shot in the back of their heads and pushed into long ditches that served as mass graves. Many corpses were still in Polish uniforms and had personal documents in their pockets. The United States and Britain abstained from making any remarks about the massacre for fear of offending Stalin and jeopardizing Russian participation in the war against Germany. In fact, the British ordered Polish army personnel to refrain from talking, not only about the massacre, but also about their experiences in the Soviet prisons.

To the civilians in the refugee camps, the news of the massacre was shocking indeed. Many in the camps had missing husbands, fathers, brothers or other members of their family. Some had information that their relatives were indeed in one of the three camps. The Katyn revelations confirmed their worst fears that their loved ones had met a brutal death at the hands of the Soviets. Today, Katyn is revered among Polish people because it represents a symbol of the Soviet attempt to eradicate Polish culture from the face of the earth. There are a number of monuments memorializing the Katyn massacre in major Polish cities as well as in London, Paris, New York, and the latest in Baltimore.

In December 1943, Churchill, Roosevelt and Stalin met at a conference in Tehran. They secretly agreed to establish a border between Poland and the Soviet Union along the so-called Curzon Line, thus ceding the eastern part of Poland, including the cities of Lwów and Wilno, to the Soviet Union. The great majority of soldiers in the Polish Army in the Middle East and the civilians in the refugee camps, including us, effectively lost their homeland. Poles never thought that the United States and Britain would consent to another partition of Poland. Now the army questioned the purpose of going into action. Anders, however, felt that as shocking as the news was, the army's first priority was to contribute to the war effort to defeat the Germans.

In November 1943, the Polish troops were fully prepared for battle and in excellent fighting spirit after the final training exercises on Mount Sinai and near the city of Nazareth in Palestine. The Corps was transferred to Egypt in January of 1944 and to Italy in February of the same year.

In Italy, the Polish army, popularly known as the Polish II Corps, was assigned to the larger British 8th Army, under General Oliver Leese. General Anders was informed that the Polish II Corps' first action would be to capture German-occupied Monte Cassino. Monte Cassino was a Benedictine monastery located on top of a mountain overlooking a valley. The Germans fortified it to block all roads leading to Rome. The Americans bombed the abbey, leaving it in ruins. However, the military bastion stood impregnable. Attempts to capture Monte Cassino by the American Army II Corps in January of 1944 were unsuccessful, as were attempts by the New Zealanders, the Indians, and the French in February of 1944. A third attempt to capture the fortress, by the New Zealand and Indian Divisions in March of 1944, met with similar failure.

General Anders described the battle of Monte Cassino in great detail in his book, *The Army in Exile.* The preparation for the battle began in early April with the stockpiling of supplies and equipment. This was accompanied by practicing fighting against strongly fortified mountain positions. The task to capture Monte Cassino was extremely difficult because of the rough terrain and constant enemy fire. The supplies had to be carried by soldiers and mules at night to reach the final destination where the attack was to commence. The mountain of Monte Cassino with the Benedictine monastery on top and the adjacent mountain of Piedemonte were defended by specially selected and trained German crack troops who formed a defensive line called the Gustav Line, which ran 100 miles across the Italian Peninsula. Monte Cassino was considered the key position of the Gustav Line. The task assigned to the Polish II Corps by the 8th Army Commander was to "take Monte Cassino and proceed toward Piedemonte." That meant breaking through the German Gustav Line and attacking the Hitler Line behind it. The Allies consisting of British, American, Canadian and French units were assigned areas on both flanks of the Poles. It was to be a co-ordinated and simultaneous attack on the whole front. The attacks were also to be supported by the American army operating from the Anzio beachhead.

The first Polish attack occurred at 1 a.m. on May 12. The Germans immediately engaged the Polish soldiers in intense hand-to-hand fighting in the rocky terrain. The battle went on for hours. The Poles made advances, but could not hold the captured terrain due to the powerful counterattacks of the enemy reserves. The Poles had to withdraw to their original positions. Even though the Poles could not hold their positions, the Allies considered Polish action a success because it drew German artillery fire from other sectors and prevented the Germans from using their reserves there. As a result, the Allies were able to make some progress in their sectors.

The second attack occurred at 7 a.m. on May 17. The Polish battalions went into action immediately after the initial artillery barrage with complete disregard for losses from gunfire and mines.

They continued their advance through the next day and at 10:20 a.m. on the morning of May 18, 1944, the Polish 12th Lancers Regiment hoisted the white and red flag of Poland over the ruins of the Monte Cassino monastery. The fighting continued for the next few days until the Polish forces captured Piedemonte Mountain on May 25, 1944. These battles had completely tied up the German forces and prevented them from defending other objectives in the surrounding areas. Thus, the Allies were able to advance in their sectors with greater ease. The capture of Monte Cassino had opened the road to Rome, which was liberated on June 4, 1944.

The casualties in that battle were very heavy. There were 850 men killed and 2,822 wounded. The wounded included Uncle Romek. His knee was shattered when shrapnel hit him during the assault on the monastery. Józek Pietryka, a medical corpsman who turned out to be my uncle's cousin, pulled him down the mountain and brought him to a field hospital. In fact, half of Uncle Romek's platoon was killed during the assault. A number of our relatives and friends were killed or wounded in the battle. My father was injured when an artillery shell hit his bunker and buried him alive. Fortunately, his fellow comrades rescued him in time and brought him to the same hospital as my uncle. When my father was told that there was another Bąk in the hospital, he went to see him and found it was his brother. Later in life, my father wondered what would have happened to him if he had stayed in the infantry. He surmised he would have been killed or seriously wounded since so many of his former comrades had met that fate.

There were many congratulatory messages sent to General Anders and the Polish troops. General Alexander, the Commander of all Allied Forces in Italy, said, "Soldiers of the Polish II Corps, if it had been given to me to choose the soldiers I would like to command, I would have chosen the Poles." General Anders received many decorations, among them the Order of Bath from King George VI, the American Legion of Merit from President Roosevelt, and the highest Polish military award, the cross of Virtuti Military from the President of Poland, Władysław Raczkiewicz. His most cherished reward, however, was the congratulatory letter from inside occupied Poland, from the Commander of the Polish Home Army, General Bór-Komorowski.

In the camps, we followed the exploits of the Polish II Corps with great interest and pride, and were saddened by each report of someone killed in action. We attended a number of requiem masses for the dead, as well as masses of thanksgiving for the glorious exploits of the army. These events were spiritually uplifting for Poles and increased our stature in the eyes of people of other nationalities.

The Polish II Corps was moved from Monte Cassino to the Adriatic sector in June 1944, and General Anders was given command of the whole area with the objective of capturing the port city Ancona. This was a strategic port and the Allies needed a close harbor in order to bring supplies to their troops that were moving northward. The advancing Polish troops ran into German defensive positions before reaching Ancona and defeated them at the battle of Loreto. The battle of Ancona took place on July 17, 1944, and the Germans were soundly defeated resulting in the liberation of Ancona. However, the Allies' casualties were considerable. The Allies took over 3,000 prisoners. Among these were many Polish conscripts who were forced to serve in the German army. The Allies carefully screened these prisoners of Polish origin and the ones who passed the screening were assigned to the Polish II Corps. My future uncle, Piotr Krawczyk, was one of them. He married Aunt Macia after they met in England after the war.

Again, the allied commanders recognized General Anders as a brilliant military strategist and he received a number of congratulatory messages from them. Pope Pius XII received the Polish troops at a special ceremony. The Pope gave them a special blessing. In a private audience with Anders, the Pope showed his great understanding of the Polish–Soviet issues and expressed his great concern about the communist menace to the world.

In the meantime, the future of Poland was again being debated and determined, this time at a conference in Yalta, in the Crimea, held February 4–11, 1945. Poland again was not consulted. At the conference, Roosevelt, Churchill and Stalin signed a declaration about the status of post-war Poland. The main points of this declaration were: The establishment of the Polish Provisional Government of National Unity, recognition of the eastern frontier of Poland along the Curzon Line, and ascension of German territory to Poland in the north and west of the pre-war borders. The news left Poles numb and bewildered. It meant that the very Allies they counted on for support had sold them out. It meant that the eastern part of Poland, including the cities of Lwów and Wilno, a territory that had been closely connected with Poland for over 600 years and which had never had any Russian population, was to be annexed by the Soviet Union. It meant that the soldiers who fought so gallantly for freedom would never be able to return to their own free country. It meant that they were destined to further wandering in alien lands or to return to a country under communist rule.

The Polish II Corps fought their last battle of the war in Italy, helping to liberate Bologna, on April 20–21, 1945. The three best German divisions opposed the II Corps, and fighting was fierce and bitter. Again, as at Monte Cassino and Ancona, the Poles showed splendid fighting spirit, endurance and great skill. The fighting against the German crack Paratroop Division was particularly fierce. The Polish II Corps liberated Bologna on April 21, 1945. On April 28, 1945, German representatives signed the surrender of the German troops in Italy, and on May 8, 1945, Germany surrendered unconditionally to the western powers in Reims, France.

The Polish cause did not look as bright on the political side as on the military side. On June 28, 1945, the new Polish Provisional Government of National Unity was set up with three-quarters of its members imposed by the Soviet Union, many of them not even Polish citizens. On July 6, 1945, both the United States and Britain recognized the new government. The Polish government, which led Poland's struggle against Germany, and the Polish Armed Forces who fought at the side of the Allies, were both discarded like unwanted intruders. This was ironic because both Allied Superpowers had strongly supported Polish causes at the beginning of the war when Polish involvement was crucial. Churchill had assured General Sikorski that, "we are bound in this war for life or death." Roosevelt, in 1942, called Poland "the inspiration of all nations." This turned out to be political hogwash. After the western powers withdrew the recognition of the Polish Government-in-Exile, all Polish forces outside of Poland were placed under the British High Command and subsequently demobilized.

The Potsdam conference held on July 17, 1945, and attended by Stalin, Truman and Attlee marked yet another step on the part of Britain and the United States toward the appeasement of the Soviet Union. It was agreed by the Three Powers that they were going to assist the Polish Provisional Government in facilitating the return to Poland, as soon as practicable, of all Poles abroad including all civilians in the refugee camps and soldiers in the armed forces. It is significant to note that a very small percentage of soldiers in the Polish II Corps applied for repatriation to Poland and less than one percent of those were soldiers who originally joined the army in the Soviet Union. The rest were Polish ex-prisoners liberated from the German army who had joined the Polish army in the west. Most of the returning soldiers had joined the army after hostilities had already ended, and most were from central Poland and had close relatives still residing there. Thus, the Potsdam conference officially sealed the fate of Poland, soon to become a communist puppet state.

Mr. C. R. Attlee, the new Prime Minister of Britain, informed General Anders in March of 1946 that the Polish forces would be transferred to Britain and demobilized. Mr. Attlee said he hoped that as many Poles as possible would opt to return to Poland. The British government set up the Polish Resettlement Corps for those who decided not to return, in order to help the soldiers' transition from military to civilian life. To Britain's credit, it was the only country that recognized that there was a moral obligation to help these soldiers and their families provide for their future.

The transfer of the Polish II Corps to England began in June 1946, and was essentially completed in September of 1946. The troops were transported to England, mostly by ships from Naples and by trains through Germany and France. My father was transferred to England by ship in the summer of 1946. Before he left Italy, he was examined by the army medical staff and declared partially disabled due to the injuries sustained at Monte Cassino. For his participation in the war, he was awarded the Polish Cross for Valor, the Army Medal, and the Cross of Monte Cassino. In addition, he was awarded British medals, a 1939–1945 Star, the Italy Star, and the Defense Medal.

In England, my father joined the Polish Resettlement Corps on July 27, 1947. The overwhelming majority of Polish soldiers in England joined the Corps, which shocked the British authorities, who expected the majority of the soldiers to return to Poland. The Resettlement Corps afforded the soldiers the opportunity to learn new skills as carpenters, shoemakers, tailors or factory workers. Unfortunately, their education, military background, and lack of English were not suited for their new professions. Career officers had a particularly tough time adjusting to this new environment. It was not unusual for a Polish army general to work as a dishwasher or a bartender, as was the case with General Stanisław Maczek, the commander of the Polish Armor Division that fought so gallantly in Belgium and the Netherlands.

My father learned how to make briefcases and other articles from leather. Briefcases were in demand by the soldiers returning to Poland. This was a way to smuggle leather to Poland. The leather could be used later to sole shoes and it was in short supply in Poland. My father was a trader at heart. He also had a side business of buying herring in bulk and reselling it retail to his fellow soldiers. None of these ventures turned into anything substantial. Later, he had to supplement his meager army pension with work at local farms doing odd jobs as a farmhand.

On June 8, 1946, a victory parade was held in London. The Polish forces were not invited to take part. It would have been politically embarrassing for the British to invite armed forces of a government they did not recognize. Stalin was still being appeased, and the communists' demands took precedence over moral obligation to the former comrades in arms. However, an invitation was extended to the Polish airmen who played such a vital role in the Battle of Britain. The airmen declined for they did not wish to represent Poland at a ceremony from which all other Polish forces were specifically excluded. The action of the British government caused the Poles to feel more embarrassed than angry toward the British. The Poles were the first to raise arms against the Germans. They fought gallantly on all fronts—land, sea and air—to the very end. It was a humiliating exclusion.

The news from Poland was not good. There were mass arrests of Home Army soldiers and higher-level Polish political leaders by the communists. The returning servicemen from overseas, after the initial welcome, were being persecuted and discriminated against. The communists initiated vicious propaganda against what they called "Anders' Army," calling them fascists and imperialists. In September 1946, they stripped General Anders, General Sosnkowski, Władysław Raczkiewicz, the Polish president in exile, and other ranking officials in exile of their Polish citizenship, calling them traitors. Thus, Poland became a captive of the Soviet Union and its communist henchmen in Warsaw for the next half a century. The true Polish heroes were forced into exile...once again.

My father in Polish II Corps, 1944.

General Władysław Anders, Commander of Polish II Corps.

General Władysław Sikorski, Premier and Commander in Chief of Polish Armed Forces.

Polish recruits in the Soviet Union, 1941. (Ref. 10, Szmagier)

Polish recruits after induction into the army in the Soviet Union, winter 1941. (Ref. 16, PAVA)

Generals Anders and Sikorski with Polish soldiers
in the Soviet Union, winter 1941. (Ref. 10, Szmagier)

Polish Army in the Soviet Union, winter 1941.
(Ref. 16, PAVA)

The remains of Polish army officers being exhumed in Katyn Forest, spring 1943. (Ref. 16, PAVA)

Our Lady of Kozielsk, Patroness of the Polish Army and Polish Refugees, St. Ándrzej Bobola Church, London.

Polish Army in the Middle East, 1943. (Ref. 16, PAVA)

Polish soldiers (my father is front right) visiting Jerusalem, 1943.

Monte Cassino after it was captured by troops of Polish II Corps on May 19, 1944. (Ref. 2, Army in Exile)

Polish cemetery at Monte Cassino. (Ref. 13, Monte Cassino)

Pakistan
Karachi

After arriving in Karachi, we were transported from the port by army trucks to the Polish refugee camp outside Karachi. Along with us were a few other families who could not continue the journey to Africa because of an illness in the family. The rest of the passengers from our freighter were transferred to the passenger ship and sailed to Africa. The refugee camp, called "Country Club," was located 12 miles from Karachi in what was then India, and now Pakistan. The camp was a transition camp for Polish refugees going to more permanent locations in India or Africa. It was the second camp set up in the Karachi area, the first being Hajj Pilgrims Camp that was located in the bazaar section of the city.

Hajj Pilgrim Camp was previously used as temporary housing by the Muslim pilgrims making the pilgrimage to Mecca. The war interrupted these pilgrimages and the camp became vacant and a convenient place to house Polish refugees. The Hajj Pilgrim Camp, housing less than 2,000 people, proved to be inadequate to house a large number of Polish refugees so a bigger camp, "Country Club," was constructed.

The new camp consisted of about 300 large tents that could house six to ten people each. The tents were pitched in the desert. There was nothing in the area but sand, rocks, and a few cacti. The sun was unbearable with its penetrating heat, and there was no place to hide from it. The camp resembled an army base more than a place for a civilian population with children. A barbed wire fence surrounded the camp to keep the animals and strangers out. The camp was like an oasis in the desert, and we were isolated from the natives by a relatively large distance from the city. A small hill was selected as a location for a chapel. The chapel was initially in a tent, but later, Polish carpenters built a beautiful wood chapel with a row of benches on the outside for worshipers. Rev. Antoni Jankowski served as the pastor for the community. The schools were housed in several tents put together near the chapel. Wash-basins, showers and latrines were located at the opposite end at the lowest point in the camp.

The camp was under the supervision of the British authorities, and British Major Reeves was in charge. Major Reeves treated Polish refugees as if they were prisoners or conquered nationals. He maintained a military atmosphere and strict discipline in the camp and put many restrictions on the population. The food rations were skimpy, especially for a population that had starved in Russia for a long time. The Polish people protested to the British authorities and the British replaced Major Reeves with Captain Allen. Captain Allen was considerably more understanding of the needs of the civilian population and, with time, became a good friend of the Poles and even learned to speak Polish. He became a major spokesman for Polish causes when dealing with British authorities. The first change Captain Allen made was to increase the quantity of food provided to the refugees. His second change was to replace some of his British assistants with Polish nationals, thus defusing tensions that existed between the Poles and the Britons under Major Reeves' tenure. The duties in the camp were divided between the Poles and the Britons along the areas of their respective expertise. The British were responsible for the general administration and sanitary facilities. The Poles were responsible for schools, cultural events and communication among the refugees. The camaraderie among the Poles and Britons improved, and with time, the British even participated in the celebration of Polish holidays and cultural events. They particularly liked *Śmigus Dingus*, celebrated by Polish people on Easter Monday, when we doused each other with water. The British went one-up on the Poles by dunking Polish girls in the big water troughs that were placed around the mess hall. All had a good time.

We shared our tent with Aunt Macia and her children. Aniela Dereń, our cousin who joined us in Tehran when my mother became sick, and three of our friends from Poland, Danka and

Wanda Zychowicz and their aunt Cymerman, occupied an adjacent tent. The only furniture we had were beds, a clay container for water, a couple of folding chairs, mosquito nets and a lantern to provide light in the evenings. The beds were simple steel frames with rope netting and thin mattresses filled with felt stuffing. Mosquito nets were used to protect us against the mosquitoes at night, especially during the rainy season when they were particularly abundant. Snakes and scorpions were frequently seen in the area and we had to be very careful to avoid being bitten. A scorpion bit my sister and her leg became swollen and turned completely black. She had to be hospitalized but, fortunately, recovered fully. The most dangerous time was going to the latrines in the evenings. The latrines were located on the outskirts of the living areas, and to reach them, we had to pass through the deserted area that attracted these creatures.

The British provided food supplies, and meals were prepared in the communal kitchen. We were given three meals a day and ate in the mess hall, a large shed with only a metal sheet roof and a short wall to protect us from the sun and rain. On some days, the wind was very strong and moved through the mess hall creating weird sounds, scaring people who did not know what to expect next. The mess hall had a row of tables and benches, resembling picnic areas in the U.S. Meals were given at preset hours and were signaled by the ringing of a large bell. The meals were adequate although children were often hungry between meals, especially late in the evening. We were always sneaking out pieces of bread from the dining area for later snacking even though it was strictly forbidden, mainly for health reasons. Food attracted bugs, mosquitoes, animals, and in the tropical heat, it spoiled quickly. We could buy tea and cookies in a small store in the camp on the rare occasions when we had money. Sometimes my father sent us a few British pounds, but these were better spent on clothing.

We were inoculated against such infectious diseases as bubonic plague and typhoid as soon as we arrived in the camp. Malaria replaced dysentery and typhoid as the most common ailment among refugees. The conditions in the camp were ideal for the spread of this disease. The monsoon or heavy rain season lasted from June to September, creating puddles and lakes in the area, which bred mosquitoes. The lack of proper housing made it impossible to keep mosquitoes out of our living areas. The authorities introduced strict rules to minimize exposure to mosquitoes. We were required to sleep under the nets, wear long sleeve clothing in the evenings, and put anti-mosquito ointment on the exposed parts of our bodies. Tents were sprayed daily with chemicals, and food was not allowed in the tents. The authorities encouraged lots of rest, especially for those who were weak and whose systems were more susceptible to disease. Persons who were even suspected of contracting diseases were encouraged to go to the hospital immediately. Those who were seriously ill were sent to city hospital in Karachi or a British military hospital in the area. During the times when mosquitoes were plentiful, malaria hit the camp population in epidemic proportions. Extra tents had to be set up in the hospital area to deal with the high number of malaria cases.

Soon after our arrival in Karachi, I became ill with malaria. I was hospitalized for several days with a high fever and cold shakes. The hospital consisted of several tents isolated from the rest of the camp by a wire fence. Polish doctors and nurses sent by the Polish army were on the hospital staff. Malaria is a dreadful disease causing the body to have rigorous shakes, with alternating feelings of high fever and freezing cold. This condition lasts for several days. The body becomes extremely weak, even after a full recovery. The medication administered for malaria was quinine a bitter powder given to us three times a day. The taste of quinine was very bitter. The powder stuck to the roof of my mouth and aftertaste lasted a long time. A few times, when the hospital ran out of the powder form of quinine, the liquid form was used. The taste of the liquid was just as bad, but at least the aftertaste did not last as long.

Once I got better, my biggest problem in the hospital was boredom; children's books or toys were not available. We tried to make up some games but ran out of ideas in a rather short time. Occasionally we sneaked out of the hospital in the evenings, but when the nurses discovered it, they confiscated our pajamas so we had to sleep naked for a couple days as punishment. This, of course, restricted our freedom to move around. Every member of our family had malaria at one time or another and visits to the hospital were part of our daily routine.

Life in the camp became routine after our initial adjustments to the new environment. It was extremely difficult to organize proper schooling for children due to the transitory nature of the camp with a constant rotation of students as well as teachers. Some people stayed in the camp for a few weeks, others for a few months and some up to a year. Under these circumstances, it was difficult to have any sort of continuity in schooling, and as a result, we fell even further behind in our education.

Adults kept busy with the usual house chores like washing and sewing, which took a fair amount of time due to lack of proper facilities. Continuing education courses also were organized for the adults. There were a number of home economic courses to teach women new skills, such as sewing, needlework and art crafts. About 90 percent of the camp population were women and children. A large percentage of the population had only minimal education, and the continuing education courses offered them the opportunity not only to advance their education but also reduce boredom. English language courses also were offered. Some people took advantage of these opportunities. Others felt there was no need to learn English since they were going to return to Poland. This was obviously a shortsighted view, but that was the mentality of the population in the camps.

A cultural committee was established to form theatrical groups and organized cultural events, such as lectures, reviews of current events, concerts, and other presentations. Books and newspapers became more available when the ships arriving from the U.S. and Britain with army supplies brought these items with them. The camp had a library and a reading room housed in three tents combined into one. The theatrical groups made a number of presentations for the American and British soldiers as well as for the people in the camp. Also, a number of people in the camp worked on American or British military bases that were nearby. The war with the Japanese in Burma and Malaysia was at its peak at that time. The British and American air forces were flying in and out of these bases on training missions or ferrying supplies. Some of the military bases were used as rest and recreation areas for soldiers who were taking part in combat, and the bases often served as major hospitals for the wounded.

An ammunition dump and military junkyard were located a few miles from our camp. My friends and I made many excursions to the dump to collect military items, mostly useless things. One time I brought back a car battery and several small electric light bulbs I found in a wrecked army truck. I thought I would introduce electricity to our tent. I don't remember if I was successful, but when my mother found out where I got the stuff, she was horrified and made me throw it away.

We went to mass in the chapel early in the mornings, before breakfast and before the heat became too intense. There was a pet goat named *Baśka* in the camp. The goat always marched ahead of everyone on the way to the chapel. She then lay down in front of the altar and stayed there until the end of the mass. After the mass, the goat got up and led us to the mess hall for breakfast. This procedure was repeated every day without exception. We got very attached to the goat and she became a frequent topic of our conversations.

The Americans and British stationed on the nearby army bases organized movies for us. The soldiers brought films to the camp and showed them on an outdoor screen set up in an open area near the sports field. People gathered around, sitting on the ground on blankets or chairs they brought with them. Most people did not understand English, so the discussions afterwards were lengthy and, at times, heated on what was being said on the screen. These conversations often extended into wee hours of the morning and even carried into the next day.

Children participated in sporting events, such as track and field, soccer and ping-pong. Chess and checkers were very popular games with the young and adults alike. Matches were organized between the local children and the Polish children in the camp. American and British soldiers often invited children to their bases on weekends. They sent trucks to pick us up in the morning and bring us back in the evening. For us, it was a big treat, for we were showered with gifts of chocolates, candy and chewing gum. Language was a problem since we did not speak English. However, there were a number of Polish Americans who spoke Polish and they acted as interpreters for us and the soldiers. We always looked forward to these visits, especially to the American bases. On several occasions a Polish–American soldier found someone in the camp who hailed from the same region of Poland as his ancestors. A friend of ours, Wanda Zychowicz, who lived in the tent next to ours, met a Polish–American soldier, Joe Górski, whose father was from her village. They fell in love and married in India. Occasionally we went to Karachi to window-shop. Unfortunately, we couldn't buy anything since we did not have money. The camp personnel organized these trips and the army provided trucks for transportation. Once we were invited to visit the Catholic bishop of Karachi at his residence. It was a beautiful place and we were very impressed by the beautiful gardens.

The heat, sandstorms and monsoon rains were very harsh on us since we still were unaccustomed to these elements. Heat was so penetrating that we could not do very much during the day. There was no place to hide from it. We were easily dehydrated and were constantly reminded to drink lots of water and take salt tablets to reduce the possibility of dehydration. Heat strokes were fairly common. Occasional sandstorms created havoc, and cleaning up after them required a major effort. The heat became less of a problem in the monsoon season. However, the humidity became so high that it was difficult to breathe. The monsoons or heavy rains lasted for several weeks. The rains created rapidly flowing rivers that carried all sort of items with them. On occasions, we could see our articles floating off from the tents with the rapidly flowing water. One night, our tent collapsed on us. The stakes holding the tent loosened from the sandy ground and were pulled out by the tension of the tent ropes. My mother and Aunt Macia took us to the neighboring tent and tried, in a driving rain, to pound the stakes back into the ground and raise the tent, but to no avail. The tent was too big and too heavy for the two women to manage. We had to wait until morning for the maintenance people to reset the tent. We lost many small items that night because the rapidly flowing water carried them away.

We often could hear jackals howling at night. These noises were very disconcerting and made sleeping very difficult. Sometimes the jackals would approach the camp and even venture inside the tents and carry off various items. They were particularly fond of soap. After a while, we got used to the sounds of jackals but were always concerned that they might hurt us.

Christmas in the "Country Club" in 1944 was rather simple. We did not have a Christmas tree or a manger in our tent. The American soldiers invited children to their camp during the holidays, and Santa Claus brought gifts for every child. It was the first time I saw an American version of Santa Claus, the jolly fellow with a white beard and red suit, unlike the Polish version of Saint Nick dressed in bishop's robes. This Santa Claus also spoke Polish, even though it was with a heavy American accent. The *wigilia* was held at the camp mess hall. The hall was decorated with colored lights and the tables were covered with white cloth. There was *opłatek* on a plate at each table. The Christmas tree was made from a desert-jagged bush on which hung paper chains, candy and homemade ornaments. The sharing of *opłatek* was rather somber because of the existing political situation. Things were not going well for Poland. In fact, we were not sure what would happen to us in the foreseeable future.

We had our ups and downs politically in Karachi. We learned in May 1944 about the battle of Monte Casino, and we were very proud of the achievement of the Polish II Corps in Italy, despite the large number of casualties. My father and uncle were wounded and a number of our friends had relatives or friends who were killed or wounded. It was difficult to balance the sadness on one hand and the exhilaration on the other. Later, the news of the other battles in Italy at Loreto, Ancona, and Bologna generated similar feelings. In

August 1944, we learned about the Warsaw Uprising, when the Polish Home Army took up arms against the Germans in Warsaw. For two months we agonized every day about the outcome of the Uprising and the large number of casualties. We heard how the Soviets refused to grant permission for Allied planes trying to supply the Polish Home Army to land and refuel on Soviet controlled soil. We also learned how the Soviets stood idly on the outskirts of Warsaw and did not assist the Home Army, allowing the Germans to slaughter thousands of civilians and army personnel and to completely destroy the city. To us, this was a stark reminder of the Soviet treachery and what happened to us only four short years before.

The camp in Karachi was a transition camp like the camp in Ahvaz. About 18,000 people passed through this camp on their way to more permanent locations. Since the camp could hold only about 2,500 people, the turnover at the camp was very high. At the peak of the influx of refugees to the "Country Club," the authorities had to transfer some of the people to an empty American military base in Malir, some 30 miles from Karachi. Most of the transferred refugees were orphans. Conditions in that camp were so severe that the children had to be moved very quickly to Valivade in India, and to Santa Rosa in Mexico.

Polish refugees were sent from Karachi to Valivade and Balachadi in India, or to Lebanon, New Zealand, Mexico, and various countries in Africa. Kenya and Tanganyika (Tanzania) had the largest Polish refugee population on the African continent with each country hosting about 8,000 refugees scattered in small camps. There were about 4,800 refugees in camps in Uganda and a smaller number in Northern Rhodesia (Zambia), Southern Rhodesia (Zimbabwe), and South Africa.

Our stay in Karachi was just another stopover in the long journey on what we thought was the trip back to Poland. The conditions in Karachi were primitive, the climate at times was extremely hot, and there were frequent bouts with malaria, but things weren't all bad. We were free, relatively well-fed, and hopeful about returning home to Poland. We children had good care, and there was a group of teachers dedicated to giving us a decent education and firm guidance in moral values.

In August 1945, our family went from Karachi to Valivade located in the province of Kolhapur, India. We were glad to leave Karachi for the more stable situation that awaited us in Valivade. The trip to Valivade took two days. We traveled by land, first by army trucks from the camp to the railway station in Karachi, then by train through Bombay and Pune to Valivade. The train ride took us through breathtaking scenery. We crossed the Hindu holy river, Indus. The river was very wide and the bridge across it was a wooden structure that swayed uneasily as the train moved slowly across it, creating an eerie feeling of insecurity. We stopped several times at small railway stations to receive meals, and we were very impressed by the variety of trees and rich vegetation at these stops compared to the barren countryside in Ahvaz and Karachi. There were hundreds of monkeys and exotic birds in the trees. The monkeys were not afraid of people and approached the train looking for food. We changed trains in Pune because the railroad between Pune and Kolhapur was narrow gauge. The scenery between Pune and Kolhapur was equally beautiful. We crossed the mountains and traveled through several tunnels. We saw many waterfalls flowing in the distance. Again the foliage was breathtaking. Two days later we reached our destination in Valivade—our home for the next two years.

Polish refugee camp “Country Club” near Karachi, 1944.

Chapel in Polish refugee camp near Karachi, 1944.

Our family in front of "our home" in the
refugee camp outside of Karachi, 1944.

Dining hall in the refugee camp in Karachi, 1944.

INDIA
Valivade

Valivade was the largest camp in India for Polish refugees who had escaped from Soviet Russia. There were two smaller permanent camps in India. One was in Balachadi near Jamnagar, north of Bombay. It had about 700 residents, mostly orphans. Another was in the mountains in Panchgani near Pune, about 30 miles from the coast of the Arabian Sea. Panchgani was mainly for people recuperating from serious illnesses, like tuberculosis.

Valivade was located about six miles from the city of Kolhapur, about 300 miles south of Bombay and a 100 miles from the shores of the Arabian Sea. The landscape was varied with some hills, trees and rich vegetation. The climate was more moderate than in Karachi or Bombay. The Panchganga River flowed several hundred yards from the camp.

The camp was constructed in 1943 to house Polish refugees from the Soviet Union for the duration of the war. It consisted of about 200 long barracks built from cheap construction materials because the camp was not planned to be used for very long. However, some of the barracks have survived to this day. The beams and posts were made from wood, and the walls were made from thin mats that, while not very pleasing to the eye, offered sufficient protection against wind and rain. The roofs were red clay tiles. There were no solid doors or glass windows, only holes in the walls covered by sliding mats. The floor was barren ground coated with a thin layer of a mud-like substance made of clay, cow manure and sand. This substance dried into an odor-free thin crust that kept the dust down. The floor had to be resurfaced about once a month and the local Hindu women were hired to do the job. The local population used this practice extensively.

Each barrack was divided into eight single family quarters, each family having two rooms and a small kitchen. The toilet facilities were simple latrines located on the outskirts of the camp. The baths were in a single communal shower area located in the middle of the camp. There was no warm water in the showers. The camp was divided into five sections for administrative purposes. There were approximately 5,000 residents in the town-like camp. Polish authorities administered the camp, but the British and, later, Hindu authorities supervised financial and legal matters. They also served as the liaison between Polish, British and Indian authorities. The Poles were responsible for general administration, educational system, health services, police and security, fire department, and minor construction. Valivade was like a microcosm of Poland inside the vast domain of India. Inside that microcosm, we could actually believe that we were in a small town in Poland. This feeling quickly evaporated once we ventured outside the camp boundaries. There the language, culture, people and tropical landscape were quick reminders of how far from Poland we truly were.

Upon arrival, each family received a kitchen table, chairs, dresser with mirror, and a portable charcoal stove for cooking. We also received lamps, mattresses, mosquito nets, wash basins, buckets for water, pots and pans, kitchen utensils, sheets, towels and blankets. Each member of the family was given a set of clothing, shoes, and a tropical hat made of cork that was mandatory for protection against the sun. It must be said that we had been equipped with everything essential for our existence. This certainly was very helpful in restoring our physical and psychological balance after the Soviet nightmare. We felt like we finally had something resembling a stable home for the first time since leaving the Soviet Union. With time, we all added personal touches to "our homes" by decorating the living areas and planting flowers and plants on porches and on the narrow strip of land by the barracks. Some people planted little gardens, including their own banana or papaya trees. Soon, crawling vines covered the walls and the posts of our barracks, greatly improving their appearance. The climate in Valivade was favorable for rapid growth of vegetation, and the camp took on the appearance of a beautifully maintained residential area.

Each family in the camp was provided with a monthly stipend of 52 rupees, equivalent to about 10 dollars, per person for food and incidental expenses. We did our own shopping in stores in the camp or at the Hindu market outside the camp perimeter. Each family cooked for themselves, but after a while, some joined together in preparing their meals since it was more economical. The meals were cooked on a camping type kerosene heater or on a small coal grill.

We prepared our main meal with Aunt Macia. The allotted funds were adequate for food purchases and we never felt hungry. We received allotted clothing from the general services store upon our arrival in the camp. Later, the authorities provided additional funds to each family for the purchase of clothing. The amount was 60 rupees, or about 12 dollars per year per person. This allowance, modest on the first glance, was sufficient, especially since we did not have to purchase winter clothing. We were able to purchase most items in camp stores where prices were reasonable. We did not have to purchase cork hats since they were issued upon our arrival, but we had to buy rubber raincoats needed during the monsoon season. Occasionally, we experienced shortages of clothing because of the war. The war effort always had first priority. In these cases the Indian government provided an invaluable assistance by directing Polish authorities to go outside the province of Kolhapur to procure additional clothing.

After a while, life in the camp began to resemble a normal life, considering the circumstances. Most activities centered around church, school, scouting, and cultural and recreational activities. The community built a beautiful wooden church funded by the donations of residents. The whole community celebrated all church and national holidays with mass and appropriate rallies. One of the most beautiful celebrations was *Boże Ciało* or Corpus Christi. The procession from altar to altar through the alleys of the camp was beautiful with girls dressed in white, throwing flowers at the priest carrying the Blessed Sacrament while the whole congregation sang religious songs. This was especially impressive to the native Hindus who gathered around to watch the procession. At Easter, the Boy Scouts, myself included, stood guard at "Christ's grave" that was set up in our church. The grave was guarded for 24 hours, half an hour at a time for each scouting detail, from Holy Friday until the Easter Sunday mass of the Resurrection. The faithful prayed in the adoration of the Blessed Sacrament without interruption for those three days and nights. Other church holidays were celebrated with equal enthusiasm. It was a demonstration of the same unshakable faith, which carried us through the Soviet nightmare and sustained us in other camps. The church provided the stability and security for a population of mainly women and children whose husbands and fathers were dead or fighting the war in faraway places.

Schooling in the camp finally began to resemble a normal academic environment. Children comprised half of the camp's population so it was important to organize a school system that could address our educational needs. We needed to make up for lost time since we had little concrete schooling while living in the previous camps. Valivade had three kindergartens, four primary schools, and one secondary school. In addition, there were a number of trade schools offering courses to children as well as adults. After arriving in Valivade, I went to third grade. By that time, I was already three years behind in my schooling.

The schools were in separate barracks and each classroom was furnished with tables and benches for the students. Textbooks were available, but we had to share them with other students, usually two to three students for each textbook. We received a number of school supplies such as maps, globes, posters and laboratory equipment from the National Catholic Relief Organization in the United States. Students were responsible for keeping the classrooms clean and maintaining the grounds outside the classrooms by planting and watering flowers and maintaining the flowerbeds. The school year was from June 15 to March 31, and classes were held only in the morning. The temperature in the afternoon was too high for any effective studying, as was the period from April 1 to June 15. The schools had excellent and experienced teachers; all educated in Poland, some were even university professors. There were about 120 teachers, so the ratio of students to favorable twenty to one. The educational level of the schools was quite good despite the difficult conditions: The tropical climate, no air conditioning, primitive buildings, and a shortage of books and school supplies.

We had not been in regular schools for almost four years and many students and teachers were still in a weakened physical condition. It was also difficult to study in the evenings due to the lack of proper lighting. On the positive side, the maturity level of students was well beyond their age and they had a great desire to learn. The teachers were dedicated and felt that they had an almost sacred duty to overcome the obstacles and teach the children entrusted to their care. The schools in Valivade trained us in the best traditions of Polish culture and prepared us well for the challenges of the future.

A number of children were offered opportunities to study outside the camp. There were about 30 boys who were sent to the United States to Orchard Lake, Michigan, to study for the priesthood. About 70 girls were invited to study at St. Joseph's Convent in Panchgani; my cousin Anulka was one of them. Instructions at the convent were in English and the girls were forced to learn the English language quickly, which later proved to be very advantageous for them.

The Polish authorities organized many adult education courses, including arts and crafts, secretarial studies, agricultural studies, sewing, carpentry, cooking, and baking. There was also a special course on reading and writing for those who were illiterate. It was the intention of the authorities to give all residents an opportunity to improve themselves and to acquire new skills if they were so inclined. These opportunities also helped to reduce the boredom among the population. One of the negative aspects of our existence was that it deprived people of the initiative to earn a living. The educational opportunities presented at the camp offered a chance to regain that initiative. As a result of these courses graduates were able to work in the camp using their newly acquired skills. For example, the sewing group made uniforms for camp firemen and security personnel and repaired uniforms for the British army. The arts and crafts group made Polish dolls for the Italian manufacturer Bata. The camp cooperative *Zgoda* managed the commercial part of the group's work. I have to admit with some degree of pride that the educational system in the camp was excellent and greatly benefited the entire camp population.

The orphanage in Valivade was very large with over 400 children. These children were housed together in a separate section of the camp. They were grouped according to age, although siblings were never separated. The orphans were given three meals a day and went to school in their section of the camp. They required They presented a great challenge to the administrators and teachers alike. However, most of them received a solid foundation to build on for the future.

Scouting became a favorite activity among the children in Valivade as it provided an outlet for our energies. It enabled contact with other children in and outside the camp, it embodied discipline and exposed us to organizational structure resembling military bearing, which we admired. Almost half of the children who lived in the camp belonged to the Boy Scouts, the Girl Scouts, or for the very young, *Zuchy* or *Zuszki*, the equivalent of Brownies. Scouting activities included field trips, sports, and taking part in religious and national festivities. For me, the highlight of being in the Boy Scouts was a two-week camping trip to the outskirts of the Indian jungle in a place called Chandoli. We slept in tents, gathered dry leaves and placed them on the ground to serve as mattresses, cooked our own meals, swam in the nearby river and made daily trips to the jungle. In the evening, we made a huge bonfire and the entire troop sat around the fire singing songs and listening to stories told by our scoutmasters. The major challenge for each scout was to earn merit badges. The most cherished badge called "three feathers." To earn it we had to spend 24 hours in the jungle alone and survive only on food that we could find in the jungle. To the best of my knowledge, no one was attacked by a tiger, elephant or snake during this time, but the threat was on our minds during those 24 hours.

The local Hindu scouting groups from Kolhapur invited us often for sporting competition and holiday festivities. The two trips that come to mind were the coronation of the young Maharaja of Kolhapur in 1947, culminating with a colorful parade that included beautifully decorated elephants carrying various dignitaries. The other celebration was when India gained its independence from Britain on August 15, 1947. The Polish community was well represented at the independence festivities, with all Polish organizations participating in the celebration. After the ceremonies, we were treated to a lunch—Indian style. It was a very festive day for the Hindus and Poles alike, and the show prepared by the Hindu Scouts that evening was very beautiful and touching. Somehow Hindu people understood our predicament better than others did because they also were subjected to domination by a foreign country. They always wished us to return to a free and independent Poland. The ties between the two scouting organizations were so close that when we departed India, the Polish Scouts left all their equipment to the Hindu contingent.

The cultural life in the camp revolved around religious and national holidays. These holidays were celebrated with masses, parades and evening shows or recitals. A theater group performed several times during the year, staging plays for adults and especially children. The group was invited to perform in Kolhapur and Bombay in front of foreign audiences and received rave reviews. There were many recitals, lectures and "concerts" via radio or phonograph. We had several reading rooms and recreational centers in the camp where we could find newspapers, periodicals, magazines and books, or play chess or checkers. On some weekends, we went to movies showing English and Indian films. One of the children's favorite films was an Indian movie showing the Hindu king Shivaji who fought against oppression and for freedom of the Hindu people from the Moslems.

Many sporting activities were organized for the children in the camp. We had three athletic fields where we participated in track and field, volleyball, soccer, basketball, and other events. Matches were set up among the schools, different camp sections, various scouting groups, and occasionally against the Hindu children from Kolhapur. We had swimming and kayaking competitions on the Panchganga River. In fact, the river was an attraction for children during the hot summer days. There were some treacherous spots in the river with fast currents and whirlpools, so we had to be very careful about where we swam. Once I fell into one of those whirlpools and was pulled out, unconscious, by a friend. When my mother heard about this she was furious and told me that she did not get me through Siberia and other camps to have me drown in some unheard of place in India. We also were able to rent bicycles from the local store. There were designated areas where we were allowed to ride the bikes, but it was forbidden to ride on the road. Once I went on the road and was "arrested" by a camp policeman. My mother was duly informed and was shocked and embarrassed to be raising a "criminal." After she bailed me out, I fully expected a spanking, my normal punishment. When we arrived at our barrack, my mother was getting ready to apply the punishment when I suddenly darted out of an open window and did not return until evening. My punishment later was reduced to kneeling for half an hour, which was preferable to spanking.

The health situation of the population in the camp became more stable. Proper nutrition, rest and better psychological disposition played a major part in this improvement. The camp also had good health care facilities including a hospital with 200 beds. The Polish army sent six doctors, a dentist and 32 nurses. People still experienced bouts with malaria with over 600 cases per year and a total of 70 deaths during our stay in Valivade. I became sick with malaria for the second time and had to spend three weeks in the hospital undergoing the dreaded quinine treatment. The camp authorities were extremely strict in monitoring the health and related matters. An inspection team was set up by the hospital staff to check the living quarters and hygiene of the residents and assure mosquito nets were being used at all times. A special sanitary team was set up to fumigate the living quarters. We were required to steam our beds once a month at specially designed troughs. The sanitary team also checked camp sanitary facilities to be sure that they functioned well. The latrines were treated with lime regularly and, overall, were kept clean.

Life in India had many interesting light moments. During the monsoon season, the river overflowed its banks and formed a huge lake. We were concerned that the planners of the camp had not taken the monsoon effect into account and the camp would flood. The barracks closest to the river came within a few feet of being flooded, but the water never reached all the way to the barracks. The heavy winds during the monsoon season often tore off clay tiles from the roof. On occasion, when the winds were strong, we had to hide under the table to avoid being hit by the falling tiles.

The mosquito nets protected us not only from the mosquitoes but also from snakes, scorpions and other bugs. Occasionally, someone would wake up in the morning to find a snake or scorpion on top of the mosquito net. Some boys kept mongooses as pets, thinking the mongoose would protect them against snakes. Not many people were bitten by snakes, but there were occasional incidences and it made us a little skittish about these reptiles. Sometimes boys played pranks on women by placing a heavy rope on the road to the latrines. In the dark, the rope look alike snake usually would scare the women and make them scream, "Snake! Snake!"

The Indian population, especially the young adults and children, learned Polish quickly. Many were very fluent in it so there was little need to learn the local language. There was a young Indian boy who went to Polish school without his mother's knowledge. Many times when his mother called him to go home, he would swear at her in Polish. The few words of Hindu that we had learned, of course, were the swear words. Children enjoyed Indian food consisting of various curries and tandoori dishes, and "naan," the tortilla-like pancakes. We could purchase these dishes from local merchants who set up their stands in the Hindu market outside the camp. We also enjoyed the sugar cane that grew in the fields around the camp and various kinds of fruits, like mangoes, papaya and bananas that we could pick off the trees or purchase at the market.

Children played simple games that they created on their own since there were no toys available. We played soccer with a ball made from rags. We played hide and seek and a game called "*kiczki*" played with two sticks, one short and one long. The object of the game was to get the small stick in the air and hit it with the large stick as far as possible. We played make-believe army using sticks as horses. When the weather was bad, we played war games using paper soldiers made by folding paper into little figures that looked like grasshoppers. Stamp collecting also was very popular among the older boys.

We had a hard time getting used to some aspects of Indian life. Indian women did most of the heavy work. For example, women pulled a plough and men walked behind holding the plough and guiding it through the soil. Women carried heavy loads on their heads while men walked behind empty handed. All these things were very strange to us since we were accustomed to men being chivalrous to women. The natives ate their meals by sitting on the ground and using their fingers rather than utensils. The Hindu religion and worship of various deities such as Shiva and Vishnu, and the wearing of distinguishing marks on their foreheads seemed strange to us Catholics. The sacred cows roaming the streets of Kolhapur and nearby villages, stopping all traffic, were another strange custom to us.

Occasionally, we visited Kolhapur, about six miles from camp, usually walking to town or sometimes taking a train or riding bicycles. In Kolhapur, we visited a number of historic sites and Buddhist temples. The camp cemetery also was located in Kolhapur. We left 70 fellow refugees behind in that cemetery, among them our friend from Poland, J. Czarny. On my return to Valivade in 1998, I visited his grave. I found the cemetery in a run-down condition and it was hard to recognize some of the graves but at least the cemetery was still there. The Polish embassy in India installed a plaque in the cemetery commemorating the 70 deceased Polish refugees.

The cordial atmosphere that existed among the camp residents struck anyone visiting Valivade. It really seemed like one big family. There was evidence of a genuine group effort to cooperate in order to raise the level of life for everyone. The difficulties were enormous. The foreign environment, single parent families, two years of recent hardship in Siberia and various transitory camps, an ongoing war and casualties, and an unknown future were just a few of the challenges and uncertainties we faced. Yet the whole community worked together. We strove to improve our educational level. We respected individual beliefs and maintained a high degree of patriotism. We felt Polish deep down to our bones and developed a sense of belonging to a large Polish family scattered around the globe. No wonder people on the outside considered Valivade to be a model refugee camp that may never be duplicated. The best illustration of the close ties among the camp residents is that the refugees from Valivade hold reunions in various parts of the world, to this day, fifty years after we left India. These meetings, held every other year, draw participants from Australia, Canada, New Zealand, Poland, the United States, Britain, and Africa.

To be sure, Siberia left its mark on those who experienced the *Nieludzka Ziemia*. Some people who survived continued to suffer physically for many years, while others continued to face emotional problems. It appeared to them that no one would ever fully appreciate what they had to endure during those horrible days. The Soviets forced upon them hunger and horrific living and working conditions. The Soviets sent them to areas with extreme climates and surrounded them with people who acted more like animals than human beings. They were exposed to terror and watched their loved ones die. These are things not easily forgotten. However, there were also positive effects of the Soviet experience. People returned with a reinforced faith in God because they personally witnessed miracles. They were almost certainly destined to die, yet somehow they survived. People who survived the Soviet camps developed strong moral character, because they had already experienced hell here on earth. They became better patriots and better citizens because they had lost their country. They gained an immense respect for individual freedom, for they witnessed the evil of the totalitarian system. They valued the importance of education, because they experienced a cultural darkness. People who survived became hard workers because any work was easy compared to the work they did in the Soviet Union.

A number of organizations were formed after the war to embrace the Siberian survivors. These organizations were formed initially outside Poland, in the United States, France, and England, due to political realities. Poland was under communist domination and the subject of the Siberian experience could not be discussed openly in Poland. The members of these organizations wanted to perpetuate the memory of all those who suffered and died in Siberia and pass that memory on to future generations. The Jewish people who wanted to perpetuate the memory of the Holocaust chose the slogan "Never Again." The Poles who wanted to memorialize the Siberian experience borrowed an expression from the famous Polish poet Adam Mickiewicz who wrote in *Dziady*, Part III: "*Jeśli zapomnę o nich, Ty Boże na niebie, zapomnij o mnie*" or "Should I forget about them, You oh God in heaven, forget about me."

The international situation for Poland deteriorated rapidly after the war with Germany. The Potsdam Conference in July 17, 1945, essentially sealed our fate eliminating the possibility for us to return to our homeland that was now behind the Curzon Line in the Soviet Union. The establishment of the Provisional Government in Poland that was dominated by the communists guaranteed a communist rule in Poland. If we were to return there, we would be forced to live under a government that was a clone of the regime that deported us just five short years earlier. The recognition of the Provisional Government by the Allies left the Polish Government-in-Exile without international recognition and without any means to support the refugees. The biggest question for us was who was going to take care of us in the camps. Who was going to provide for our existence and what were our options? The decision about our future did not rest any longer with the Polish authorities but was transferred to the British and international organizations.

The financial responsibility for caring for the refugees in Valivade was passed to the United Nations Relief and Rehabilitation Administration, or UNRRA, on August 1, 1946. The British informed us that they had supported the refugees as long as they could and that they were no longer able to continue that support. UNRRA was charged by the United Nations to help millions of war refugees return to their native lands or resettle in other countries. UNRRA operated on a very limited budget and immediately reduced payments for the upkeep of the refugees by 25 percent; consequently, all Polish camps were forced to cut costs dramatically. Various camps were consolidated, the educational options for the children reduced, and the pay for the Polish workers employed in the camps eliminated. UNRRA personnel visited Valivade to assess the situation. They ordered registration of all refugees in the camp to help them plan their future. The population in Valivade became immediately suspicious about the purpose of the registration. We all feared being returned to the Soviet Union by force, for that was where our homes were under the new international agreements. We refused to submit to the registration. UNRRA personnel were chased out of the camp; some were even beaten by angry women. The camp was in chaos and we were not sure what to do next or whom to trust.

The Polish camp authorities asked the Polish government in London for instructions. Urgent letters were written to husbands and other relatives in the Polish II Corps seeking advice. The situation calmed down somewhat after assurances from UNRRA that only they and no other agency would use the information submitted on registration cards. However, the calmness we displayed over the years in Valivade never returned. Also, various foreign political leaders suggested that we should return to Poland now that the war was over. These people saw no reason why we should continue to live in the refugee camps. The government of India formally requested that Polish refugees leave India as soon as possible. At the same time the communist government in Poland initiated a propaganda barrage to convince us to return to Poland. The communists were not very successful. Less than 500 people chose to return to Poland from Valivade and most of them were from the western part of Poland.

The British also were concerned about our safety in India since the political situation in India was becoming very unstable. Shortly before gaining independence from Britain, India was on the verge of a civil war between Hindus and Moslems. Riots and demonstrations were commonplace in the entire country. The Polish population became a problem for all sides in the political arena. One year later, on July 1, 1947, UNRRA stopped its funding for the Valivade camp. Again, we were in limbo and did not know what would happen to us. Finally, The International Refugee Organization, IRO, took over the responsibility for maintaining the camps. Not much changed after IRO took over, however, it became obvious to all of us in the camp that we would soon have to leave India. In July 1947, it was announced that families whose husbands and fathers were in the Polish armed forces could join them in Great Britain. The rest of the refugees would be resettled to other parts of the world, mainly to the countries comprising the British Commonwealth.

Our family, minus Aunt Macia and her children, left Valivade on September 4, 1947. This was the first time our two families were separated from each other. No arguments were strong enough with the authorities to keep us together. They stated that the decision was out of their hands. The instructions were very specific; only immediate families of the soldiers could leave on the first transport. Our separation was very difficult.

We left Valivade in the evening and traveled all night to Pune where we changed trains. We arrived in Bombay the next morning and got off the train at the port. There were 960 refugees in the first transport out of Valivade. We boarded a British ship named the *Empire Brent*. It was an old troop transport and looked very large and impressive to us watching from the dock. In fact, it was relatively small compared to other passenger ships with a displacement weight of about 10,000 tons. We were assigned cabins alphabetically, boys separate from girls and women. There were cabins with four to ten berths. I was assigned to a cabin that had four berths and my mates were the Birecki brothers and another boy whose name escapes me. Our cabin was comfortable but very small. The bathrooms were in the hallway and were shared by boys from several cabins. Meals were served in shifts in the mess hall. Boys were allowed to visit their mothers during the daytime.

We sailed from Bombay on September 5, 1947. We left India with a degree of sadness. The hospitality and the understanding extended to us by the local population were greatly appreciated by everyone. A number of ex-residents returned to India in recent years and were greatly saddened by the changes they saw. Our little camp in Valivade had become a city of 100,000 people. The group of Polish orphans who returned to Balachadi in 1995 left a memorial plaque there with the following inscription, "Blessed be the land afar, the friendly land, the human land, and a good land." Another group that went to Valivade and Kolhapur in 1998, on the fiftieth anniversary of our departure from India, dedicated a monument in one of the parks in Kolhapur. The dedication, inscribed in three languages, Polish, English and Hindi, reads, "In the years 1943–1948, thanks to the hospitality of Kolhapur State, 5,000 Polish refugees found shelter in Valivade Camp. Dispersed throughout the world we remember India with heartfelt gratitude."

Shortly after we sailed into the open sea, we hit a big storm. Many people became very seasick, including my mother and sister. Somehow I avoided the seasickness, although I felt somewhat queasy moving about the ship. The storm lasted three or four days. We had daily emergency evacuation practice sessions during the first few days of our trip. We were instructed on how to put on life jackets and how to get into designated lifeboats. These drills became boring after a while, and the boys played tricks on women by tying loose straps of the life preservers to women standing next to each other. When the drill was over, the women who were tied together could not get separated and, of course, became extremely angry. All were rather careful to hold on to their loose straps during the next drill.

The first port we reached after leaving Bombay was Aden, located at the south end of the Red Sea. We stopped in the port to refuel and to take on new supplies. There were many Arab merchants in small boats around the ship who were touting their merchandise. Buckets tied to ropes were hoisted to the ship's deck to transfer the merchandise from the small boats to customers on the ship. The Arabs were very skilled at this. Sign language was adequate to consummate a deal.

We left Aden that evening and sailed into the Red Sea. Somehow we all expected to see red colors in the water, but this was not to be. The water was still a beautiful aqua green color. The Red Sea was calm, but the days were very hot. There was no air conditioning in the cabins and we stayed on deck as much as possible. A few days later we reached Suez (El Sewis), then Ismailia, at the southern tip of the Suez Canal. We sailed through the Suez Canal at night. Most of us stayed up all night, watching the lights on the shores of Egypt and the ships that were docked on the side of the canal as we passed. We reached Port Said (Bur Said) the next morning and again docked to refuel and take on fresh supplies. General Wiatr, the commander of Polish forces in the Middle East, paid us a visit on the ship during our stay in Port Said. After taking on supplies, we sailed into the Mediterranean Sea. The seas were calm and the rest of the voyage was uneventful. Three weeks on the ship was a long time and there wasn't much to do. We played some games, but mostly we gazed at the sea and watched fish swim behind the ship. I learned to play bridge when I was asked by an older foursome to substitute when one of the regulars was sick or couldn't play.

We reached Gibraltar at the west end of the Mediterranean on September 20, 1947. All passengers poured onto the deck looking toward the shore to pay respects to General Sikorski, who had been killed on that very spot on July 5, 1943. Most of us cried and wondered how things would have turned out were General Sikorski still alive. Somehow, we all felt that we would have been sailing to a free and independent Poland instead of into the unknown future. The *Empire Brent* docked in Southampton in southern England on September 25, 1947.

Polish refugee camp in Valivade, India, 1944.

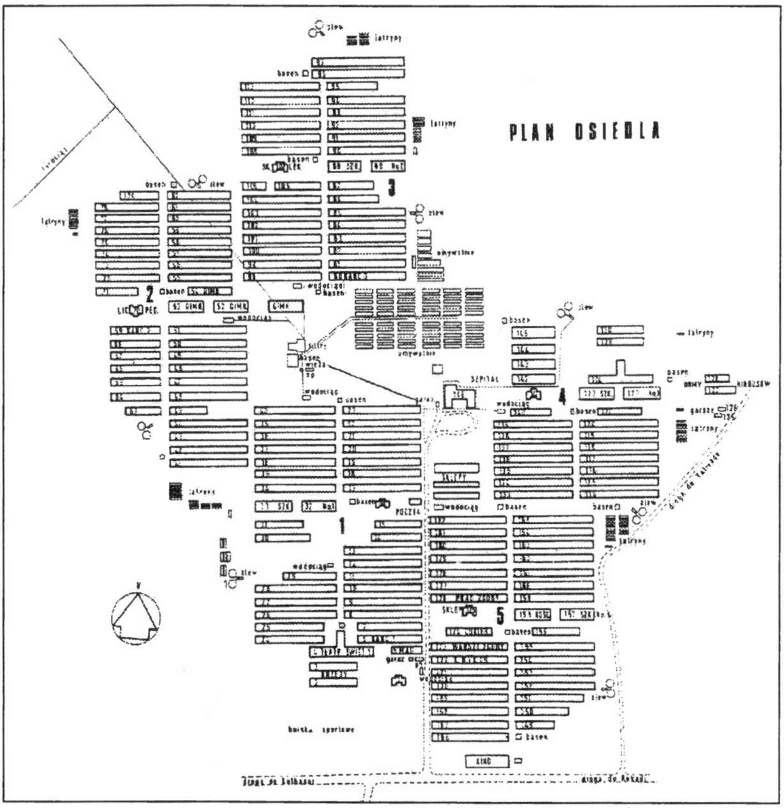

Map of Polish refugee camp in Valivade. (Ref. 19, Exiled Children)

Church in Valivade.

Interior of Church in Valivade. (Ref. 19, Exiled Children)

Corpus Christi celebration in Valivade.

Holiday parade in Valivade. (Ref. 19, Exiled Children)

School children (I am on the far right) welcome a school inspector in front of our classroom in Valivade, 1946.

Typical classroom in school in Valivade. (Ref. 8, Z. Kresów)

Our family under a Papaya tree in Valivade, 1945
(In front: Leszek and Alina. In back: Macia, Mother, J. Czechowicz, Anulka, A. Dereń and me).

I as a boy scout in Chandoli, India, 1947.

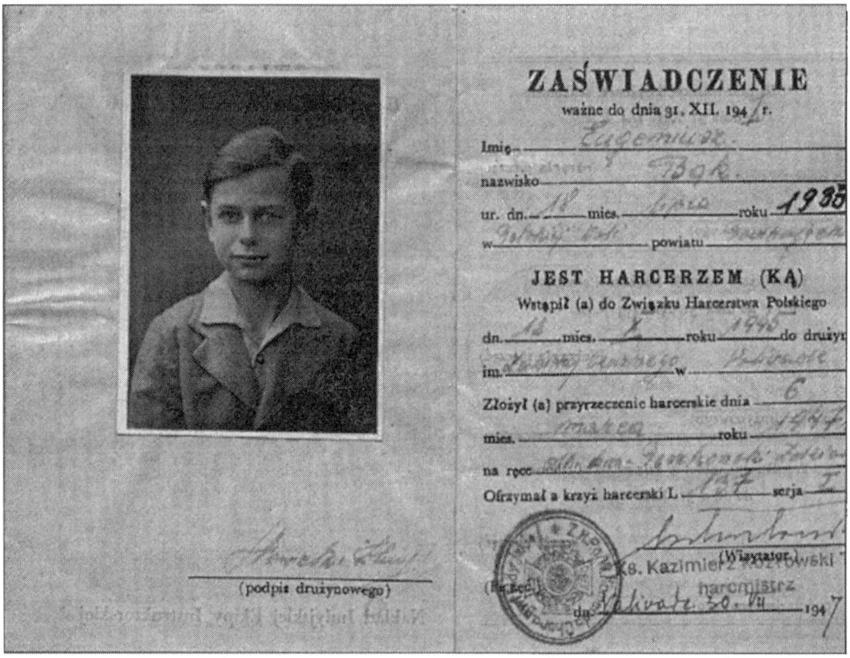

ZAŚWIADCZENIE

ważne do dnia 31. XII. 194_ r.

Imię Eugeniusz

nazwisko Bok

ur. dn. 18 mies. lipca roku 1935

w ____ powiatu ____

JEST HARCERZEM (KĄ)

Wstąpił (a) do Związku Harcerstwa Polskiego

dn. 12 mies. X roku 1945 do drużyny

im. ____ w ____

Złożył (a) przyrzeczenie harcerskie dnia 6

mies. marca roku 1947

na ręce ____

Otrzymał a krzyż harcerski L. 137 serja I

(Wizytator)

Ks. Kazimierz Kozłowski

harcmistrz

dn. Valivade 30. VII 1947

(podpis drużynowego)

Boy scout identification certificate, 1947.

Boy scout camp in Chandoli, India, 1947. (I am third from the right.)

Our departure from Valivade, 1947. (Ref. 18, Polacy W Indiach)

T.S.S. *Empire Brent*. Ship that transported us to England from India, 1947.

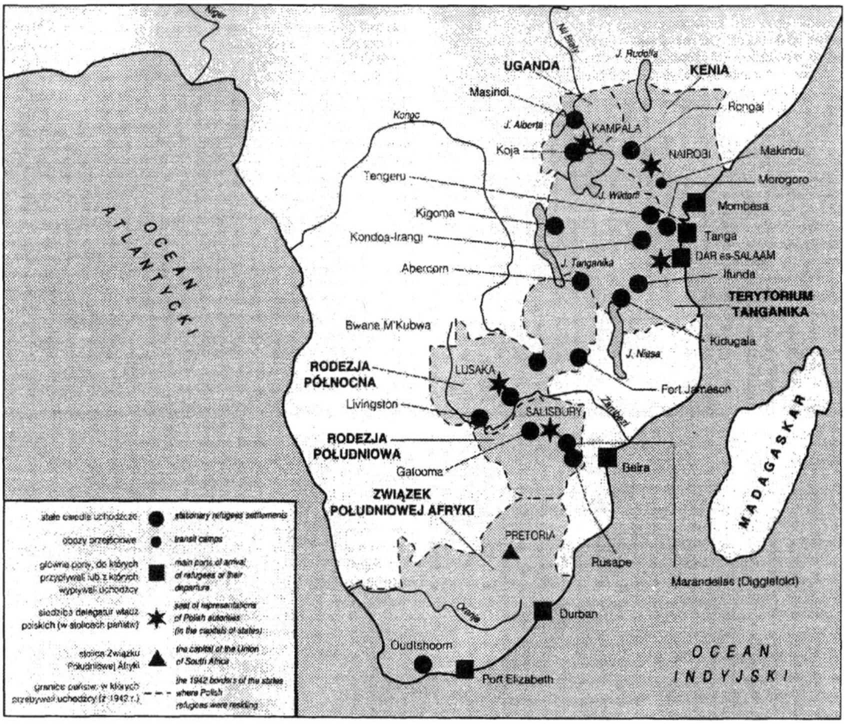

Location of Polish refugees on the African continent 1944-1948.
(Ref. 19, Exiled Children)

Polish refugee camp in Lusaka, Zambia. (Ref. 11, Szujecki)

ENGLAND

We were transferred from the port of Southampton to a transit camp called Possingworth West Camp in Sussex, south of London. The camp was used as a quarantine area and staging place to process the refugees and issue them the necessary documents.

The reunion between the soldiers and their families after so many years of separation was very joyous and emotional. We had not seen our father for five years and were very anxious to "meet him again." We did not know exactly when he would arrive at the camp. One day, I was walking through the camp when I literally ran into him. He did not recognize me at first. However, I hugged him immediately. The reunion is hard to describe, but I remember we both cried with joy. I took him to our barrack to "meet the rest of the family." The most difficult part of our reunion was that we could not leave the camp with him. We had to wait for the British authorities to release us after an adequate quarantine period and the completion of proper documentation.

Possingworth was an old British army camp. We were housed in Quonset huts, which we called *beczki śmiechu* or barrels of laughs. They looked like a half of a barrel lying on its open side—certainly a funny thing to live in. We were given meals three times a day in the mess hall. The biggest problem we had was adjusting to the weather. The end of September could be very cold in England, especially by comparison to India. We had no appropriate clothing for this type of weather. The authorities in India were to issue us warm clothing before we departed, but the clothing did not arrive in time. I did not even own a single pair of full-length pants, only shorts, and I had no warm jacket or sweater. My father took us to town, and the first items he bought for us were sweaters, coats and pants for me.

We left Possingworth two weeks after our arrival in England when the authorities were satisfied that we posed no health risk to the British population. We went by train to Rednall, a camp where my father was stationed. Rednall was located near Oswestry in Shropshire, about 60 miles south of Chester, and was a resettlement camp for soldiers from the Polish II Corps. My father joined the Resettlement Corps on July 27, 1947, about two months before we arrived in England. As I mentioned previously, the British government formed the Polish Resettlement Corps to help Polish soldiers not returning to Poland after the war assimilate into civilian life in Great Britain. The members of the Resettlement Corps were still, at least theoretically, in the armed forces under British command.

When the Polish II Corps arrived in England, the British authorities made available to the Polish soldiers and refugees a number of ex-army and air force military camps called hostels. These hostels were available to refugees who had no intention of returning to Poland mainly for political reasons. The hostels afforded us Poles a transition from the conditions we had lived in since leaving the Soviet Union. For over five years we had lived in tents, barracks, or other temporary housing. Others had organized our lives for us; usually we were placed in Polish enclaves, isolated from outside influences. We had few worries about food or clothing; the essentials had been provided for us. The hostels were designed to serve as temporary housing for Poles trying to assimilate into British society or for those who were waiting to immigrate to other countries.

Another purpose of staying in the hostels was to teach refugees the language and get them acclimated to British customs and their way of life. Staying in hostels enabled the residents to raise their educational level if they had missed the opportunity because of the war or because they had inadequate education in Poland in the first place. The hostels offered courses where Poles could acquire useful trades or other skills. They resembled an independent society that was part of British society but still a part of the Polish way of life.

There was a housing shortage in England after the war. The hostels helped to ease that shortage and reduce the tensions that developed between the Polish people and the Britons. The British were resentful that the Poles did not return to their own country. They felt that the Poles competed with them for the same jobs and housing. British men even resented Polish chivalry toward the British women. Nonetheless the Poles quickly gained a reputation as valuable and dependable workers in factories and on farms. Overall, they were generally successful in getting back on their feet and becoming independent citizens again. Many were able to develop or upgrade their newly discovered talents in commerce, business, trade or technical areas.

Some soldiers were able to get jobs quickly and left the army immediately. Others chose to immigrate to different countries, including Canada, Australia and the United States. Uncle Romek, who was sent from Italy to England to recuperate from the wounds he received at Monte Cassino, stayed in England until 1946 when he decided to immigrate to Argentina and join his brother Ludwik, who immigrated there from Poland in 1936. Uncle Romek told my father that he would go to Argentina, scout out the living conditions there, and let my father know if it was a good place to settle.

My father stayed in the Resettlement Corps for two years, the maximum allowed, and was discharged on July 26, 1949. The army provided support for the soldiers who were members of the Resettlement Corps as well as their families. The British government and the communist government in Poland exerted many pressures on us living in England to return to Poland. British politicians and the general British population urged us to return. This was the time when the British were very sympathetic towards the Soviet Union and communism in general. The communist government in Poland used various means of propaganda to persuade us to return. It was embarrassing to the communists that such a high percentage of Poles elected to remain in Britain.

However, the news from Poland was not very encouraging to us. There were letters from relatives, some written in pre-agreed codes, describing the harsh conditions in Poland. There were about 266,000 Poles who returned to communist Poland from the Soviet Union after the hostilities ended. This number included the members of the Kościuszko Division that fought on the Russian front. Many returning Poles from the Soviet Union were temporarily settled in the Ukraine, mainly to improve their physical condition. This was done more for propaganda than humanitarian reasons. The Soviets did not want to be embarrassed by the appearance of the returning deportees.

Most of the deportees eventually settled in the western part of Poland, on the lands acquired from Germany after the war. Their return was a mixed blessing for them. They were happy to be back in Poland and were welcomed by many Poles, especially friends and family. However, not all Poles welcomed them back with open arms. The Polish communists implied that there must have been a good reason why these people were deported in the first place and even questioned the loyalty of the new arrivals.

The UB (*Urząd Bezpieczeństwa*), the Polish internal security, now replaced the NKVD as the new defenders of communism. The UB, in some cases, tried to outdo the NKVD. They questioned the new arrivals, indiscriminately arresting those who appeared to be suspicious, and in some instances deporting them back to Siberia. The new arrivals often were blacklisted, preventing them from holding jobs or getting higher education. The UB also arrested the members of *Armia Krajowa* or the Home Army, as well as many returning officers and soldiers from the Polish II Corps. Many of these ex-soldiers were imprisoned for the second time and some were sent to Siberia again.

We read with dismay about how the Polish communists and the Soviet government invited 12 prominent representatives of the Polish political and military establishment to Moscow supposedly to negotiate the structure of the future Polish government. These representatives were arrested upon arrival in Moscow, tried for treason and many of them executed. Later, Mr. Stanisław Mikołajczyk, the former Prime Minister of the Government-in-Exile, returned to Poland, at the insistence of the Western governments and with the consent of the communists, to take part in the newly formed Provincial government. Shortly after he arrived in Poland, his political party was subjected to persecution, and he, himself, became concerned about his safety and escaped to Great Britain to avoid arrest. There was no question in the minds of us Poles remaining in Britain and other parts of the free world that the communist regime in Poland was determined to finish the job of eliminating the free and independent Polish society, a job started by the Soviet Union when it invaded Poland in 1939. No way would we return to Poland under those conditions. It was time for us to organize our lives in exile.

Life in Rednall was similar to the life we led in other refugee camps, except that we were together with our father. We lived in the army barracks. We were given two meals a day, lunch and dinner. We picked up the meals at the army kitchen and brought them back to the barracks where we warmed them on small electric plates. Father supplemented his small army pension by making leather suitcases and briefcases, selling them mainly to the people returning to Poland. I got my first bicycle in Rednall. It was put together from old parts purchased in the bicycle junkyard. I cherished it since it was my first possession. Unfortunately, in my eagerness to try the bicycle, I had an accident and ended up in the hospital with a severe concussion. I was in and out of consciousness for two days, but fortunately recovered fully—at least I think I did. My sister and I went to grammar school in the camp; I was 14 at the time and one of the oldest children in the sixth grade. One day my father said to me, "You are too old to be in grammar school. You should consider skipping a grade and going to *gimnazjum*." *Gimnazjum* is equivalent to high school in the U.S. This meant going to a boarding school in another city. I was not too anxious to leave my parents, but I also realized that in order to continue my education I would have to leave home eventually.

I applied to Polish Nicolas Copernicus Gimnazjum and Lyceum, an all-boys boarding school in Riddlesworth, near Norfolk on the east coast of England. I arrived in Riddlesworth after Christmas break in January 1948. The school year was half over and I had a lot of catching up to do. This was especially difficult with subjects like Latin, which I had never studied before. I was never able to fully catch up to the level my classmates had achieved; it seemed that I was always one step behind them. As a result, I was not a very good student in high school.

The school was located in an old army camp and we were housed in the Quonset huts, the famous *beczki śmiechu.* We were required to do the housekeeping chores like cleaning the barracks, maintaining flowerbeds, keeping the barracks warm in the winter by tending to the coal stoves, and doing KP duty in the kitchen. All in all, we were kept busy and there was very little time for play. All instructions were in Polish; English was offered only as a foreign language. About 450 students were in the school. Tuition was free for students who could not afford to pay. In the summer of 1948, the school was transferred to Ellough near Beckles, also an old army camp, and then in November 1948, to Bottisham near Cambridge. The number of students increased to 500 as a result of the influx of refugees arriving from Italy, India, Africa, Germany and the Middle East. The Superintendent of the school was Dr. Gemborek, and later, Dr. T. Bornholtz. There were about 30 teachers in school, all well-trained and experienced professionals. A number of teachers had doctorates and had been university professors in Poland before the war. The school graduated over 1,000 students during its six years of existence. Many students, myself included, did not graduate from Bottisham, but we received an excellent education from that institution.

Three teachers in the Nicolas Copernicus School had a profound impact on my thinking and life in general. One was Professor Łucki who taught history and political science. Prof. Łucki had a great talent for making the subject of history interesting and meaningful. History and political science were always favorite subjects of mine and continue to be so to this day. One day, I expressed an interest to Prof. Łucki to pursue a career in history and political science. He dissuaded me from going in that direction, stating that in my nomadic life, I should choose a profession that would be equally applicable no matter where I went. I must say this was the general feeling among many Polish students in England. They chose mostly technical fields like engineering, medicine, architecture and sciences. Many avoided arts and humanities for pragmatic reasons since technical fields were more portable and applied equally well regardless of where one chose to settle. Prof. Łucki also suggested we consider immigrating to the United States. He told me that the United States offered more opportunities, especially for young people.

Another teacher who influenced my life was an instructor of Polish language, Professor Fierla. Prof. Fierla was a writer, poet, and somewhat of a romantic. He taught us to appreciate literature, poetry and classics, how to interpret these readings, and how to get the most joy out of literature.

The third teacher who left an imprint on my life was a priest, Father Walczak, who made us appreciate religion, not in the blind sense of the word, but how to rationalize religion and mesh it with our daily lives. Father Walczak also taught the history of the church, its involvement in the arts, and its impact on world history.

These three individuals greatly influenced my life and my thinking, and they helped shape my mind. I will always be grateful to them.

Life in the school in Bottisham was simple and harsh. It was not much different from the life in Riddlesworth and Beckles where the school was previously located. We also lived in Quonset huts, 10 students to each barrack. We did our own housekeeping, cleaned and polished the floors, maintained the fire in the coal stove, cleaned the classrooms, heated the classrooms in the morning before the classes started, and performed various chores in the kitchen. Most of these duties were done on a rotating basis among the students in each class or barrack. We had three meals a day in the mess hall, although I must admit I did not always make it to breakfast. The classes were held from 8 a.m. to 5 p.m. on weekdays, with a one-hour break for lunch, and 8 a.m. to 12 p.m. on Saturdays. We had free time between 5 p.m. and 6 p.m. and had our dinner at 6 o'clock. A compulsory study period was between 7 p.m. and 9 p.m. and lights went out at 10 o'clock. There wasn't much time to play on the weekdays, but weekends were free from Saturday afternoon through Sundays. A mass was offered every Sunday morning in the school chapel. There was a good library with Polish books and we read ravenously in our spare time, probably to make up for lost time when books were not available to us. There were a number of shows, concerts, and recitals given during the school year. We participated in many sports activities. Soccer was very popular, as was basketball and volleyball. We had physical education class twice a week; we played games outdoors when the weather was good and performed exercises on the various gymnastic equipment during winter and inclement weather. Individual grades organized their own soccer teams and played against each other in school tournaments. The school representative teams in soccer, basketball and volleyball played against other schools, Polish as well as English.

The instructions in school were in Polish, except for the English language class, which was offered as a required foreign language. The curriculum was switched to all English in the 1951 school year although the Polish language, religion and Polish geography classes continued to be taught in Polish. The Polish Committee for the Education of Poles in Great Britain was responsible for all Polish schools in England. The Committee decided that school instructions must be switched to all English if we were to assimilate into the British society quickly, and in order to help us prepare for the final examinations required for British certification and admission to the universities. Initially, the percentage of Polish students passing these final examinations was low, mainly due to the poor knowledge of English. However, with time, these percentages matched and even exceeded those of the British students.

Several Polish schools existed in Great Britain after the war. My sister attended the all-girls school in Stowell Park near Oxford. These schools were slowly consolidated between 1951 and 1957. By 1957, all Polish schools in Great Britain had closed.

I first showed an inclination toward business while I was in school in Bottisham. I became an amateur photographer and a self-appointed unofficial photographer for the students. I took pictures of school teams, classes, and students and sold these pictures to the students. Not too many students in school had cameras at that time. I built my own darkroom in an old chimney in an abandoned powerhouse which had no electricity, so I developed the pictures in daylight, using a sliding window covered with red glass to provide light in the darkroom. It was a very primitive set-up but it gave me a lot of satisfaction because I used my own resources to accomplish it. Students didn't have much money, and I didn't sell too many pictures. The other business I developed was selling cigarettes to students. I owned a bicycle in school, and on weekends, I went to the local villages and towns and bought different brands of cigarettes to resell to students and, on occasion, even to teachers. Most of the students could not afford to buy full packs of cigarettes, so they bought a few cigarettes at a time from me. Smoking was very popular after the war. People smoked everywhere, in homes, in the movies, on buses. There were no restrictions on smoking; smoking was the "in thing." A great number of our students were older, in their twenties. Many had served in the armed forces and were now in school trying to catch up with studies missed because of the war. Smoking for them was a habit carried over their the days in the army. The school authorities discouraged smoking, but never strictly enforced the rules. Selling of cigarettes, of course, was not an "approved curriculum." Even though it might have been a good education in business, I could have been suspended, or even expelled, from the school. The buying and selling of cigarettes was a much more successful venture than photography and I made enough money to cover my pocket expenses.

The food provided by the school was adequate but not plentiful. Most items in England, food included, were sold on rations after the war. Most students felt hungry and were always looking for something to eat. I often brought bread and other food items from my trips to buy cigarettes, and resold these items to students. However, this part of the business did not always pay off. Many times I was hungry on the way back from my "business trip" and ate the extra food before I returned to school.

I went home in the summertime to be with my parents. I spent my first summer in Oulton Park near Chester where my parents had moved after Rednall was closed. I worked during summer vacations on the local farms. Several big farms were in the area and the local farmers hired Polish workers from the camps to help them during busy summer months. We were considered migrant workers. People wishing to work that day congregated in a designated spot, usually in front of the camp, and were picked up by the farmers in trucks that morning and brought back that evening. The workers were paid each day in cash. Most of the work was seasonal. However, a few people had steady jobs on the farms.

Work on a farm was hard. My back and other muscles hurt so much in the evenings after a full day's work that I could not sleep at night. We picked potatoes, carrots, beets, strawberries, and other farm products. Some of the work was piecework, meaning we were paid by the unit of output. The more we produced, the more money we earned. We also helped in harvesting various crops at the end of the summer. This work included sheaving crops, stacking the sheaves in the fields to let them dry in the sun, and then bringing the dry sheaves to the farm by tractor. When the weather was bad, we pulled weeds from the fields of beets, cabbage and other produce. There was a lot more to farm work that I initially realized, and I gained a lot of respect for farmers from my summer experiences.

In summertime when I was home, I collected canned foods from friends and relatives. We received these goods regularly as part of our food allotment from the camp kitchen. I took these canned goods to the country stores in surrounding villages and exchanged them for butter, eggs and other fresh produce, which we received only in limited amounts. I sort of picked up where my father left off in Poland, being a local trader. My father and I joked about this, saying that some day we would open a business together.

We moved to East Moor, near Sutton-on-Forest, about six miles from York, after my father was discharged from the Resettlement Corps in July 1949. East Moor was one of the largest hostels assigned to Poles in Britain. It was also one that lasted the longest. There were people still living in East Moor as late as 1961 or more than 15 years after the war ended. Many refugees did not want to leave these Polish enclaves. It took a certain amount of courage to do so. The British accused the Polish authorities of prolonging the existence of these hostels, of spoon-feeding and babying the refugees. To their credit, the British allowed the assimilation and the camps to continue despite the griping.

Many Poles, like my parents, did not want to give up the hostels. The hostels were relatively inexpensive even for those who worked and had to pay for room and board. They were located outside the big cities, around farmlands, often reminding the residents of the Polish countryside. The hostels provided good health facilities, Polish–English grammar schools, and even a daycare center for mothers who wished to work. The common kitchen often was supplemented with vegetables grown in their own gardens, and they could buy fresh eggs, butter and fruit in season on the nearby farms.

The hostels were also religious and cultural centers. The larger hostels had their own chapel with a Polish priest. Dances and social events were held on weekends, where young people could meet and have a good time. The Polish community had a large number of unmarried men and women who had no opportunity to meet members of the opposite sex during the long years of war. Now they could meet at these various social events. The hostels had Polish libraries, held concerts, showed Polish movies, and sponsored shows by the Polish traveling theater. Even a Polish store on wheels traveled from one hostel to another bringing Polish goods like kiełbasa, Polish ham, and baked goods.

My father had a job working for a local farmer, and my mother worked at Rowntree Chocolate Factory in York. My father bicycled to work and my mother took a bus to York. Aunt Macia and Cousin Aniela were able to come to England as well. Aunt Macia lived in East Moor, but later, after she married Piotr Krawczyk, moved to a hostel in Wales. My cousin Aniela got a job in a textile factory in Oldham near Manchester. She married a former Polish soldier.

Slowly, we were able to acclimate to the western lifestyle, to the atmosphere of freedom. We were able to develop a generally wholesome philosophy on life. This was extremely important and sometimes difficult after our traumatic wartime experiences in the Soviet Union and the refugee camps. At the same time, we were able to avoid culture shock and psychological conflicts by living within our own culture, traditions and religious beliefs, and even maintaining some degree of independence from British society within the hostels. London served as a cultural center for the British Polonia. The Government-in-Exile was still functioning there. London had a Polish University that was part of the University of London.

The Polish community in England was a closely-knit group bonded together by past experiences. A Polish daily newspaper called *Dziennik Polski i Dziennik Żołnierza* was published. We also had Polish radio programs, book publishers, and guest speakers who visited the various Polish communities. I had an opportunity to hear General Anders speak in Leeds. The hall where General Anders spoke was packed with veterans. The General walked down the main aisle, and when he reached the stage, he shouted, "*Czołem Żołnierze*," which loosely translated means "I salute you my soldiers." The soldiers responded, "*Czołem Panie Generale*," or "We salute you, General." The response was so forceful that the entire building shook and the atmosphere in the hall became charged with electricity. This exchange of greetings between the General and his soldiers best illustrated the great love and respect the soldiers had for their General and vice versa.

The Poles in England formed a unified group, many thousands strong, a microcosm of a society within a society. There was a Government-in-Exile, cultural structure, and religious organization with a bishop assigned by the Pope to attend to the needs of the emigrants. It was a mini country in exile. The Polish exiles even collected taxes, though voluntary, to maintain the Government-in-Exile. Many Polish exiles still considered Britain only a stopover on a long journey back to a free and independent Poland.

While in England, I had the opportunity to visit London with a school tour. We went to the Festival of Britain or World's Fair and many other tourist sites. On other occasions, I visited such historic places as Cambridge, Eli, York, Chester and Manchester. At the end of the 1951 school year, I rode a bicycle from Bottisham to York, a 150-mile trip that took two days, riding through the beautiful English countryside.

We had a family get-together in the summer of 1951, and came to a decision to emigrate from England. The question of where to go was answered when we received a letter from Uncle Romek in Argentina. He wrote that the situation in Argentina was politically unstable and that he would not recommend we move there. My mother's half-sister Felka, who lived in Cleveland, sent us an invitation to come to the United States. Aunt Felka came to the United States in the 1920's at the invitation of one of her uncles who had immigrated to the United States earlier. She settled in southeastern Ohio, near Wheeling, West Virginia, in the same area my grandfather lived when he was in the United States before the war. She moved to Cleveland after she got married and my mother lost track of her. When we moved to India, my mother made inquiries about Aunt Felka through the Red Cross. My mother did not know her sister's married name or where she lived, so she used their maiden name and the place of their birth to make connections. A friend of Aunt Felka, Mrs. Szmyd, who lived in Pittsburgh and was from Haczów, the village of my mother's birth, read in a Polish newspaper that my mother was looking for her sister. She immediately telephoned Aunt Felka and told her about my mother's inquiry. Aunt Felka wrote to my mother and they began corresponding with each other.

The United States Congress passed a law in 1950 allowing Polish Displaced Persons and Polish World War II Veterans living outside of Poland to be admitted to the United States, provided these people had a sponsor in the United States who would guarantee them a job and provide housing. Many Polish–Americans volunteered, to their credit, to sponsor Polish refugees to come to the United States. In many cases, these sponsors were not related, nor did they even know these refugees. Aunt Felka offered to sponsor us, and a complete stranger from New Hampshire sponsored Aunt Macia and her family.

The preparations to immigrate to the United States were not very complicated, but we had to pass rigorous screenings and health examinations by the American authorities. Once those formalities were completed, we received passage tickets from the British government for the voyage to the United States on the *Queen Mary*. The ship was scheduled to sail from Southampton to New York on January 15, 1952. We packed our few possessions in suitcases, and with $100 in cash, we left East Moor on January 14, 1952, taking the train to London. We stayed overnight in a hostel in London and very early the next morning we took a train to Southampton. We boarded the *Queen Mary* that morning and began our voyage to America in the afternoon.

The *Queen Mary* was a beautiful ship with a displacement of 81,000 tons. The *Queen Mary* and the *Queen Elizabeth* were the two jewels in the Cunard Shipping Line at that time. However, airplanes already were providing tough competition for the trans-atlantic passenger travel, and these ships were underutilized and soon would be taken out of the Atlantic crossing service. The *Queen Mary* sailed the Atlantic for the last time in September 1967. Our voyage was quite spectacular, at least by our standards. It took five days. The seas were rough at times but the ship's large size made the passage very tolerable and no one got too sick to enjoy the crossing. The ship had many amenities, such as theaters, movies, bars, and other entertainment sources. We had access to most of these amenities and were very impressed by it all. We ate in a beautiful dining room and although we did not understand the menu, our waiter was accustomed to this. Once he had figured out what food we liked, he made the choices for us. He practically read my father's mind and always brought him food my father liked, especially freshly brewed coffee.

We sailed into New York City on January 20, 1952. It was a beautiful site. As we sailed past the Statue of Liberty, we realized we were to begin a new life in a country that was free and full of opportunities. We docked at the 34th Street Cunard Line docks on the Hudson River at mid-morning.

Our family in England, 1949.

My parents in England, 1951.

In front of school dorm in Bottisham, England, 1950.

Studying in the dorm in Bottisham, England, 1950.

In England with my prize possession, 1950.

High school classmates in Bottisham, England, 1950. (I am bottom right.)

Polish refugee camp in England, 1947.

The *Queen Mary*.

UNITED STATES (1952–1970)

The immigration officials boarded the ship as soon as it docked at the pier and processed the passengers on board. Because of the number of people, this procedure took a long time. Our turn was around mid-afternoon. We all were waiting anxiously to see what America was like. After the immigration officials cleared us, we left the ship and a porter helped get our luggage to the taxi stand. He was a big black man, very imposing in appearance. Once he loaded the luggage into the taxi, he extended a hand demanding "two bits." He repeated "two bits" several times. I was intimidated by the whole situation and had no idea what "two bits" meant. I told him I did not understand English too well. Finally he asked me for 25 cents and I gave him the quarter he requested. That was my first impression of America.

A taxi took us to the Pennsylvania Rail Station on 8th Avenue and 34th Street and we went to the platform where we waited for the Penn Central train to take us to Cleveland. Aunt Felka had sent us the tickets ahead of time. The train arrived at eight o'clock that evening. It was night so we couldn't see much of the country. We tried to get some sleep lying down on the benches, but there wasn't enough space for all of us in one compartment, so I went to an empty adjacent compartment. Soon a man, who obviously had been drinking but was still well-behaved, joined me. He asked me a few questions about where I was from and where I was heading, and then proceeded to tell me about himself. He was a bricklayer from some small town in Pennsylvania and had gone to New York for a trial. He won a compensation case for the injuries he sustained in a fall at a construction site. He then proceeded to stuff money in my pockets, claiming he had lots of it. He showed me his pockets that were full of money, so I believed him. I politely refused his money and he left me alone. That was my second impression of America. What a contrast! One man demanding money, and another throwing it at me.

We arrived in Cleveland in the morning. We left the train and went to the main lobby of the Cleveland railway station, today's Terminal Tower, where Aunt Felka was waiting for us. I had never met her, and the last time my mother saw her was when they were little girls before the war. The reception was polite but not emotional. We loaded our few belongings into a single taxi. We had only a couple of suitcases and $100 dollars in cash with us and these were our only possessions. We drove to Aunt Felka's home in Parma. Her house impressed us very much; it appeared to be very spacious and well-furnished with all present day amenities including a large pleasant yard, well-maintained and with fruit trees.

Aunt Felka's husband, Frank, came home from work late that afternoon and her children returned early in the evening. We were introduced to Uncle Frank, their daughter, Genevie, and son Frank Jr. The other two sons, Marion and Eugene, were away from home. That evening, we had supper together with the Wilkosz family, a very sumptuous meal by our standards.

All of Aunt Felka's family spoke some Polish so the communication between us was reasonably good. Their Polish however, was laced with English words containing Polish prefixes and Polish suffixes. This at times led to misunderstanding or hilarious situations. For example, Aunt Felka was trying to tell us that her boys occasionally got into fights in the streets and she used the following phrase, "boys*y po*fight*ali się na* street*cie*," which is totally meaningless to a Polish speaking person. After a while, we got used to this pidgin-Polish, and now, some of the made-up words occasionally gravitate into our own Polish.

That evening, cousin Frank took me for a ride, to show me some Cleveland sites. We drove downtown and around Cleveland and at the end of the ride he took me to a Dairy Queen and treated me to a banana split. I greatly appreciated the gesture, even though I was not used to eating ice cream in the middle of winter. Impression number three about America: Family bonds are as strong here as everywhere else, and it doesn't take long to get them renewed.

We stayed with Aunt Felka for about a week, then moved to an apartment on Jefferson Avenue in Cleveland's Tremont section. It was difficult to find apartments at that time and Aunt Felka rented one a few months before we arrived and held it for us. The apartment was sparsely furnished but had the basic necessities: Beds, mattresses, some chairs, and the essential kitchen utensils, most of the items donated by Aunt Felka's friends. A number of people stepped forward after we arrived and gave us many items for our apartment. It was embarrassing to accept these gifts, but the items were very helpful at the early stages of our lives here in the United States and we were very appreciative. Impression number four about America: People are very friendly and very generous.

When we moved into our apartment, we set out to fulfill our dream of having enough bread and butter until we were completely satisfied. We went to the nearby bakery, bought several loaves of bread and two pounds of butter. We returned to our apartment and sat in chairs around a makeshift table made out of orange crates. We began to eat bread covered with thick layers of butter. We ate and ate until we could no longer take another bite, thankful that we could finally fulfill a dream.

The area of Cleveland we moved to was considered the Polish and Ukrainian section of the city. There was a Polish Catholic Church, St. John Cantius, a Polish bank, stores with Polish-speaking clerks, and a library with Polish books. One could get by reasonably well here with very little knowledge of English. In fact, my parents had only a very rudimentary knowledge of English, just enough to get by. My father got a job at Ferry Cap on Scranton Road in Cleveland, arranged by Aunt Felka. He started working the day after we moved into our apartment. His job was to carry crates of nuts and bolts to storage from the machines that were stamping them out. It was hard work, but the pay was good (less than $1.00 per hour) and the work was steady. Initially our life was difficult. We had a lot of catching up to do but did not have the money to do it. We relied on my father's meager earnings for our living. We were very frugal and watched carefully how we spent our money. For example, we walked to the West Side Market some two miles away to buy groceries, or walked downtown rather than pay the fare to ride a bus. It was a great way to get acquainted with Cleveland. Later, my mother got a job as a cleaning woman for Ostendorf Morris Company in downtown Cleveland. Between the two of them they made enough money to provide for the family and even save a few dollars.

Aunt Macia and her family immigrated to the United States in 1953. A complete stranger from New Hampshire sponsored them. Their beginning was much harsher than ours. They had no family or friends to help them out. They lived in a one-bedroom apartment and could not find steady jobs. They really had to struggle to make ends meet. We received a letter from them asking if they could join us in Cleveland. We found an apartment for them and invited them to come. They moved to Cleveland and settled not too far from us, also in the Tremont section of Cleveland. Uncle Piotr found a job at Republic Steel and Cousin Anulka at Marymount Hospital. We were fortunate and very happy to be together again.

After we arrived in the United States, we found that there were also some less pleasant sides to this country. Prejudice was evident—in some cases subtle and in some not so subtle. Children and some grown-ups called us DPs or Displaced Persons, name usually followed with the catcall, "Why don't you go back to your own country?" There were similar signs scribbled on walls, on buildings and sidewalks. Our first reaction was that this harassment was no big deal. So we're Displaced Persons. However, at times the name-calling became ugly with some nasty adjectives added for good measure. Some of the prejudice was motivated by the poor job situation in the United States at that time. The economy was in a recession in 1952 and the job market was tight. Many people blamed the poor job market on the influx of immigrants as they felt the newcomers took jobs away from American citizens. Impression number five about America: Prejudice exists even in the country with the greatest democracy in the world.

Our first Christmas in the United States was so very different from the Christmases we celebrated several years before. Father was laid off from work and, even though mother was still employed as a cleaning woman, her job did not pay very well and our means were very limited. We managed however to be self-sufficient and did not seek outside assistance. The *Wigilia* on our first Christmas on United States soil was modest by today's standards but sumptuous by comparison to all Christmases since we left Poland. We went to the midnight mass at St. John Cantius Church. The church was packed and the mass was beautiful. The choir sang Polish carols. Several members of The Cleveland Orchestra accompanied the choir and the music was spectacular. I still remember that first midnight mass to this day. I have gained a lot of respect for the immigrants who came to the United States in the early 20th century and, in spite of their modest means, built beautiful churches. These immigrants were very proud of their Polish heritage; they maintained the knowledge of the Polish language and practiced Polish traditions.

Alina and I went to St. John Cantius High School. I skipped a grade again, upon urging from my father, and went to the 12th grade instead of the 11th, which I was attending before leaving England. The principal of St. John Cantius High School, Sister Dulcia of Sisters of St. Joseph, interviewed me to determine which grade I should be assigned. Since the principal taught Latin, which I knew rather well, she concluded I was ahead of her 12th grade Latin class. Therefore, she assumed that the rest of my subjects must be on an equal level and she assigned me to the 12th grade. She cautioned me, however, that if I could not keep up with the rest of the class she would be forced to reassign me back to the 11th grade. I was 18 at the time and the prospect of going back to the 11th grade did not sit well with me. I had no problems keeping up with the rest of the class except in English and American History of which I had only a rudimentary knowledge. I was able to catch up in American History very quickly, but English, well, I am still working on it. I graduated Cum Laude in June 1952 to the great surprise of my relatives and friends.

The Sisters, the lay teachers and most of my classmates were very friendly and understanding of my difficulties and tried to help. They often gave me food leftovers from the cafeteria to take home. This gesture embarrassed me greatly even though I realized they were just trying to be helpful. However, since at that time I was rather shy and at times withdrawn, I did not reach out to take full advantage of their support. About the middle of the semester, I realized I had a lot of free time on my hands. I was able to do all my homework at school, therefore, I decided to get a full-time job. I found work at a window manufacturing company, on the four to midnight shift, which did not interfere with my schooling. Business became slow, however, and I was laid off after two months.

After graduating from high school, I got a job at White Sewing Machine Company in Cleveland. The job consisted of sanding wood sewing machine cabinets. I was paid according to the number of cabinets I cleaned and sanded. The job was hard and my hands were always raw from the sandpaper I used. When I got home after work, I often did not feel like doing anything else but resting. My father kept telling me that if I did not want to work that hard for the rest of my life, I had better think about a college education. Aunt Felka's tenant, Woody Turner, was a college graduate in mechanical engineering. I went to him to seek advice. He encouraged me to go to college, suggesting Case Technology or Ohio State University as two possible options. I went to Case first and applied for admission. The admissions director discouraged me from enrolling at Case because of my language problems and because I lacked a few basic subjects that were prerequisites for enrollment in an engineering school. The admissions director recommended I apply to Ohio State. It was already late in August when I found out that I would not be going to Case. I took a bus to Columbus and went to Ohio State to inquire about admission. The classes were starting in a week and I didn't have much time. The admissions office at Ohio State told me I needed to take the SAT test before I could enroll at the school. However, they were willing to accept me conditionally if I agreed to take the test when it was offered in the fall. The prerequisites for the engineering school, algebra and trigonometry, I could make up at the university. I enrolled on the spot.

I found lodging in the stadium dormitories; the rooms were located under the stadium stands. The rooms in the dormitories were large, housing 15 to 20 students each. There were bunk beds, multiple toilets and shower facilities, study halls, a cafeteria, and lots of noise on Saturdays, the days of the football games. Coincidentally, the band also practiced just outside the stadium every afternoon of the fall semester. The large rooms afforded me the opportunity to be with a variety of students, to practice my English, and to make new friends. It was hard at first to be in a totally English environment after a lifetime of mainly Polish surroundings. My fellow classmates and roommates like Tom Sashihara, Bill Bates and Mike Huddle were very friendly and tried helping me adjust to the American way of life. I was invited to visit several friends at their homes in a number of different cities. The studies did not present too many difficulties, except for the English language. My first paper in English class was a disaster and the instructor could not understand how I could have graduated from high school with such a poor knowledge of English. She called me in for a conference, and after hearing my story, promised to grade me on the progress I made rather than on absolute knowledge of the language. I passed the course.

English was not the only difficulty I had encountered while at Ohio State. I had to overcome a number of other problems. The Siberian experience, the years in the refugee camps left their scars on my psyche. I was shy and had a low level of confidence and self-esteem. I felt inferior to the American students and unsure how to behave in the new environment. For example when I was invited to my friends' homes I didn't know how to act. When my friends' parents offered me food or something to drink, my initial response was, "no, thank you," even though I would have liked to accept the offer. I learned quickly that in this country, if someone offers you something, they mean it, and you may not get another chance if you refuse. I was also very unsure of myself when speaking in front of a large group of people. My first attempts at public speaking were not very pleasant, usually accompanied by a good dose of jitters. With time, however, I began to overcome these difficulties by observing, listening and learning.

At Ohio State, I came across a teacher who left a lasting impression on me just like the teachers from high school in England. He was Dr. Joseph Koffolt, Chairman of the Chemical Engineering Department, who embraced me and ushered me through the maze of university life. He called his students "his jewels" and made everyone feel like they were the most important person on earth. He knew all his students by their first names and made it a point to remember as much as possible about each student. He also kept in touch with everyone after their graduation. He claimed that if you gave him the name of a student, he could tell you their age, their hometown, and the color of their eyes; and he could. From him, I learned to treat every person as a unique individual and to respect him or her for their uniqueness. He also showed me the value of networking. He seemed to know everybody in the chemical industry.

After graduating from high school, I had to register for the army draft with our friendly Selective Service Board in Cleveland. Soon afterwards, I was summoned for a physical examination and received a notice for induction into the army in April 1953. I was to report for induction on May 19, 1953. The notice shocked my parents and me. We had been in the United States for slightly over a year, and I was to go off to the army. My mother was particularly upset, for she had not been too keen about coming to the United States in the first place. These were the times of the 1950–1953 Korean conflict, which meant a possible combat—not a very appealing thought. Since, at that time, there was a shortage of engineers and scientists in the United States, the local draft boards were inclined toward granting deferments to students pursuing engineering degrees. I wrote a letter to the draft board seeking a deferment stating I wanted to pursue a chemical engineering degree. A week later, miraculously, my call for induction was cancelled. I got my deferment, which was, as I understood, unprecedented after one received a notice for induction.

At Ohio State I decided to enroll in the ROTC program, thinking that if I had to serve in the army, I might as well do it as an officer. The Army ROTC did not accept non-citizens to the program. However, the Air Force ROTC did take in students who were non-citizens, but only for the first two years of the program. In the last two years the same US. citizen rule applied. A five-year residency was required to qualify for U.S. citizenship. Therefore, even after two years of basic ROTC I still would not have the residency qualification for the advanced ROTC program. I was caught between a rock and a hard place. I decided to enroll in the basic Air Force ROTC anyway.

While in ROTC, I met an Air Force major who was a ROTC instructor and soccer coach. Major Wagner invited me to try out for the soccer team. I made the team. At that time, there wasn't much interest in soccer in the United States and the attendance at our games was sparse. Occasionally, we were allowed to play our matches in football stadiums. It was strange to play in front of 70,000...empty seats. About 30 students were on the team and about half of them came from foreign countries. It was truly an international representation from Europe, Asia, Africa and both Americas. I played soccer at Ohio State for four years, earning an honorable mention on the All-American team in my third year.

I enjoyed my stay at Ohio State. The school was large but divided into small colleges. Many activities at the school fascinated me such as a variety of sporting events one could attend with the purchase of a single athletic card, homecoming activities, the student week with float parades, elections for student offices, and many others. While in school, I got a job as a dishwasher in a local restaurant to earn some spending money. In the summertime, I found jobs in Cleveland, usually earning enough money to pay for tuition and room and board at the university. One summer I worked at the Republic Steel strip mill. The job was demanding, consisting of trimming rough edges from large coils of steel. We were paid according to the tonnage we trimmed, so the more we trimmed the more money we made. Another summer I worked at the Harshaw Chemical Company making various chemical salts from different metals. Again the work was backbreaking labor, in an area contaminated with fumes, but the pay was good. My foreman appreciated my financial situation and let me work double shifts on many occasions. The extra money I earned working two shifts enabled me to buy my first car, a seven-year-old Ford, for $200. The last summer while in school, I worked at the University Agricultural Experimental Station in Columbus and in Wooster, Ohio. The job involved analyzing soil samples. This work was relatively easy by comparison to the other jobs, but the pay was not as good. However, that job carried over into the school year and provided me with spending money for my last year in school. My third year at Ohio State was the most difficult. I worked part time, played soccer, and consequently, my grades suffered. I was very discouraged and contemplated quitting school. I told my father what I was thinking; he took the news calmly and asked if I wanted to have him check job openings at Ferry Cap. His calmness and common sense hit me like a ton of bricks. I certainly did not want to work like he did for the rest of my life. I returned to school, determined to finish my studies no matter what it took.

I graduated from Ohio State in June of 1957 with a Bachelor's degree in Chemical Engineering and got a job with the Diamond Alkali Company in Cleveland. I was assigned to the central engineering department in Cleveland. My first assignment was a preparation of flow sheets for purifying trona, a naturally occurring soda ash, for a plant to be constructed in Wyoming. The work was not very challenging but I figured I had to pay my dues. I had a fair amount of time on my hands and I started to explore some business ideas that would expand my horizon. One idea was to manufacture inflatable PVC seat cushions that could be used at sporting events. I made several prototype cushions with school logos imprinted on them. I had several hundred cushions made and sent the samples to many major schools' athletic departments, asking if they would be interested in selling them through school athletic stores and at sporting events. These were the early days of PVC plastics, and inflatable items were not yet very common. I received several positive responses from a number of universities but not in large enough quantities to make the business worthwhile. This venture was a lot closer to real business situation than my photography or cigarette-selling.

The recession of 1957 was difficult for the United States and the working environment was very slow. Diamond established a training program for their young engineers to take advantage of the slow period by getting additional training. I was chosen to participate in the new training program. The new engineers were assigned to three six-month rotations at three different divisions of the company. My first assignment was the Soda Ash Division in Painesville, Ohio, about 30 miles east of Cleveland. I stayed five days at the local YMCA in Painesville while working at the plant, and on weekends I came home to Cleveland. My second assignment was in the Chlorinated Products Division, also in Painesville, where I worked in the polyvinyl chloride experimental group. As a final assignment also in the Chlorinated Products Division I worked with a group of engineers developing a crab grass killer called Dacthal. The group was sent to Texas in 1959 to start up a small plant to produce the newly developed product. I went to Texas as one of the engineers and later stayed on as a plant supervisor for the new unit. In Texas I was surprised to see many signs of discrimination, especially against Blacks and Mexicans. Particularly revolting were the separate facilities for the white and "colored" people in public places such as restaurants and motels. The public toilet facilities also were segregated. There was noticeable discrimination against Catholics and even the "Yankees." Strangely enough, I was exempted because I was Polish. Here was a country that espoused freedom for all, and yet, not all were equal. This was a big paradox for me.

Diamond Alkali had a plant in Mexico City and I had the opportunity to visit it in 1959. While there, I visited the typical tourist sites in Mexico City and the surrounding areas, like the pyramids, the Xochimilco floating gardens, the archeological museum, and the bullfights. One of the fellows in the plant knew a matador, who presented me at the end of the bullfight with the set of banderillas from the bull he just killed. We then exchanged drinks of rum and wine from the traditional leather sack, right in front of 50,000 applauding people. That evening we went to a square where mariachis entertained the crowds. The whole trip was an enjoyable experience.

In the summer of 1960, I made my first trip back to Poland since being forced to leave the country in 1940. I was apprehensive to go at first. I still harbored bad memories of deportation to the Soviet Union and did not know what to expect. I arranged a one-week tour of Poland with the Polish tourist agency "Orbis" and set aside another week to visit my relatives. Before the trip, I had a hard time visualizing a country where everyone spoke only Polish. As soon as I checked into a hotel, I took a tram ride in order to immediately become surrounded by native Poles. It was a very emotional experience for me. The tour of Poland included historical places like Kraków, Częstochowa, and Oświęcim (Auschwitz). The trip to Częstochowa, the most holy place in Poland with the miraculous Black Madonna, was particularly emotional. I was able to thank Our Lady of Częstochowa for all the favors and, yes, the miracles of which we were beneficiaries during our journeys. I also visited Zakopane, the winter resort in southern Poland. I hired a guide and hiked into the mountains and down to Morskie Oko, a lake in the midst of the mountains. I also went rafting on the Dunajec River through the very colorful canyons in the Pieniny Mountains. The American dollar went a long way in communist Poland. One could exchange dollars on the black market equivalent to five to 10 times the purchasing power in the United States. The Polish government fixed the official exchange rate artificially low in relation to actual market conditions. The cost of hiring a guide or treating people to a dinner was minimal in U.S. dollars

I visited relatives, some of whom I had never met, others whom I barely remembered from the pre-war days. The realities of the political situation in Poland became apparent to me very quickly. My grandmother told me stories about life during the war under German occupation. My two aunts participated in the Polish underground movement as communication messengers and smugglers of ammunition to the partisans. My aunt Jania was so affected by the war experience that she joined a cloistered order of nuns, *Norbertanki*, after the war. She later became the Mother Superior of the convent and devoted most of her time to restoring a church in Imbrowice, near Kraków. The church is famous for having the only Brueger painting in Poland.

My uncle Władek told me stories about their experiences in the Soviet Union after we were evacuated. He described my grandfather's suffering and death. He told me he was drafted into the Tadeusz Kościuszko Division, saw action at the battle of Lenino and was wounded. He returned to Siberia after he was discharged from the army. He and his family were repatriated to kolhoz near Kiev in the Ukraine in 1945. They returned to Poland in 1946 along with a large group of Poles who were being repatriated at that time. Uncle Władek and his family settled in Ząbkowice near Wrocław on lands acquired from Germany in what is now a western part of Poland. He told me about the difficulties they experienced in the early days after returning to Poland from the Soviet Union. They were discriminated against, could not get decent jobs, and barely were able to make ends meet. I also witnessed the sad results of the communist indoctrination of Polish youth by listening to my cousin's espousing communist theories and their distorted claims that the Soviets liberated Poland not only from the Germans but also from the Polish bourgeois class.

I drove through Legnica, a large city in southwestern Poland, to visit my cousins. All of a sudden, I heard Russian patriotic songs coming from the windows of the apartments by the road. My whole body shuddered. The nightmare of Siberia passed in front of me. Later, I learned from my cousins that a large garrison of Russian troops was stationed in Legnica. There were similar garrisons of Russian troops stationed in several other Polish cities. Many other signs of Soviet domination were evident all over Poland. Red banners with communist slogans hung on most major buildings, schools and overpasses. It seemed one could not go even a few yards without running into some sort of communist propaganda.

I visited Uncle Staszek who was a pastor of a church in suburban Kraków. He and several other priests took me to a basement of the rectory, closed all doors and windows, and quizzed me about the political situation in the West. They told me they listened to Radio Free Europe, but wanted to hear information firsthand. They wanted to know the possibilities of the West's liberating Poland from the communists. They were particularly interested if John Kennedy, a Catholic, had a chance to become president of the United States.

I returned from Poland rejuvenated in my Polish heritage but at the same time confident that we made the right decision to stay in the west. Poland in 1960 was a depressed and oppressed country with limited freedoms and lack of opportunities. It was very sad.

In June 1961, I was transferred by Diamond to Newark, New Jersey, to head up a project to improve the process of making a weed and brush killer. The compound was used to kill vegetation on utility right-of-ways, for clearing brush along railroad tracks and as a weed killer in a number of agricultural applications. I was to head a small group of three engineers to investigate the new methods of making the compound. The investigation was successful and Diamond built a new unit in Newark. The compound was later used to make Agent Orange for the Vietnam War. Initially, we at Diamond were not aware that these compounds contained dioxin, classified as the most toxic chemical known to mankind. However, even early on, there were indications that the compound caused severe acne in many workers. Dow Chemical, our competitor in the manufacturing and marketing of the product, identified dioxin and its toxic nature and shared the information with all its competitors. However, it was up to the individual companies to devise the means of removing dioxin from the products. We made extensive efforts to clean the compound containing dioxin; however, our efforts were only marginally successful. Diamond shut down the plant for economic reasons in 1969. Personally, I strongly suspected that the dioxin issue weighed heavily on the decision to close the plant.

Another negative facet of working at the Newark plant was the strong odor of phenol that permeated the plant and penetrated into everything that was exposed to the plant environment. Our books, clothing, cars, and even our bodies smelled of phenol. No amount of cleaning, washing or showering could remove the persistent odor. It was embarrassing to have people sniff around in my presence inquiring from where the smell of medicine was coming. (Sometimes I also sniffed around to divert the attention away from me.)

My career at Diamond was beginning to look very promising. I became a unit supervisor after a successful start-up of the Dacthal unit in Greens Bayou, Texas. On my recommendations, we made a number of changes in the production unit that helped production workers reduce their workload, for which they were very appreciative. I always tried to involve as many people as possible at every level, when evaluating changes that affected them. As a result, I received a great number of suggestions from many individuals and good cooperation when the changes were implemented. I always made a point to listen to all sides of the discussion and be considerate of other people's opinions, and as a result, gained their confidence. This approach resulted in improved morale and better efficiency for the company, a win–win situation.

I moved to Newark on a special project assignment, and when that project was completed, I was asked to stay on as part of the plant engineering staff. In 1964 I was promoted to technical superintendent, and in 1967, to production superintendent although there were other equally competent candidates. The reason I was selected to fill both positions were my positive attitude, the enthusiasm I displayed in performing my job, and the cooperation I received from associates who worked with me.

Diamond acquired Nopco Company in 1965 with a plant in Harrison, New Jersey. The Harrison plant, unlike Diamond was unionized which created some anxiety among Diamond workers. We wondered how long it would be before the union activity disrupted the congenial atmosphere at our plant. Great pressure was exerted by the Electrical Workers Union from the Nopco facility to organize the workers in the Newark plant. The organizing effort was bitter and antagonized many people, but eventually, the Newark plant was unionized in 1968. I had witnessed a transformation of a friendly and cooperative group of people into a confrontational environment not only between the management and workers, but also among the workers themselves. It became more difficult for supervisors to deal directly with the production people without interference from the union. I felt unionization could have been avoided if our plant manager had made himself more accessible to the people at the plant. I came to the conclusion that any manager who lets the situation deteriorate to the point where workers have to seek an outside voice to speak for them deserved the union. Bob Connoles, who worked at the unionized plant in Harrison, replaced our plant manager, Mike Kennedy, after the plant was unionized. The confrontational environment at the plant did not change much with the change in management. However, I continued to have excellent relationships with all of our associates. Again, they recognized my accessibility, my openness and my appreciation for their contributions.

My social life in the Newark area looked brighter because there was a large Polish community in the New York metropolitan area. Upon my arrival in Newark, I purchased a Polish newspaper to get a feel for the Polish community there. An announcement in the paper stated that a picnic would be held on the Fourth of July at the Bud Lake picnic grounds, so I went to the picnic. I found a large number of Polish people enjoying the holiday with good Polish food and dancing, so I had a good time. A number of young people were dancing, and I asked some of the girls for a dance. One of them was Barbara Wiśniewska, a young girl who seemed to be having a good time. At the end of the day, I offered Basia (diminutive of Barbara in Polish) and her girlfriend a ride back to Jersey City. A week later, I called Basia and asked her if she would go with me to see the Broadway play *Camelot*. She agreed. During the evening, she commented that it was nice of me to take her out on her birthday and asked how I knew it was her birthday. I responded, "What do you mean it's your birthday? It's *my* birthday!" We had a big laugh about having birthdays on the same day, although she kept reminding me that our birthdays were five years apart. There were many things Basia and I had in common. Of course we were both Polish, and we both enjoyed music, dancing and travel. We fell in love and became engaged at Christmastime. I wrote a letter to Basia's father asking him for permission to marry her, just as the Polish tradition dictated. We were married on August 4, 1962. Our only sorrow was that no one from Basia's immediate family was able to attend the wedding. Here again the political situation in Poland did not allow families to be united even at such a joyous occasion as a wedding.

Basia had came to the United States in 1959 at the invitation of her uncle, Jan Jaworowski. Her uncle, a wonderful man, was married to the sister of Basia's father. Jan Jaworowski sponsored numerous families to come to the United States after the war, some of which were complete strangers to him. Basia was born in the village of Jaskółowo, near the city of Nasielsk, about 40 kilometers northeast of Warsaw. She and her three sisters spent the war years in German-occupied Poland and the post-war years in communist dominated Poland. She can best attest to the horrible atrocities committed by the Nazis during the war and to the communist indoctrination of the Polish society, especially children, after the war. On the positive side, she appreciated the formal education she received in Poland. She received a degree of *Felczer of Medicine.* A shortage of doctors existed in Poland after the war, and Felczer of Medicine was a shortened version of a Medical Doctor degree. When she came to the United States, she worked as a scrub nurse technician in the operating room at Saint Francis Hospital in Jersey City, since the U.S. medical profession did not recognize her degree. Later, Basia attended Clarion State University, graduating with Bachelor of Science in Nursing. She earned a second degree in school nursing and also obtained a Professional Nursing license.

Basia met a number of Polish people in the New Jersey area and introduced them to me. Some of them had been friends of mine from Iran, India and England. I ran into Wanda and Danka Zychowicz, who stayed with us in Tehran, Ahvaz, Karachi and Valivade. I found several classmates from my high school in England, among them, Jan and Zygmunt Birecki and Witek Łukaszewski. We also met many new friends whom we became very close to over the years, such as the Jachnas and Wandyczes. We took full advantage of the entertainment opportunities available to us while living in the New York area. We went to Broadway plays, concerts, dances, nightclubs, and many sporting events. We saw Yankees baseball games, championship boxing fights in Madison Square Garden, New York Giants football games, and soccer matches including Milan of Italy vs. Santos of Brazil with the great Pele.

Our son Mark was born May 8, 1963. When I picked up Basia and Mark at the hospital, I was so nervous that I had forgotten to buy gas beforehand and, needless to say, ran out of gas on the way home. Three years later, Mark got a birthday present in the form of our second son, Tom. It certainly saved the cost of birthday cakes with four birthdays within two days. The boys added a tremendous amount of joy to our lives but also changed our lifestyle somewhat. Now we did more things as family. We camped in places like Wildwood, New Jersey; Lake George, New York; and the Thousand Islands area of the St. Lawrence River and in Canada. We spent weekends on the New Jersey shore in Clifwood Beach where Basia's uncle had a cottage. Basia quit working when Mark was born and devoted her energy to raising and educating the boys. She taught them to speak, read and write Polish. Basia and Mark went to Poland for three weeks in 1965 when Basia's father became terminally ill. I didn't care for the separation, but I also understood Basia's need to fulfill an obligation to herself and her father. Later that year, Basia's sister Irena came to the United States, and two years later Basia's other sister Teresa joined us as well. Their mother came to the United States in 1969 and eventually married Basia's Uncle Jan Jaworowski (not a blood relative).

I enrolled in the MBA program at Seton Hall University in 1963. It took me four years to complete the program since I was employed and could only attend school in the evenings, taking two courses a semester. I received my MBA degree in June of 1967.

Diamond management asked me in 1965 if I would be interested in going to Poland to help solve production problems the

Poles were experiencing with an acetylene plant. The Poles bought the process to manufacture acetylene from an Italian company but the process had many technical problems. Diamond also had purchased the process from the Italians and spent millions of dollars improving it. The Poles were interested in Diamond's know-how and Diamond agreed to send a team of technicians to work with their Polish counterparts. I was chosen as a liaison person for the project. Basia and I were very exited about the possibility of going to Poland, but the project fell through because the Poles did not have sufficient foreign exchange currency to pay for Diamond's know-how.

Diamond built a new production unit in Greens Bayou, Texas in 1968 to increase the production of Dacthal, the compound used as a crab grass killer. The plant was based on a technology similar to the original process I was involved in when I worked in Texas. There were many problems with the new process and I was asked to go to Texas in 1969 for a three-month period to help out as a troubleshooter. Diamond also agreed to send my family with me. At the end of the assignment, we went to Mexico City for a 10-day vacation. I had been in Mexico City before, but this was the first trip for Basia and the boys. We visited many typical tourist sites and had a good time. There were two incidents from the trip that stuck in my mind: our trip to the pyramids and shopping in downtown Mexico City. We went to see the pyramids, but to save money, we decided to go by bus. We asked for directions to the bus station at the hotel but we got lost and had to ask a local in Spanish for new directions. The Mexican must have misunderstood me because he gave us directions to a bus repair garage. So much for my Spanish! The garage personnel were greatly surprised to see two gringos with small children show up at the garage. An English-speaking supervisor showed us where the bus stop was. The bus that arrived was an old, dilapidated bus filled to the brim with native Mexicans, some holding cages with live chickens, others holding goods they were apparently taking to the market at the pyramids. All passengers were gaping at us like we were from Mars. A couple of natives gave up their seats for us.

It was a beautiful day, not a cloud in the sky. As we looked out of the window we saw what we thought were raindrops on the windows. After looking around, bewildered, we saw a little boy urinating through a window in front of us. It all seemed so perfectly natural.

We arrived at the pyramids and did the usual tourist things. We climbed up to the top of the pyramids, had a nice lunch in a restaurant underneath the pyramids, and returned to Mexico City. This time we took a taxi.

The shopping was much more traumatic. We went to a basement shoe store in downtown Mexico City to purchase sandals for Basia. While she was trying on the sandals, the boys and I wandered about the store. After we paid for the shoes Basia turned to me and asked where Tom was. We looked around the store; Tom was nowhere to be seen. We ran outside, and still no Tom. It was noontime and the streets were packed with people. Basia and I split up and circled the block hoping that Tom did not cross the street. Basia was crying. We were trying, with the help of an English–Spanish dictionary, to ask people around us if they had seen a little boy. No one has seen him. On the second trip around the block, I spotted Tom standing on the corner of the street holding on to a lamppost. When I asked him where he went, his reply was, "You told me to stand on the corner if I got lost." Our joy was beyond description; we did not even dare to think what could have happened to him.

The situation at the Newark Diamond plant became more tenuous after Bill Bricker became the president of Diamond. Bricker decided to shut down the operation in Newark. After the decision was made to shut down the plant, Diamond offered me a position at their Greens Bayou plant in Texas.

While in New Jersey I had met a fellow Pole, Włodek Ginilewicz, who formed a small chemical company called Radom Chemical. Włodek asked me to assist him in building a chemical production unit in the building he purchased. I helped him in the evenings and on weekends to design and construct the production facility that would produce specialty chemicals. When Diamond offered me a position in Texas my friend Włodek asked if I would join him as a partner in his firm. I chose the partnership because I always had a desire to own a business, or at least have a stake in a business.

The new firm was too small and unprofitable to pay me a salary at first, but I saw potential. We worked hard to make the firm successful, sometimes working as many as 80 hours a week. We were making some progress. The two main products we produced were coatings to protect printing on PVC printed fabrics and pipe sealer for threaded pipe joints. We had four full-time employees and hired part-time people to help when the workload was heavy. The business was too small, however, for two strong-minded individuals, and differences between my partner and me were beginning to emerge, mainly about quality and safety issues. Finally these differences became too large for me to take, and I resigned from Radom Chemical in February of 1970. A year later, an explosion at the plant killed four people, including my partner, and leveled the entire plant. I wonder to this day what would have happened if I had remained with that firm. I doubt I would be writing this autobiography.

The search for a new job in 1970 wasn't easy. It was a recession year and people were being laid off, not hired. I had several interviews, but no firm offers. A family, two small children, minimal savings, a recession and no job—the situation was not a desirable one. Here again, my faith and positive outlook carried me through. One day I received a phone call from a friend in Cleveland, who told me Jim Mooney of Mooney Chemicals was looking for a plant manager for his plant in Franklin, Pennsylvania. I sent Jim Mooney a resume and he invited me for an interview. The interview took place in his Cleveland office. Afterwards, Jim invited Basia and me for a dinner at his house. We were impressed by his family, its religious beliefs, and the close relationships among the siblings. Jim was a very gracious host and we left his house feeling cheerful and optimistic.

Our first Christmas in the USA, 1952.

Wilkosz, Suchey and Bąk families, 1953, (front: Alina, Marion Wilkosz; back: St. Suchey, Sophie Suchey, Mother, me, Aunt Felka, Father, Frank Wilkosz, Frank Jr. and Genevie Wilkosz).

Macia's and our families with my grandmother when she visited us in 1959.

Uncle Romek (standing) and Uncle Ludwik with his family in Argentina, 1953.

Approval of Budget Bureau not required.

SELECTIVE SERVICE SYSTEM

ORDER TO REPORT FOR INDUCTION

Local Board No. 28
[illegible] County
[illegible] Street
Cleveland 9, Ohio

(Local Board Date Stamp With Code)

April 23, 1953.
(Date of mailing)

The President of the United States,

To Eugene (First name) (Middle name) Bak (Last name) | 33 | 28 | 33 | 165 | (Selective Service Number)

511 Jefferson Ave.,
(Street and number)

Cleveland (City) Ohio (State)

GREETING:

Having submitted yourself to a Local Board composed of your neighbors for the purpose of determining your availability for service in the armed forces of the United States, you are hereby ordered to

report to ~~[illegible]~~ The Standard Bldg. 1370 Ontario St., Cleveland, O.
(Place of reporting)

at 8:00 a. m. (Hour of reporting), on the 19th day of May, 19 53, for forwarding to an induction station.

This Local Board will furnish transportation to the induction station where you will be examined, and, if accepted for service, you will then be inducted into a branch of the armed forces.

Persons reporting to the induction station in some instances are found to have developed disqualifying defects since being examined and may be rejected for these or other reasons. It is well to keep this in mind in arranging your affairs, to prevent any undue hardship if you are rejected at the induction station. If you are employed, you should advise your employer of this notice and of the possibility that you may not be accepted at the induction station. Your employer can then be prepared to replace you if you are accepted, or to continue your employment if you are rejected.

If you are not accepted, return transportation will be provided.

Willful failure to report promptly to this Local Board at the place specified above and at the hour and on the day named in this notice is a violation of the Selective Service Act of 1948, and subjects the violator to fine and imprisonment.

You must keep this form and bring it with you when you report to the Local Board. Bring with you sufficient clothing for 3 days.

If you are so far removed from your own Local Board that reporting in compliance with this Order will be a serious hardship and you desire to report to a Local Board in the area of which you are now located, go immediately to that Local Board and make written request for transfer of your delivery for induction, taking this Order with you.

L. A. Hanford
Member of Local Board.

SSS Form No. 252

U.S. GOVERNMENT PRINTING OFFICE : 1948 O - 799811

SELECTIVE SERVICE SYSTEM

Local Board No. 28
Cuyahoga County
3804 West 25th Street
Cleveland 9, Ohio
(Stamp of Local Board)

Eugene Bak
511 Jefferson Ave.,
Cleveland, Ohio

Dear Sir:

In accordance with Selective Service Regulations, Section 1622.15 Paragraph B, your induction is hereby cancelled.

Very truly yours,

C. L. Dempsey EW

C. L. Dempsey, Clerk

CLD:ew

Order to report for induction into the US army and cancellation of the same.

Another Buckeye On All-American: Booter Gene Bak

Gene Bak, Ohio State booter, was given honorable mention on the All-American soccer team, Buck mentor Skip Knuttgen announced yesterday.

The first and second teams and the honorable mentions were selected by the National Soccer Coaches of America. Men were chosen from a cross section of 40 colleges and universities.

Bak, who was named to the second All-Midwest squad, had played consistent soccer through the entire season.

"Gene is one of the steadiest players I've ever seen, and it will sure help to have him around next season," commented Knuttgen.

Soccer at Ohio State University, 1954.

In ROTC uniform at Ohio State, 1953.

THE UNITED STATES OF AMERICA

ORIGINAL
TO BE GIVEN TO
THE PERSON NATURALIZED

No. 7798906

CERTIFICATE OF NATURALIZATION

Petition No. 127368

Personal description of holder as of date of naturalization: Date of birth July 18, 1933 sex male complexion fair color of eyes hazel color of hair brown height 5 feet 10 inches; weight 140 pounds; visible distinctive marks none
Marital status single former nationality Poland
I certify that the description above given is true, and that the photograph affixed hereto is a likeness of me.

Eugene Bak
(Complete and true signature of holder)

THE UNITED STATES OF AMERICA
Northern District of Ohio } ss:

Be it known, that at a term of the District Court of Northern District of Ohio held pursuant to law at Cleveland, Ohio on April 12th, 1957 the Court having found that Eugene Bak then residing at 805 Jefferson Avenue, Cleveland, Ohio intends to reside permanently in the United States (when so required by the Naturalization Laws of the United States), had in all other respects complied with the applicable provisions of such naturalization laws, and was entitled to be admitted to citizenship, thereupon ordered that such person be and (s)he was admitted as a citizen of the United States of America.

In testimony whereof the seal of the court is hereunto affixed this 12th day of April in the year of our Lord nineteen hundred and fifty-seven and of our Independence the one hundred and eighty-one.

It is a violation of the U.S. Code (and punishable as such) to copy, print, photograph, or otherwise illegally use this certificate.

C.B. WATKINS,
Clerk of the U.S. District Court.
By [signature] Deputy Clerk.

DEPARTMENT OF JUSTICE

Copy of my US citizenship certificate.

Graduation from Ohio State, June 1957.

At Diamond Alkali Company in Greens Bayou, Texas, 1959.

Our wedding picture, August 4, 1962.

Bak side of the family at our wedding.

Basia (front) with parents and sisters Irena,Teresa and Regina, 1947.

Mark and I at my graduation from Seton Hall University, June 1967.

FRANKLIN (1970–1991)

Basia and I stopped in Franklin on the way home to see what this Mooney Chemical facility looked like. The factory was an old Mobil Oil plant that was used to manufacture block greases. The plant experienced a fire in 1963 that destroyed a major part of the facility. Mobil Oil decided to shut down the plant and Jim Mooney bought it for $70,000. The plant appeared old and in disrepair. It would require a lot of work to get it into a suitable working condition. I certainly had doubts about the long-term viability of the business and told Basia, "A good thing about this place is it can't get much worse, but it sure as heck can get better." Compared to the plants I worked in with Diamond, this plant seemed like a relic from the past century.

The day after we got home, Jim Mooney called and offered me a job as the plant manager. I told him I needed a couple of days to think about it but he insisted on my decision right away. I accepted the job after Jim agreed to let me take a month off to go to Poland during the summer. I started working at Mooney Chemicals on April 1, 1970. I spent two weeks in the office and the laboratory in Cleveland getting familiar with the company's business and then moved on to Franklin. Basia and I decided that she and the boys would stay in New Jersey until the end of the school year.

The plant employed 20 people and did not have any technically trained personnel. I became the plant manager, plant engineer, and plant chemist, all in one. At least I did not have too many people to blame when things went wrong. I did have two wonderful supervisors, Iggy Pataki, who was in charge of production, and Bill Exley, in charge of maintenance. These two individuals helped me immensely during the early stages of my assignment. The company's sales were approximately $2,000,000 dollars. We made around 14,000,000 pounds of products per year, mostly lead-based oil additives and lead- and cobalt-based paint driers. The company made $100,000 in gross profit that year. All technical work, development of new formulations, and technical service were performed in the Cleveland laboratory, which employed eight people. The Cleveland office was also small, with a staff of only 12 people. Mooney Chemicals sold its products through a direct sales force consisting of three salesmen. Most of the sales were east of the Mississippi River.

Jim Mooney was a tough but fair businessman, a very focused and results-oriented individual. He founded the company in 1946 with his brother-in-law, Carl Reusser. Carl ran the Franklin plant until he died in 1967. Initially, Jim put many restrictions on my activities. I had stringent limits on how much money I could spend on each new item ($25), the exception being emergency repairs. As one can imagine, I happened to need many emergency repairs. I also was required to check with him about every change I wanted to implement in the plant. This made managing the plant very challenging. Jim eased some of these restrictions as he gained confidence in my abilities, but he continued to quiz me in detail about all facets of plant operations for a long time. Jim had developed tremendous networking with people in the chemical industry and was constantly pushing the so-called "experts" to advise me on how to do things. This, at times, was very helpful, but at other times, it was very annoying.

Jim Mooney was also a very people-oriented person. He played a father role to all his employees, or associates, as he used to call them. Maybe this image was acquired as a result the large family he had of his own (he had 13 children) but without question he had a genuine interest in all his employees. He was concerned about their welfare, especially in the areas of health and long-term security. He had one of the most progressive health insurance plans and a profit sharing plan for long-term security. The profit sharing was particularly impressive since each person received 15 percent of his or her earnings at the end of each year. The money was deposited into a trust account and invested in safe securities. The investment options were later modified to include other securities and OMG stock. The gains from these investments became quite impressive, especially for people with a long tenure with the company.

After moving to Franklin, I lived temporarily in a cottage located on the plant property. The Cleveland personnel who came to the plant for business used this cottage for an overnight stay, but otherwise the cottage was empty until I moved in. I would like to say I lived alone, but that would be ignoring my housemates—the rats and a black snake that also seemed to have keys to the cottage. A broken down cottage in the woods by a stream made a nice home for many creatures, but I didn't mind the company since I was otherwise alone. I got used to the snake poking his head up through the floorboards looking for a rat for dinner.

I found western Pennsylvania very picturesque and the people very friendly. On one occasion when I was looking for a house to rent, I drove very slowly looking for a street address. A pick-up truck ahead of me pulled over and the driver got out to ask if I was lost and if he could help. When this sort of thing happened in New Jersey you were likely to be shot. The incident left me with a warm feeling about the people of Franklin.

I had to adjust to the lifestyle of Pennsylvanians. People in rural Pennsylvania passionately love hunting and fishing. All schools, many businesses, and public workplaces shut down on the first day of deer season. This way all members of the family can go hunting together. Hunting is a serious business, which I found out during my first hunting season in Pennsylvania. We had to deliver an order to a customer on Monday after Thanksgiving, the first day of deer season. I asked one of our truck drivers to deliver the load. He told me that he could not go because it was the first day of deer season and he was going hunting. I pointed out that the season was two weeks long and offered him a different day off during the two weeks if he delivered the load. He finally agreed. That was, he agreed until 6 a.m. Monday morning, when I received a phone call from him informing me that he was sick and could not deliver the load. Later, I found out he went hunting. I confronted him, stating that he could be fired for lying and flagrantly disobeying what I perceived was our agreement that he would deliver material to the customer. His response was, yes, he understood the infraction could get him fired but he took the chance anyway. I realized that since this man had risked his employment for the sake of being able to hunt on the first day of deer season, it must be very important to him. He had tried to convey that message to me. I heard the words, but the message didn't sink in. I learned a very important lesson that day. I needed to be attentive not only to the words of my associates but also to the music behind those words. I did not fire the individual who turned out to be one of the best drivers we had.

I found the people of rural Pennsylvania to be good people, good workers, very conscientious, and very dependable. I always treated my associates with respect and frequently expressed my appreciation for their work.

Western Pennsylvania was a hotbed of unionized companies. The Steelworkers, the Mineworkers, the Oil and Chemical Workers, the Teamsters, and the Teachers Union represented workers in plants and institutions in our area. I did not believe in unions, or for that matter, for the need of any outside organization to represent the working people as long as they were treated fairly and with respect. Of course, I did not question their right to be represented by a union if they chose, but it was up to management to make employees feel that it was unnecessary for them to seek outside help. For this situation to exist, there had to be a mutual respect, sharing of information, fair treatment, and above all, expression of appreciation for the contributions the employees made toward achieving common goals. I had an opportunity to observe confrontations between unions and management first as a steelworker at Republic Steel, then as a manager at Diamond Shamrock in Newark, and finally, as a board member in the Franklin Area School District. The atmosphere in these cases was always confrontational with "we–they" situations between the members of the union and the management. We at Mooney Chemicals had made a conscientious effort to eliminate the confrontational atmosphere and to promote a concept of one team regardless of the job function each person performed. I believe we were quite successful. We became a very productive plant, with a trouble-free environment, where every individual was given an opportunity to perform up to his or her potential. The plant became one of the safest in the industry, working many years without any workers being injured. This was very unusual in an industry like chemical manufacturing. People enjoyed coming to work because they felt they were needed and appreciated. We had some problems of course, but they were resolved within the plant walls in one-on-one discussions and with mutual respect for each other's positions. Many people in the community approached me saying they had never heard anyone complain about working at Mooney Chemicals. This was one of the highest compliments I could have received.

It was a difficult beginning in Franklin. Our plant was not a choice place to work. It was dirty, smelly, and running on a very limited budget. The plant initially was like a revolving door for people looking for other employment. We had one individual who started his first day of work in the morning, went out for lunch, and never came back. He never even bothered to ask to be paid for the hours that he did work. However, there was a core of good people at the plant who made up the backbone of our work force. Occasionally, a person from that group would come to me, asking my opinion as to whether he should leave for better job opportunities. Some of these individuals wanted to leave for better paying jobs at Joy or Pennzoil, some wanted to buy farms, others wanted to change careers (one engineer wanted to become a dentist). My answer was always the same—look to the future, look at the progress we have made already. Are you happy with what you are doing? If the answer is yes, then stick around and financial rewards will follow. Most stayed and had very successful careers.

I had lots of help during my early days at the plant from people like Iggy Pataki, who preached to everyone that work was very serious business and should be done well and conscientiously. Bill Exley, our maintenance supervisor, was the hardest working and most conscientious mechanic I have ever known. Tony Alkaitis, the formulation chemist from Cleveland who spent a lot of time in Franklin, was very innovative and extremely enthusiastic. He also gave me the biggest headaches with his uncontrollable passion for perfection. He was always changing formulations and making messes trying to improve on a formula. Many times I felt like strangling him, but each time he convinced me that his new idea would work, and it usually did. Tony came up with most of our new formulations. Rick Ditzenberger, an operator and later a production supervisor, was the hardest worker and could not understand why everyone did not measure up to his standards. He set an example for all our production people. I always will be grateful to these men for setting good examples for others to follow. The management team we eventually assembled was a dedicated group of people with Steve Flinchbaugh, Randy Amsler, Mike Vincler, and Fred Duncan. They dedicated themselves to making the plant not only a productive and safe place to work but a place where people were proud to work. We worked as a team. My philosophy was that no one had a monopoly when it came to brains. We encouraged participation by everyone in discussions. Original ideas were often modified by group participation to the point that everyone felt they had contributed to the plan that was finally adopted. The implementation became a lot easier since many signed on to the idea. I did not appreciate a negative attitude. I did not want to hear why things could not be done, but rather wanted to know how things could be done. As a result of this approach, our associates developed a "can-do attitude."

We initiated several programs at the plant to increase productivity, improve the quality of our products, safeguard the environment, and ensure the safety of every associate. We made education and the improvement of individual skills our top priority. We introduced DuPont's safety program at the plant. DuPont's philosophy was that all accidents can be prevented. They were very successful in preventing accidents at their workplaces and were considered one of the safest companies in the chemical industry. We made DuPont's program the cornerstone of our safety program. People were put to task to eliminate all unsafe conditions in the plant. In spite of this effort, we had some serious accidents early on. Mike Vincler was seriously hurt when an explosion occurred in a small-scale production unit. One of the most traumatic experiences was when hot material overflowed from a tank and seriously burned Rick Walbourn, one of our production workers. I received a phone call that evening from my son Mark who was working at the plant as summer help. Mark told me to go to the hospital because Rick had been seriously hurt. I went to the emergency room and saw Rick lying on the emergency room table, his body completely black. At first I thought that his skin was burned. The attending physician told me that Rick's body was covered with the material, which had overflowed from the tank. Underneath that material, Rick's skin had second and third degree burns. The doctors were not sure if Rick would pull through the ordeal. Fortunately, he recovered fully and continues to work at OMG, holding a very responsible position. These incidents furthered my resolve to make sure all our associates went home in as good or better condition as they came to work that day.

Throughout the years, Mooney Chemicals continued to produce the block grease that had been originally made by Mobil Oil. The production of grease helped keep our overhead costs down but it did have its drawbacks. The grease plant dated back to the '20s and still had wooden tanks that leaked, wooden platforms that were in disrepair, and open production kettles that were heated by open flame and occasionally caught fire. The plant had a direct telephone line to the Rocky Grove Volunteer Fire Department. We became a joke at the fire department because our fire alarms were sent out to the fire department so frequently. I was often awakened in the middle of the night by telephone calls informing me about the fire. I then would drive to the plant to address the situation. After each fire, we made modifications to the equipment to reduce the possibility of another fire, but we were never successful in completely eliminating them. The reputation that Mooney Chemicals had as a company with frequent fires lingered on for many years, even after we discontinued making the block grease in 1985.

The housekeeping at the plant was a big challenge during the early days of my tenure. It was impossible to walk through the plant without shoes sticking to the floor. There were large lumps of sticky chemicals on the floor that made walking hazardous. These lumps were so bad that they had to be removed with scrapers attached to forklifts. We solved the problem by washing floors with weak caustic solution after every shift change.

There were also a number of environmental issues early on. The plant had no waste treatment facilities. It relied on a septic tank for the treatment of human and industrial waste, which was legal under the existing laws. The tank overflowed on many occasions with these waste materials. The state inspectors that policed the area could not understand why the spring water coming from the ground was so warm. The reason was that it wasn't spring water, but an overflow from the septic tank. There were several incidences of chemicals being discharged onto the ground and into nearby streams. Some were serious, others were minor and some even resulted in small fines by the Pennsylvania Department of Environmental Resources. Eventually we separated the industrial waste from the sewage, shipped the industrial waste off site for treatment and connected the sewage into the municipal sewage system. An open pit on the plant property, used for burning garbage and waste chemicals, was definitely a fire hazard and an environmental problem. We discontinued the practice and completely cleaned up the site by hauling tons of contaminated soil to an approved hazardous industrial waste site.

We had a few incidents with our trucks on their way to deliver products to customers. One night, the State Police informed me that one of our trucks was pulled over into a rest area because it was leaking chemicals. Denny McNany, our shipping supervisor who also doubled as a spare driver, and I drove 100 miles in the middle of night to Snow Shoe, Pennsylvania. Several State Police cars were there, with red lights flashing, anxiously awaiting our arrival. The truck was cordoned off in a remote area in the rest stop. Dan Wimer, our truck driver, had some exposure to fumes, but was otherwise OK. We opened the door of the trailer and found a loose cover on top of a small tank in the trailer. The tank contained a product that had flammable solvent, and apparently the solvent had splashed out when the truck was going over a bumpy road. We secured the cover and aired out the trailer. Denny went on to deliver the load to the customer, and Dan and I returned home.

Several incidents occurred when irate citizens called me in the middle of the night to complain about the odor coming from the plant. The air scrubbing system failed or was inadequate to remove the odorous materials present in the air coming from the plant. It required some degree of skill to calm down these upset citizens. Another time, state and local police converged on the plant because someone reported that the plant was discharging radioactive cobalt into the atmosphere. Of course, the form of cobalt we used was not radioactive at all and the police reassured the citizen that the area was perfectly safe. An operator called me one night informing me that there was a blasting cap in one of the drums containing raw materials. We called the police and the fire department for assistance. They removed the drum from the premises without an incident, but we at the plant experienced some tense moments in the process.

We were very determined to operate our facility in a safe and environmentally acceptable manner. We were not satisfied to just meet the minimum law requirements; we wanted to exceed them and continue to raise our standards. Mooney Chemicals signed on to "Responsible Care," a program set up by the Chemical Manufacturers Association. The program set up rigid standards of safety and environmental requirements and demanded that each participant meet these standards on a predetermined schedule. The representatives of the Chemical Manufacturers Association, the citizens living in the community, and representatives from other chemical companies conducted the audit to ensure that these standards were met. We passed the audit, and the chemical community recognized us as one of the most safe and environmentally responsible companies in our industry.

There were a number of incidents at the plant for which I was totally unprepared. One of our associates died on top of a railroad tank car. He climbed to the top of the car, opened the cover to take a sample and collapsed. The initial suspicion was that he died as a result of inhaling fumes from the car. Local, state, and federal agencies showed up at the plant to investigate, and radio and TV reporters wanted to know what had happened. We were very cooperative, but refrained from making any conclusions until the autopsy was completed. The autopsy revealed that the associate's coronary arteries were completely clogged and he had died of a heart attack. Another associate committed suicide, put a gun into his mouth and pulled the trigger. He was experiencing emotional problems and was undergoing psychiatric treatment at the time. Still another associate died watching TV and his body was not discovered until three days later. One day, one of the production operators walked into my office and informed me that he was going to shoot a construction worker who ran away with his wife. It took me several hours to convince the associate that he was not going to accomplish anything by shooting the fellow except wind up in jail for the rest of his life. Later we even became good friends. He was diagnosed with cancer a few years later and was hospitalized. While in the hospital, he asked the hospital staff to take him to a Tiffany lamp shop in Oil City. He wanted to buy Basia and me a Tiffany lamp, and he wanted to select it personally. The hospital staff was reluctant to transport a dying patient, but he insisted and the staff finally arranged for an ambulance to take him to the shop. The gesture was extremely touching for both Basia and me.

Somehow we survived through the hard times and grew better and stronger each year, working together with all associates. It was truly a team effort, with the managers, the technical and office staff, the production people, and the shipping and maintenance staff all contributing. There were no departmental lines in emergencies; all associates pitched in wherever help was needed. We faced the adversities together: The emergencies, the floods, and the accidents. Little did the associates know how much my past experiences helped me deal with these adverse situations. I knew from past experiences that evil did not last forever; things always turned around as long as I didn't give up. I tried always to be optimistic, cheerful and to project a conviction that the future would be better. My positive outlook had a steadying effect on the associates during some of the dark days we experienced.

I got great satisfaction from providing our associates with the opportunity to perform up to their potential, regardless of the job they performed. The associates earned a good living, had excellent benefits, and had bright prospects for a secure future. We stressed the educational aspects of the job and provided opportunities to improve their skills. Today, all of our associates at the plant are computer literate; many are excellent laboratory technicians or possess good mechanical skills. These are learned skills that will accompany them for life, regardless of where they end up.

Quality was another area in which we struggled initially but moved aggressively to correct. Young Jim Mooney and I met Dr. W. Edwards Deming at a seminar in Iowa. Dr. Deming was well-known for transforming Japan from a nation that produced junk products to a nation that made some of the world's best, be it cars or electronics. The Japanese were so grateful to Dr. Deming for helping them that they established an award in his honor. It was called the Dr. Deming Prize and was awarded to an individual or company that contributed most to the advancement of quality. The Emperor of Japan bestowed the Medal of Sacred Measure on Dr. Deming in 1960, the only foreign national to receive such a distinction. Dr. Deming was a statistician and he believed that statistical analysis of quality problems was the best tool to improve quality. He also believed that working people in general wanted to do a good job and the two things that stood in their way were bad management and defective systems. Dr. Deming was a consultant to many large American and Japanese companies such as Ford, ITT and International Paper. Jim and I asked Dr. Deming to help us improve the quality of our systems but he told us we could not afford him. His next seminar was in Cleveland and we offered him a ride to Cleveland on our company plane. During the trip, we told him about our company and how we worked together with associates to achieve common goals. Dr. Deming liked our approach and agreed to be a consultant for us. He had two stipulations before agreeing. One was that we pay him in advance and the other that we come and see him on weekends and holidays. This way, he would be able to charge us a more modest fee. Steve Flinchbaugh, Randy Amsler, our statistics consultant Smitty Haller, and I visited Dr. Deming on a number of occasions in his home in Washington, DC. Dr. Deming also came to Franklin to give a seminar for our associates. We eventually worked out most of the quality problems with his help and the hard work of all our associates. Mooney Chemicals became known as the company that produced the best products in our industry. We received numerous awards for quality from such customers as Ford, Goodyear, and Shell. We were one of the first companies in our industry to receive an ISO 9000 rating, an international rating system signifying that we maintained excellent quality standards.

Jim Mooney's health slowly began to deteriorate (he had Lou Gehrig's disease) and it was hard for him to carry out his duties as president. He turned over the day-to-day running of the company to his son, James P. Mooney. Senior Jim believed Mooney Chemicals should be run like a publicly held corporation. He hired a number of consultants to advise him how to make this transition. Boy, did he love consultants. We had a consultant for every area of our business: management, quality, technology, marketing, etc., etc., etc. The two management consultants who advised him how to transform Mooney Chemicals into an organization resembling a publicly held company were Leon Danco and Don Sharp. Dr. Danco and Mr. Sharp recommended that Mooney's appoint an independent Board of Directors and hire professional managers. They agreed to do this, and to their credit, they appointed some very capable people to the Board. These board members were independent thinkers, smart, experienced, and experts in their respective fields. I worked closely with them and we became friends. Some, like Lee Brodeur, became not only my friend but an advisor and confidant. When the company was reorganized along the lines outlined by Dr. Danco and Mr. Sharp I became vice president in charge of operations, research and development in 1974. I began to spend more time in Cleveland directing our research and development effort and attending management meetings.

Senior Jim Mooney moved to Florida in 1976, where he continued to function as the Chairman of the Board. His son Jim took over as the president. Younger Jim had been the marketing manager for our company before being named the president. He started with the company in 1971 as a sales representative for the southwestern territory based in Houston, Texas. Jim's younger brother John started working for the company in 1974 as a purchasing manager. John was given additional responsibilities as

Chief Financial Officer in 1976. The three of us became the management team of Mooney Chemicals. We visited the senior Jim Mooney in Florida frequently and reported on the status of the company. Jim grilled us about the details of the way we conducted business and we often walked away from these meetings wondering if we were fit for our positions. However, when the time came for raises, Jim was always very generous. I had always had a good rapport with him over the many years of our association. Basia and I became very fond of the whole Mooney family. They have always showed their appreciation for our contribution to the success of the business. They treated us like one of their own. We were included not only in the company business but also in many Mooney family functions.

Basia, Mark and Tom moved to Franklin in June 1970. We rented a house on Oak Hill in Franklin and settled into the routine of small town living. The boys joined Little League, swim teams, and a number of other activities that kept them busy during the summer. They had no problems adjusting to small town living. Basia enrolled at Clarion State College to pursue a nursing degree. I was kept busy at the plant, spending many hours during the week and on weekends working.

We went to Europe in 1970. We bought a car through a local Volkswagen dealer before we left, and picked it up in Paris. Driving through Paris was an experience, especially around the Arc de Triomphe. From Paris we went on to Lille, Brussels, and then to West Berlin. We crossed into communist East Berlin at the famous border crossing, Checkpoint Charlie, where we were subject to a thorough search by the East German border guards. They searched our luggage and the car thoroughly; they even poked a stick into the gas tank to see if it had a false bottom for smuggling something. The guards made us change the West German license plates to East German plates. All this lasted for several hours. When I asked the guard why we had to go through this long procedure, he smiled and responded, "Higher politics."

We finally crossed into East Germany and drove on a deserted highway toward Poland. The only traffic we encountered was the occasional Russian or East German military vehicle. The surrounding countryside was very dreary, and the boys kept asking where all the cars were. We crossed into Poland after a two-hour ride. We changed the license plates back to the original West German plates. The crossing at the East German–Polish border was uneventful.

Driving through Poland was an interesting experience. People stared at us and treated us with a cold shoulder whenever we stopped. Later, we found out that there was still great resentment and continued fear of the Germans, especially the West Germans, from the war. The West German car and the West German plates made people think that we were Germans. Once they found out we were Polish and that we came from the United States, our reception quickly changed and they became friendly, almost affectionate. The resentment against the Germans was not the only source of tension in Poland in 1970. The strain between the communist regime and the population was felt throughout the country. There were food riots in various cities in Poland and the army was called to restore order. Forty-five people died that year in these riots in several Polish cities on the coast. Although we were not overly concerned about our safety, the atmosphere in Poland was not conducive to a relaxed visit.

We had the opportunity to visit Basia's family; it was the first time I had ever met them. They met me with open arms and vodka. I had never drank so much alcohol in my entire life. One evening we had so much to drink that the next morning I awoke with alcohol poisoning. I went to the emergency room at a local hospital where I was treated with powdered carbon to absorb the alcohol from my system. That was the last time I consumed such large quantities of alcohol.

We visited a number of historical sights, trying to show Poland to Mark and Tom. We also visited my relatives in Rzeszów and Uncle Staszek in Bytom. We made the pilgrimage to the Shrine of the Black Madonna in Częstochowa. I always make it a point to visit the Shrine whenever I am in Poland to thank the Madonna for the many blessings my family and I have received due to Her intercession on our behalf. I always walk away from the

Shrine rejuvenated and reinforced in my beliefs in God's benevolence. It is always an emotional and spiritual experience for me.

On the return trip, we wanted to visit Prague in Czechoslovakia, but the guards at the Polish border informed us that we had to cross the border at the same location we entered. Why, I had no idea. It seemed to us like just another roadblock the communist regime put up to make life of ordinary citizens more difficult. We had to go to Słubice, the town where we crossed the border when entering Poland, which added another 200 miles to our trip and prevented us from visiting Prague. We drove from Słubice straight through East Germany to Nuremberg in West Germany where we stayed overnight and did some sightseeing. The following day we went to Switzerland where we stayed a couple days before returning to Paris. In Paris we arranged for our car to be shipped to the United States and we returned to the States by air the next day.

In 1972 we moved to a rented house in Seneca, a small community about 10 miles from the plant. The move prompted us to start looking seriously for a permanent home. The search was accelerated by the fact that we were expecting another child. Ewa was born on May 19, 1973 and in August we moved to a new home outside of Polk. Polk was an even smaller community than Seneca but we found a house with a fair bit of land and a stunning view. This was the first home we'd ever owned. The location was so beautiful that we bought the house even though it was too small for our family. We expanded the house in 1977. We designed the expansion ourselves with the help of my good friend from the Diamond days, Don DiNezza. We subcontracted the work, doing many projects ourselves mainly as helpers to the skilled craftsmen we hired. Mark was especially involved; he was 14 at the time, and he worked with every contractor and craftsman who was on the job. However it was the tennis court that was the first major item we added after moving to our new house. Our house was in a remote area, seven miles from Franklin, and the closest neighbors were a quarter of a mile on either side. We felt our children needed a focal point that would keep them at home and tennis was a very popular sport at the time. Building the tennis court turned out to be a great idea. The children liked tennis and our whole family enjoyed the game. Our friends and my associates from the plant came over to our house to join us in the game. Tennis became an integral part of our lives; it was good exercise, it kept the whole family together, and it gave the children a sense of competitiveness.

I was slowly being sucked into civic work in Franklin. Bill White, a local attorney who later became the county judge, asked me to serve on the school board as an appointed member when one of the elected members moved out of town. I agreed and was appointed to the school board in 1979 to serve out the unexpired term. I also agreed to run for the seat in the next general election. I attended my first few board meetings saying very little and observing a lot. The meetings usually dragged on for hours and accomplished very little. Most of the discussions centered on sports, bus routes or complaints from irate parents rather than items of importance like curriculum, planning or academics. Agendas were only loosely adhered to and everyone was allowed to speak at length. My first recommendation was to limit discussions only to topics on the agenda, except for any emergency items that arose occasionally. We put limits to the length of the discussions and encouraged members to concentrate on the matters of substance and leave the administrative items to the school administrators. I also made an effort to introduce MBOs, management by objectives, to make the school administrators more accountable. We tried to develop better rating systems for the teachers. We were successful in streamlining the meetings, and the implementation of MBOs lasted only while I was on the board. Teachers' ratings were vehemently opposed by the teachers' union and never got off the ground. Dr. Bob Morris, the school superintendent, had some success in weeding out teachers that were not performing up to the minimum standards, but it was not an easy task. Teachers' contract negotiations were an interesting experience for me. The two sides were polarized by the "us–them" attitude and the negotiations became very confrontational. The teachers voted to go on strike. Wages were the main issues but there were also a few minor items that obscured the total picture. The big item of discussion at the board meeting was whether the sports teams would be allowed to practice during the strike. The board agreed to allow the teams to practice. The strike was settled after one week, so there was no significant disruption in academics or sports activities. The boys had an extra week of vacation, for which they kept thanking me.

One of the school board members was convicted of embezzlement at his company. He would not resign from the school board, and the situation became an embarrassment for us. We found a loophole in the Pennsylvania school code that allowed the dismissal of an individual for not attending school board meetings without a valid excuse. We determined that being in jail was not a valid excuse and we voted to dismiss the individual. However, the decision was not unanimous (the vote was 5–3). I was a very vocal proponent for the member's dismissal, and as a result I made some enemies on the school board. When I was a candidate for the school board in the 1980 election, I lost. I did not campaign very hard for the office assuming I would be elected even though my name was not well-recognized in the community at that time. Another vacancy arose on the board in 1981 and the president of the school board asked if I would be willing to serve again. I agreed, but the vote to appoint me was a split 4–4. The board members who were against the dismissal of the convicted embezzler voted against me. The case went to the county judge, Bill White, who re-appointed me. I served a total of five years on the board, two of them as secretary, and I must admit I valued the experience. It showed me what it was like to be in the public eye, and how different it was from life in the business world. It taught me to be more diplomatic and also showed me the value of a compromise. As secretary, I also got to sign my boys' high school graduation diplomas.

My experience on the school board introduced me to life of public service. I had an excellent management team and could rely on them to run things at the plant. Consequently, I had more time to devote to the community. I was appointed to the Venango County Industrial Board and served as its chairman for one year. I was a member of the Northwest Pennsylvania Planning Commission (NWPPC) that dealt with long range planning for development of industry in the northwest counties of Pennsylvania. My participation in NWPPC exposed me to concepts involved in planning for expansion, attracting new industries, and setting educational programs for the entire region. The Commission worked together with the legislative representatives such as U.S. Congressmen Ammerman, Clinger, and Peterson, as well as a number of State Representatives. I also served on the Vo-Tech School Board where I helped set up educational programs for students who had no plans to go to college.

I was a member of the First National Bank Board of Advisors. The board advised the bank on local issues affecting citizens as well as the bank. It gave me many insights into the mentality of banking people. I also was appointed to the Franklin–Oil City Hospital Foundation Board. The board's function was to raise money to finance special projects for the hospital. The board also administered a local pharmacy as a means of generating money for the foundation.

I served as a co-chairman of the United Way campaign in 1991. It was an interesting experience to take part in a major fund drive. We organized various committees each in charge of different sections of the community such as industrial, residential, commercial, professional and educational. The drive was successful and we raised about $100,000. We had the cooperation of many individuals and it was gratifying to see so many people working together for a common cause. It was by far the most successful community group effort of which I have been part. The United Way campaign demonstrated that if you ask people for help and you organize the effort well, you get good results.

Public service gave me a lot of satisfaction. I was able to directly help people. I began to realize that after I retired, I wanted to be involved in some activity that would use my skills to help people in some measure.

Our family took another trip to Poland in August of 1980. It had been 10 years since our last visit to Poland, and Ewa had never been there. Little did we know that we would be witnesses to history in the making. *Solidarność* (Solidarity) was born in Poland in August of 1980, the exact time we were there. The euphoria that transcended the country was difficult to describe. The winds of freedom were blowing from every direction. Wałęsa scaled the walls of the Gdańsk shipyard. Gierek, the premier and the Secretary of the Communist Party, was forced to resign. The church was given access to the media and was allowed for the first time to broadcast religious programs. Opposing views were freely expressed on the street and in the media. One had to be in Poland to fully appreciate the significance of these events. We were somewhat apprehensive about our safety since we could not anticipate the direction these events would take. The threat of a Soviet invasion was very real. We went to the American embassy to seek their opinion about how safe it was to stay in Poland. They could not offer any concrete advice, as they too were caught off-guard by these events. We decided to stay and were rewarded by witnessing some of the most remarkable events in recent history.

All the euphoria of Solidarity's early gains came to a screeching halt on December 13, 1981, when the Polish government declared martial law in Poland. The military arrested all prominent Solidarity activists and imposed severe restrictions on the entire population. Shortages of goods became common; restrictions were imposed on all imported goods, and the Western governments imposed embargoes on imports and exports of Polish goods. Long lines developed in front of stores, as people waited in shifts, sometimes through the entire night or even for several days. The shortages of medicine and medical supplies became particularly acute. Several organizations in the United States got involved in helping Polish people in this crisis.

The Americares Foundation in Connecticut was one of the first to organize a drive to send medicine and medical supplies to Poland. The Foundation established Americares for Poland with Zbigniew Brzezinski as the Honorary Chairman to funnel donations to the Polish people. Jim Mooney had worked with Americares in the past when the Foundation was involved in organizing help for Guatemala. Jim introduced me to Bob Macauley who headed the Foundation and I volunteered to help. Bob Macauley's many connections with the pharmaceutical industry were very helpful in obtaining donations of medicine. I helped raise funds to pay for the air freight. We were able to get enough medicine and medical supplies to fill an entire DC–8 Flying Tiger cargo plane. This amounted to almost 40 tons of supplies. We were also able to collect enough funds to pay for the air freight to Poland. Representatives from Americares and Polonia, among them Ed Piszek, Jan Wydro and I, accompanied the plane to Poland. We left LaGuardia Airport on December 4, 1982, and arrived in Warsaw the following day. The plane ride was not the most comfortable. We sat on boxes and slept in sleeping bags among the tons of crates that filled the plane. We landed at Warsaw airport in the morning and were immediately surrounded by military personnel armed with submachine guns. Ours was the first and only plane from the West. The atmosphere at the airport was dreary, spooky and intimidating. The Polish authorities wanted to unload the supplies and store them in a government warehouse. We did not trust the authorities for we feared they would appropriate the cargo and use it for their own needs rather than distribute it to the general public. The Catholic Church helped us find volunteers who transported the supplies to a basement in one of the churches in Warsaw. The supplies were later distributed to the needy by the Catholic charitable organizations. Ed Piszek, who knew Archbishop Glemp, the Primate of Poland, was able to arrange a meeting for our group with the Archbishop. Primate Glemp expressed his appreciation for our efforts to help the Polish people in those difficult times. Americares also received letters of praise for this effort from Pope John Paul II, President Ronald Reagan, and Vice President George Bush.

I had an opportunity to ride with Bishop Domin, the President of the Charities Commission of the Polish Catholic Church, to Katowice. This city is in southern Poland, about a five-hour drive from Warsaw. Bishop Domin provided me with many insights about the situation in Poland, especially about martial law. He explained the role the church played in calming down the explosive situation that existed in Poland. The church tried very hard to avoid confrontation between the members of Solidarity and the government and wanted to avoid bloodshed at all cost. A deep concern also existed in Poland about a potential invasion by the

Soviet Union. The atmosphere was extremely tense and we could see the evidence of this tension everywhere. Kraków, normally a very vibrant and lovely city, was almost deserted. The faces of people on the city streets were serious, with no laughter to be heard anywhere. I flew from Rzeszów to Warsaw on a commercial plane, which had two military guards armed with submachine guns on board. We were required to remain seated and could move only after obtaining prior permission from the guards. The streets of Warsaw were deserted and there were roadblocks set up at all major intersections. All telephone conversations were monitored. The written media was censored and the military manned the TV stations, with all announcers being military personnel. Nearly all food was rationed, and many items were scarce or completely unavailable. These were not good times for the Polish people. I stayed in Poland for 10 days and returned home convinced that I was very fortunate to live in the United States.

Life in Franklin was peaceful and quiet but occasionally we had some exciting moments. Former President Ford visited Franklin in 1986. I attended a reception in his honor and had an opportunity to exchange a few words with him. We talked about the Ohio State–Michigan football rivalry. He told me that he and Woody Hayes, OSU's football coach, were best of friends, except on one particular Saturday in November. President Ford was a very charming and gracious man.

I continued my education to improve my skills, as well as to demonstrate to my children and associates that the education process never stops. I attended Syracuse University for six weeks to study sales and marketing. I spent two weeks at the University of Michigan to study manufacturing strategies and for another two weeks studying managing managers. I spent three weeks at Harvard University studying operations management. These courses enabled me to interact with many individuals from other businesses and benefit from their experiences. One of the most interesting seminars I attended was put together by an organization called the Council of Union-Free Environment or CUE, later renamed the Council of Positive Employee Relations. The authors of these presentations shared with us their experiences of dealing with people at their work places. I usually took one of our managers and a supervisor to these seminars so they also could benefit from these presentations. It was gratifying to note that our approach to employee relations was, in many cases, similar to the more successful approaches presented at these meetings. Often we were ahead of our times. These seminars were given at various locations throughout the country, and Basia and I had an opportunity to enjoy many beautiful resort areas.

The children were busy with their schoolwork; all three were good students, and all were involved in many extra curricular activities. All three played in the marching band and stage orchestra, played varsity tennis, skied, and took part in school plays and talent shows. Mark and Tom played Little League baseball, and Ewa took piano lessons becoming a very accomplished pianist and winning the Pennsylvania State piano competition. She was selected to be an accompanist for the state choir concert at Heinz Hall in Pittsburgh. She received a scholarship from Chautauqua Institute for piano, and we spent many summer days driving her to the Institute where she had piano lessons and took part in a masters for piano program. We spent many summers vacationing in Oglebay Park in Wheeling, West Virginia. The Mooney family rented cottages in the park for their family and friends, and we joined them. These were fun times for the children. Close to 100 children were in the group with many activities organized for them, such as tennis, golf, swimming, boat rides, and private fireworks in the evenings. Our children always looked forward to these vacations.

Living in the country had its advantages for our children, especially in the way of outdoor activities. Besides summer activities, there was tobogganing and snow-mobiling in the winter. One winter, Mark had an unfortunate accident with the snowmobile. He was outside playing with the snowmobile when he accidentally pressed the accelerator instead of the brake and drove the snowmobile right through the front door into the living room where Tom was watching TV—coincidentally, a show called "Emergency One." Fortunately no one was hurt, but we had to board up the front door to keep the cold out until it was repaired.

Many other incidents happened, moments that only parents remember and cherish.

Mark graduated from high school in 1981 and went to Case Western Reserve to study Chemical Engineering. He worked summers at the plant and got the flavor of what hard work was about. He always was handy with mechanical things, and engineering looked like a good fit for him. He graduated in 1985 and went to work for International Nickel Company in West Virginia as a salesman. He moved to Houston in 1986. In 1987 Mark joined SACHEM, a small specialty chemicals company run by John Mooney, Jim's brother. Mooney Chemicals acquired this privately held company in 1984 from Cecil Hale. The Mooney family spun off the business into two separate companies in 1989 to reduce the risk of having all eggs in one basket. Mark was hired as a sales representative and moved to Austin, Texas, where the company was located. He became a manager of safety and environmental affairs for the company in 1991. Mark married Nancy Nunez in 1988, but unfortunately, their marriage did not work out and they divorced in 1999.

Tom graduated from high school in 1984 and enrolled at the University of Texas to study pre-med. He graduated in 1988 and went on to Tulane Medical School in New Orleans. He graduated from Tulane in 1992, earning a degree in medicine, his lifetime ambition. Tom completed residency in general surgery at the University of Colorado. After finishing the residency, he subspecialized in transplant surgery, which he continues to do in Denver. Tom and Mary Koegler married in 1989 after meeting in college in Texas. They have three lovely children, Alexandra, Meagan, and Michael, who are now the joys of our life.

Ewa graduated from high school in 1991 and went to the University of Notre Dame where she studied pre-med. She graduated in 1995 and went to medical school in Poznań, Poland. She earned her medical degree in 1999 and is doing her residency at the University of Kentucky Medical Center. Ewa and Dan Lewis were married in May of 2001.

It was interesting to watch the children grow. They were three different individuals with three different personalities. Basia and I are extremely proud of their accomplishments. We have always encouraged them to do their best and praised them for their efforts and accomplishments. Initially, it required a lot of effort and attention to guide them through their lives. A lot of credit goes to Basia. She spent endless hours teaching them the Polish language, taking them to piano lessons, to tennis, baseball and basketball practice, to swimming and gymnastics. Our house became a gathering point for the friends of our children. I am sure Basia's cooking had something to do with that. Basia's contributions cannot be overstated. She was always supportive and understanding of my approach to the business needs and was never jealous of the time I put into business activities. For that I will be always grateful to her.

My father died in December 1990. It was a great loss for me personally. We were very close and I respected and admired him for the way he brought the family through all the difficult times we faced. I respected him for his common sense and for the advice he offered me over the years. I have missed his presence over the past years, and on numerous occasions, I have wished he were alive to witness some of the successes I have achieved, which in great measure I owe to him. After my father died, Mother became the head of our family once again, the role she performed so admirably during the early days of my life. The pain of my father's death was somewhat eased when our first granddaughter, Alexandra, was born on Christmas Eve in 1990. We were all overjoyed by her arrival, and our lives were tremendously enriched.

Our good friends the Cenedellas, Basia and I established a small medical device company called CenBak in 1984. Dr. Cenedella had an idea that cooling the scalp during chemotherapy treatment of cancer patients would prevent or greatly retard the loss of hair, a very common and traumatic experience for cancer patients. Sufficient scientific evidence existed to suggest that cooling the scalp reduced the chances of hair falling out, but the methods used in the investigations were very crude. The researchers used ice packs and chilled chemical packs, which were heavy and cumbersome. We devised a cooling machine, a two-layer plastic cap placed on the patient's head, and a system that pumped chilled water through the cap. Many nights were spent cooling Mark and Tom's heads while analyzing the machine's effectiveness. The Federal Drug Administration gave us the approval to market the device. However, the long-term effects on Mark and Tom's heads are still unclear.

We made some progress marketing the machines. We sold over 70 units throughout the country to such institutions as the Cleveland Clinic, Sloan Kettering Cancer Center in New York City, Rush Presbyterian Hospital in Chicago and many others. We employed two full-time people, an office manager and a sales representative who also helped to assemble the machines. The boys and Ewa also helped, working for us during summers. We appeared at several cancer treatment shows to demonstrate the effectiveness of the device, and it was favorably received. The Federal Drug Administration rescinded the approval to market the device in January 1991 because they claimed the original approval was based on insufficient data. They requested more information about the efficacy and safety of the treatment method. We could not understand the FDA's logic of requesting additional information and we appealed the decision on the grounds that scalp cooling was used for many years and it was effective and safe. We learned that federal bureaucracy is not that easy to overcome. It would cost several million dollars to generate the additional data. We and the Cenedellas invested substantial amounts of money into the project and the business had not been profitable. We decided to discontinue the business in December of 1991. We got a great deal of personal satisfaction knowing we were helping many people in spite of the fact that we lost a fair amount of money. The method is now being used in Israel and in some European countries. Maybe it was the wrong time or the wrong place, but we had to at least try doing what we believed was the right thing.

Mooney Chemicals continued to flourish and the company made good profits. Many members of the Mooney family wanted to cash in on the value of the company and use the proceeds for their own needs. A friction developed between some members of the family and Jim Mooney as to the direction Mooney Chemicals should take. Jim wanted to expand the company and target the earnings to fuel growth; others wanted an immediate payoff. The sale of the company seemed like a good compromise. A Finnish firm, Outokumpu OY, and a Finnish Insurance company acquired Mooney Chemicals in 1991. Outokumpu, after acquiring Mooney Chemicals, combined our company with their chemical division, Kokkola Chemicals, and renamed the new company OMG. Jim Mooney became the President of the new company. Jim asked me in August 1991 if I would be interested in moving to Cleveland to take his place as President of Mooney Chemicals. The offer presented an interesting challenge and an opportunity for me. I accepted the offer and moved to Cleveland in September 1991.

Franklin Plant in 1970.

Franklin Plant in 1991.

With Mark at Brandenburg Gate in Berlin in 1970.

Our family at Niagara Falls, 1971.

On Dunajec River, Pieniny Mountains, August 1980,
(l to r: Mark, Basia, Ewa, Basia's sister Regina, Tom).

Our family on my parents' wedding anniversary, June 1982.

A 50th birthday present from my friends??? July 18, 1983.

Franklin associates at safety awards ceremony, October 1982.

Meeting with Archbishop Glemp in Warsaw in December 1982 during Americares for Poland Airlift.

With Cenedellas in London, 1984.

Family reunion on Alina's 25th wedding anniversary,
Franklin, 1984.

Tom and Mary's wedding, June 1989.

CLEVELAND (1991–1999)

The move to Cleveland presented a whole set of new challenges for me, both personally and professionally. We hated to leave Franklin, where we had spent a good part of our lives and developed many friends. On the other hand, Cleveland was where my family lived and where I spent the first years after coming to the United States.

Professionally, I was moving into a new business arena that involved total responsibility for the profitability of the company. That meant overseeing manufacturing, marketing, research and development, and support services. Mooney Chemicals was, at that stage, a very successful company with sales in excess of $60 million a year. It had good management such as Tom Fleming who was in charge of marketing, Mike Scott in charge of legal and human resources, and Burn Tinker in charge of research and development. I did not have any doubts that we would continue to grow and be successful.

My first challenge was to find a new plant manager for the Franklin plant. There were good people at Franklin, but I felt they needed more seasoning and, therefore, I decided to go outside to hire a new manager. I hired Arun Mehan, a highly qualified, well-experienced professional. Unfortunately, Arun did not fit into the OMG culture. He was not a people's manager, as numerous complaints were voiced by our associates about his style of management and his lack of consideration for the people of lower rank. I decided to replace Arun after two years on the job. In retrospect, going outside to hire a new plant manager was a flawed decision. I should have known better; good people respond well to new challenges and I should have picked one of our own associates. I selected Mark, my son, to replace Arun as the new plant manager. I felt Mark was the best person at that time to bring back stability and regain the confidence of the associates in Franklin. Mark came to Mooney Chemicals in 1992 from SACHEM as the Quality Manager. He knew Franklin people well; he understood the plant issues, and the associates in Franklin received him warmly.

Outokumpu proceeded to put its imprint on OMG after they purchased Mooney Chemicals. Jim Mooney was the President, but Outokumpu appointed Mark Toivanen as the Chairman of the Board and Kari Muuraiskangas as a Board Member. We were subjected to many requests from Outokumpu for information, documentation, business plans, etc. It seemed to us that Outokumpu was more interested in creating a hierarchy and preparing sophisticated plans rather than in the profitability of the company. We at Mooney were not used to the workings of a large corporation, a metal based company, and a foreign company, all at the same time. It was a bit of a cultural shock for us. Also, Outokumpu did not show any interest in expanding the chemical business. The budget for capital expenditures allocated to OMG was low, and it was obvious that their priorities were elsewhere.

Outokumpu needed cash to expand their nickel refinery, and in 1992, they decided to sell OMG through a public offering. Donaldson, Lufkin & Jenrette (DLJ), a financial advisor firm, managed the public offering. The offering was very successful and the company was sold for $250 million. The process of the public offering was very interesting. There were intense negotiations between Outokumpu, DLJ and Jim Mooney as to how the new entity would be structured, how it would be managed, and how much stake Outokumpu would continue to have in the new company. In the end, Outokumpu did not retain any ownership in OMG and OMG was free to pursue its own strategy for the future. DLJ was charged with the job of presenting and selling OMG to potential investors. OMG management participated in the preparation of the literature and we took part in the so-called "road show." The road show consisted of meetings with potential investors at which OMG managers described OMG, its strategy, its financial projections, and its vision for the future. The whole process lasted two weeks. We had days when we had three or four meetings in a single day with different investors, and at the end of the day, it was hard to remember what was said where and to whom. The price of OMG stock was set at the end of the road show and the issue was oversubscribed, meaning there were more orders than available shares. OMG was listed on NASDAQ and we became an independent company responsible only to its shareholders. The stock moved to the NYSE in 1996. I might add that the price of the stock has done very well since OMG went public, increasing in value over fivefold in eight years.

Once OMG was sold, we began to pursue our own strategy. We hired Michael Robert, a consultant specializing in strategic thinking and strategic planning. Mr. Robert helped us develop vision and operating strategies for OMG and guided us through the implementation of those strategies. It was fun to be able to do the things you always dreamed of doing, that is to pursue growth, without the often arbitrary restrictions by the previous owners.

I became Executive Vice President of OMG in 1992, responsible for worldwide manufacturing and research and development. These responsibilities were in addition to my responsibilities as President of Mooney Chemicals. We began to integrate the OMG culture into all our manufacturing and marketing operations. We now had a global presence and had to blend American, European and Asian cultures and methods of doing business. We wanted to continue to recognize the individual regions and countries as unique, diverse and valuable contributors to our strategy for expanding the company.

My principal effort was to integrate the Kokkola plant, our Finnish facility, into the OMG mold. The Finns are excellent technical people; they are very proud of their capabilities, very conscientious, and very hard working people. They are somewhat introverted, at least at first glance, but they quickly warm up once they get to know you better. We couldn't contribute much technologically to what was already being done in Kokkola. We just wanted to share with them our marketing techniques and make them more outgoing in communicating with their customers and fellow associates. I had an outstanding ally in that effort in Antti

Aaltonen, the president of Kokkola Chemicals. Antti bought into our plans with enthusiasm and dedication that was hard to duplicate. The results were evident in a relatively short time. The synergy between Mooney Chemicals and Kokkola we envisioned before the merger materialized as predicted. Kokkola Chemicals, which struggled under Outokumpu and was almost shut down, began to flourish, expand and contribute to the profitability of OMG. The Kokkola associates knew the Americans were not there to take over their operation and dictate how to conduct their business, but to listen, help, and cooperate. We made a major commitment to expand Kokkola's operation and, by doing so, gained the confidence of the people in the plant. The Finns warmed up to us and began to participate aggressively in the programs to make OMG grow and flourish. The plant quadrupled its output in seven years as a result of that effort. It was a classical win–win situation.

My relationship with the Finns was always special. They considered me part European, a man who understood the European culture and who was more sensitive to their feelings than an average American. Historically, Finland always had a special relationship with Poland and that also positively influenced our relationship. I have spent numerous hours in saunas with the Finns discussing various topics from business to politics and, in the process, consumed enormous amounts of beer. I was invited to their homes, their summer cottages, and even went sailing with them. One of the highlights of my many visits to Finland was an touring the islands of the Finnish Archipelago with my business associates and their wives.

OMG made a commitment to streamline its marketing effort in Europe. We established an office in Dusseldorf, Germany, to handle all of our European marketing. The Outokumpu office in Paris initially handled OMG sales in Europe. However, we felt that it was imperative to have an independent sales organization and Dusseldorf seemed like a strategic location. The office was under the direction of my good friend and golfing partner, Kari Muuraiskangas.

Our efforts in Asia Pacific were less successful. We established an office in Taipei, Taiwan, under the direction of J. R. Hwang, to handle the marketing in that region. Our strategy for Asia Pacific was to establish strategic partnerships with the local business people. We formed a joint venture, D&O, with Dainippon of Japan in 1995, and another joint venture, J&O, with Jay Yee in Korea in 1996. These were fifty–fifty joint ventures and they did not work out well for OMG. It was difficult to convince the Japanese and Koreans to sign on to the OMG strategy of aggressive expansion. They were more interested in acquiring our technologies than in expanding the joint ventures. We could never build enough trust between us to make much progress, and both joint ventures were dissolved in 1999.

I became the President and Chief Operating Officer of OMG in July 1994 and was elected to the Board of Directors in 1995. Jim Mooney concentrated on developing the vision for OMG. He was very focused in pursuing that vision which was to grow and make OMG a multi-billion dollar company in 10 years, never losing sight of our incipient strength in specialty metals and metals-related chemicals. I was responsible for the implementation of the operating strategy. Jim Materna, our Chief Financial Officer, handled the financial matters for the company. The three of us comprised the Executive Committee of OMG. Tom Fleming, our Chief Marketing Officer, was named to the Executive Committee in 1998. We developed a very aggressive plan for expansion that included acquisitions as well as internal growth. In January 1997, OMG acquired SCM Metals Products, Inc., a copper and specialty metals powders company located in Raleigh, North Carolina. Its sales were around $100 million. Fidelity Chemical, a Newark, New Jersey, company manufacturing specialty chemicals for the electronics plating industry, was acquired in January 1998. Fidelity's annual sales were around $60 million. Dussek Chemical, a Canadian company with annual sales of around $10 million was acquired in February of 1998.

OMG signed a contract with Gecamines and Forrest Group in June 1997 to build a smelter in the Democratic Republic of Congo

(DRC). It was a major commitment on the part of OMG since the cost of the plant was estimated to be over $100 million. The smelter was to be built in the DRC, one of the most unstable parts of the world. However, we felt if OMG was to have a good supply of cobalt, a very critical raw material for us, we had to go to the DRC where the cobalt ore deposits are the richest in the world. In spite of the political turmoil in the DRC, the smelter was built and is operational.

These acquisitions, coupled with internal growth, enabled OMG to achieve sales in excess of $500 million in 1998. We have been able to increase our profits at least 15 percent per year on a consistent basis since the company went public. The performance was a far cry from the days when I started with the company in 1970 when sales were $2 million with minuscule profit.

As I stated before, my main function as president was to implement the operating strategy of OMG. The cornerstones of the operating strategy were the guiding principles I had developed over the years, first at Diamond Shamrock, then in Franklin, and finally in Cleveland. These guiding principles relied heavily on the total commitment and participation of all our associates in achieving the successful implementation of the operating strategy. These guiding principles were:

1. To create an environment for all associates to perform to their potential. I have witnessed many talents wasted because people had little opportunity to use their full potential or they were not encouraged by management to use those talents. What a waste!! No one has a monopoly on brains. People have a tremendous pool of knowledge and are eager to share that knowledge if asked. We at Mooney Chemicals in Franklin, and later at OMG in Cleveland were very successful in tapping that potential.

2. To have and to demonstrate respect for each individual. Managers have a tendency not to show sufficient respect for their subordinates. I found it essential to recognize each person as an individual who has specific needs. All our associates were treated equally, even though they held different positions. We at OMG

emphasized the need to be always respectful toward our associates, and that was the main reason they were never interested in joining a union or seeking outside representation.

3. To drive fear out of the organization and to show a tolerance for honest mistakes. Fear is a killer of innovation. People who have to look over their shoulders and worry if they are doing the right thing will always be cautious and unwilling to try new ideas. We encouraged our associates to be innovative and were very tolerant when they failed or made mistakes.

4. To maintain an environment favoring innovation. Innovation is the lifeline of an organization. Eliminating fear and providing encouragement to try new ideas promote innovation. We also developed a system to flush out innovative ideas and bring them to fruition. At least 25 percent of our revenues were derived from the products that were not in existence five years earlier.

5. To have a global perspective. Global perspective is essential for survival of a business engaged in global markets. The competition is fierce throughout the world and only the fittest survive. We made it a point to become the lowest cost producer for our specialty chemicals. We were fully aware that the cost of labor in many countries was lower but we made up the difference by being more productive and more innovative. As a result, we became the dominant producers of cobalt and nickel products worldwide.

6. To encourage continuous improvement. Continuous improvement for OMG did not mean continuous improvement for business only, but for associates as well. We encouraged our associates to strive for the best and we facilitated individual development by providing tuition reimbursement and time off for study. There was never a concern that associates might leave the company after achieving higher education or higher skills. We decided if that happened, so be it. Few left.

7. To challenge everyone to look for growth opportunities. I have already mentioned that innovation is the lifeline of an organization. Looking for new opportunities was part of our innovation

process. Our marketing people were particularly good at recognizing new opportunities, which led to substantial increases in revenues for the company.

8. To seek partnership with other associates to conserve resources and accelerate implementation. It was amazing how much time and resources we could save when we asked for help and advice from other associates, customers and suppliers. Seeking partnership meant getting the best input and acting on it. Both Jim Mooneys were particularly good at this. They had an incredible network of friends, customers and suppliers they relied on for advice.

9. To empower associates to strive for results, not meaningless activities. Results were the bottom line for which we at OMG strove. All activities did not amount to a pot of beans if they did not bring results. Sometimes people spent enormous amounts of time talking about their activities, and usually it was an attempt to disguise the fact they had not achieved the desired results. We instilled in our associates the notion that we should always focus on results. To help us get the desired results, we developed a simple chart listing all critical issues on which everyone should focus. There was never a question what was the main focus for each individual, for each department, and for the corporation.

These principles were not novel. Many individuals and organizations applied them in one form or another. I believe we at OMG applied them as a package and that was one of the reasons we were successful.

Each of these principles had a historical significance to me. My life experiences have shown me that the presence of these principles in an organization paved the way to success, and their absence led to disaster. However, the key to success was always people. The principles provided only guidance. I was extremely fortunate to have a dedicated, enthusiastic, and talented group of people working with me.

As president of OMG, I had the opportunity to visit our facilities and our customers throughout the world. I have developed friendships and have had the opportunity to see many interesting places in many corners of the world. Finland was the country I visited most frequently. Whenever I was in Europe, I usually visited Dusseldorf, our marketing office in Europe, and Paris, the location of Vasset, our metals carboxylate plant. Paris was my favorite place. The city has such a unique character that I could go there time after time without ever getting tired of it. My favorite activity after arriving in Paris was to walk up and down the Champs d'Elysees and take in the city. An evening meal at one of the Paris restaurants was always a treat.

We had a Board of Directors meeting in Kokkola in 1997. We organized a side trip with some of the Board Members and their wives to visit Stockholm, Helsinki, St. Petersburg, Dusseldorf, and Paris. The trip to St. Petersburg was somewhat emotional for me. I had not been to Russia since my days in Siberia and I admit I was a little apprehensive about going there. The Siberian experience was still etched in my mind even after all the years that had passed since I left the Soviet Union. St. Petersburg was at one time considered the Venice of the North. It was a beautiful city with many canals and 365 bridges, one for every day of the year. Unfortunately, now the city had a drab appearance. The communists had let the city run itself into the ground. The highlight of the trip was visiting the Hermitage Museum. It was beautiful and rich with precious paintings and art. Credit must be given to the Russians for restoring the museum after the city and the museum were completely destroyed by the Germans in World War II.

I have visited Japan on several occasions. Tokyo did not impress me, except for the impeccable public transportation system. However, once I got out of Tokyo, the countryside was beautiful. Ewa spent one summer in Japan as an exchange student, and Basia and I visited her. Ewa's Japanese host had a summer house in the resort town of Atami, and we spent a weekend there. Atami is a seacoast town, known for its sulfur springs. The scenery there is spectacular.

I went on a business trip to India in 1998 and had an opportunity to visit Valivade. The camp had turned into a sprawling city of over 100,000 people. I recognized a few buildings that were still standing after more than 50 years, but the area had turned into a filthy slum for the Hindu people resettled to Valivade from Pakistan. I met two men who still remembered the Polish refugees. One was a tailor who had done some work for the Polish people. He even spoke some Polish after 50 years of no contact with the Poles or Polish language. He told the group of natives assembled around us how clean the Polish people were, how beautifully they kept their areas around the barracks, and how ashamed he was to see the place deteriorate so much after the Poles left. When our agent, who was with me, translated what the tailor said, it made me proud to be Polish. I went by the banks of the river to the spot where I'd almost drowned. I went by the hospital where I spent my share of days fighting malaria. It was a nostalgic visit.

The return trip from Valivade to Bombay was a stark reminder of the past. The agent and I went from Bombay to Valivade by train and we were returning the same way. A train wreck happened ahead of us, and the conductor informed us that he did not know how long it would take to clean up the wreckage and repair the tracks. It could be hours or it could be days. I was not about to wait forever for a train in some Godforsaken town in India. We rented a taxi, actually an old jalopy with a driver, and drove all night back to Bombay. The roads were terrible, full of potholes, and the car had no shock absorbers. I thought I would end up with a broken spine from all the bouncing. I had to use my hands as shock absorbers to reduce the pressure on my spine. On one occasion, the driver stopped the car in the middle of the road, turned off the lights, turned off the engine and got out of the car without uttering a word. He got back in the car after a minute or so and explained he had to do this because a cat had run across the road and he considered it to be bad luck. The only way to avoid bad luck was to start the journey all over again. That minute, sitting in a car in the middle of the road with cars speeding by, seemed like an eternity to me. At that moment, a thought passed through my mind. If we get into an accident, its déjà vu. My chances of survival in the boondocks of India, away from a major city, are minimal at best, as they were in similar situations in the past. It was hot even at night, and the car did not have air conditioning. The windows were open, and dust was coating everything. I was covered with a thick layer of dust by the time we reached our hotel in Bombay. I'm glad I went back to Valivade in spite of the bad experience during the return trip because the visit put a sort of closure on that part of my life.

Another trip that was a little hairy was the trip to the Democratic Republic of Congo (DRC) and to Zambia. OMG was working with Gecamines, the state-owned mining company, and with the Forest Group, the local businessmen, to build a smelter in the DRC. We purchased cobalt raw materials from the DRC and Zambia. I made the trip to both countries to assess the situation and meet with representatives of both organizations. Antti Aaltonen and I flew to Johannesburg in South Africa where we leased a small plane and flew to Lubumbashi in the DRC. The airport in Lubumbashi was almost deserted. There was only one other plane at the airport and there were armed soldiers everywhere. The airport officials and the representatives of the Forrest Group escorted us through customs and drove us to the local hotel. The drive through the city opened my eyes to the unbelievable poverty that still exists in this world. Hundreds of people were sitting on the side of the road waiting for no apparent purpose. We drove by the city zoo, which had been completely destroyed with the animals slaughtered for food by the Mobutu soldiers. They rampaged the city when the government failed to pay them. We were stopped several times by army personnel for a passport check and a handout.

We stayed at the only hotel in the city. The hotel was rundown and filthy. The receptionist issued us a towel and a bar of soap when we checked in. The water was turned on only during certain hours of the day. The hotel must have been very beautiful at one time, when the DRC was a Belgian colony. One could still see the remnants of the old days. Kabila, the country's president, was in town when we were there. The hotel was full of state dignitaries and their bodyguards. It was disconcerting to see soldiers with submachine guns standing by almost every door at the hotel. In the morning, these soldiers came to the restaurant with their weapons and put their guns on the table while having breakfast. Some of the soldiers were boys, 16 to 18 years old, and I wondered what must be going through their minds watching us, we were so out of place. What would it take to make them pull that trigger? I was relieved when the meetings and discussions with the local business people were over and we could return home.

Not all the trips were as dramatic as the ones to India or the Congo. Most of the trips were pleasant experiences, especially the ones when Basia accompanied me. We visited such places as Budapest, Prague, Rome, and Monte Carlo, in addition to Warsaw, Paris, and numerous other cities in Europe. We had an opportunity to visit Monte Cassino during our visit to Italy. The trip was an emotional experience for me. I was able to see the area where the Polish II Corps fought their most famous battle of the Second World War and where my father and my uncle were wounded. The cemetery located close to the monastery is the final resting-place for over a thousand Polish soldiers who died in Monte Cassino during the battle. It is also the resting place for General Anders, who died in 1970 and, according to his wishes, was buried alongside his soldiers. At graveside, I paid my respects to the memory of General Anders who liberated us from the Soviet gulags. In Asia we visited Hong Kong, Taipei, Singapore, Seoul, and several cities in Japan. We went to Australia and visited Sidney, Brisbane and Perth. I also visited Sao Paulo in Brazil.

I have developed a liking for golf and have had the opportunity to play the game in many parts of the world that I have visited. In fact, my only golf-related claim to fame is that I have played the game on all continents that have grass—not much of a claim, but a claim nevertheless.

The number of facilities owned by OMG was growing by leaps and bounds and we decided to create a new position of Vice President of Operations to help me manage the manufacturing at OMG. I struggled with the decision of whom to appoint to the new position. I have learned that going outside was a risky move. I turned to Lee Brodeur, who was on our Board of Directors, for advice. Over the years, Lee became an advisor, consultant and good friend, and I greatly valued his opinion. I wanted to appoint Mark to the new position, but for obvious reasons did not consider my judgement to be totally objective. I presented the situation to Lee and asked for his opinion. Lee knew Mark well; he visited Franklin and had an opportunity to observe Mark's performance there. Lee was able to clarify the pros and cons of my thinking. He also understood the benefits of selecting someone from within the organization, someone of known quality, for the new position. After a lengthy discussion, we agreed that Mark was a viable candidate. Jim Mooney concurred with the recommendation, and I appointed Mark to the new position. Lee promised he would objectively monitor Mark's progress.

I have developed a great respect for Mark's abilities. He did a good job as a plant manager in Franklin during the two years he was there. He pursued his education by earning an Executive MBA at Case Western Reserve University. He was a hard worker, a good organizer and a leader. He possessed very good people skills. Mark moved to Cleveland in 1997 to assume the new responsibilities as Vice President of Operations. Steve Flinchbaugh took over as the new plant manager in Franklin. The two years Mark and I worked together in Cleveland were the most rewarding years of my career. Not only was OMG successful as a company but Mark and I developed a relationship based on no hidden agendas. We discussed issues openly and provided each other with unfiltered opinions.

Basia moved to Westlake in the spring of 1992 after the construction of our house was completed. The house we purchased did not have the scenery we had in Franklin, but it was located in a secluded development on a small man-made lake. The location was a compromise between the city and a rural location. We did not sell the house in Franklin. I guess it was a step we were not willing to take. I did not get involved in the civic life in Cleveland to the extent I was involved in Franklin. There were two reasons for this. First, OMG business required a lot of my time. The travel and many business demands did not leave much time for outside activities. Second, Cleveland is a large city and it was not as easy to get involved in civic work as it was in Franklin. As the saying goes, I was a small fish in a large pond versus a large fish in a small pond. I did join the Cleveland Society of Poles, an organization of businessmen of Polish descent. After I retired in 1999, however, I became much more involved in civic work.

After Ewa went to Notre Dame to pursue her pre-medical studies, it was just Basia and me remaining in the house. We felt lonely after Ewa's departure and the house seemed deserted. Tom and his family moved to Denver in 1992. Tom, after graduating from Tulane Medical School, accepted a residency position in surgery at the University of Colorado in Denver. Basia and I visited them as often as we could, always cherishing the time we spent with Tom, Mary and the grandchildren. Tom graduated from his residency program in 1998 and went on to sub-specialize in transplant surgery. He has achieved his lifetime ambition of becoming a surgeon after many years of hard work and endless hours at the hospital. Basia and I attended his graduation from the surgical residency and were very proud of his accomplishments. Our new granddaughter Meagan arrived in December 1993 and our grandson, Michael, was born in January of 1998. These two and Alexandra added much joy to our lives. Mary has done an outstanding job raising the children and looking after the house, since Tom was almost never home.

Ewa graduated from Notre Dame in 1995 and went on to Poland to study medicine. She enrolled at Karol Marcinkowski School Of Medicine at the University of Poznań. The school offered a program in English for English-speaking students who wanted to study medicine. I often stopped in Poznań on my business trips to Europe to visit with Ewa, which made it a lot easier for her to be so far away from home. Ewa graduated from medical school in 1999.

I organized a trip to Poland for the whole family to attend Ewa's graduation. Twenty-five people made the trip: Basia and I, Mark and his girlfriend Karen Peters, Tom, Mary, and our two granddaughters, Alex and Meagan. Also my sister, Alina, and her husband, Steve; their children, Chris, Rick with his wife, Janice, and Lisa with her children, Annette and Brian; my cousin Anulka and her husband Steve; their daughter, Susan; and their daughter-in-law Denise with her daughter, Megan. My cousins Andy Krawczyk and Genevie Wilkosz also joined us. Basia's sister Regina and Basia's classmate from college joined us in Poland. It was a trip to be remembered. We rented a bus with a driver and a tour guide to transport us around Poland for 10 days after Ewa's graduation.

The bus picked us up at the airport and we went to Poznań, stopping first in Łowicz, a very picturesque little town 60 miles west of Warsaw, known for its colorful costumes and music. From Łowicz, we went to Poznań. We attended Ewa's graduation from medical school on a Saturday afternoon. That evening, the whole group had a dinner party at Kresowa, one of the famous restaurants in the old square in Poznań. The younger generation celebrated Ewa's graduation until the wee hours of the morning. The next day, we attended early morning mass in the cathedral and afterwards left for Częstochowa. On Monday morning, we attended a mass at the Shrine of the Black Madonna in Częstochowa. The priest, who said the mass, once visited Cleveland and was very pleased to see us. He even conducted part of the mass in English and made arrangements for us to sit in the front rows during the mass—the same rows where Polish kings sat hundreds of years ago. It was a moving experience for us all, especially for those who were visiting the Shrine for the first time. After the mass, the priest took us on a private tour of the Shrine's museum and its treasury.

I had a shoulder problem before we went to Poland. I could not move my arm backwards, and I woke up often at night with a pain in my shoulder. The orthopedic doctor took X-rays of my shoulder and told me I had a slight tear in the rotator cuff. He told me to get physical therapy. If the therapy did not help, he would have to operate. The shoulder improved dramatically after the visit to the Shrine of the Black Madonna, and by the time we returned to the United States, the pain was completely gone. I do not claim it was a miraculous cure; I used all my chits for miracles long ago.

And besides, who am I to deserve such a consideration? All I know is the pain was gone, and in my heart, I knew whom to credit.

We went from Częstochowa to Oświęcim (Auschwitz) where we visited the Holocaust Museum. That evening we went to Kraków. We spent the next day touring Kraków's historical sites. Kraków was the capital of Poland until the early 17th century and is rich with historical sites such as the Wawel Castle, the cathedral with the graves of Polish kings and heroes, and the Jagiellonian University, the second oldest university in Central Europe. Kraków has to be one of the most beautiful cities in Central Europe. The next day we went to Wieliczka, the site of an underground salt mine famous for the many halls and statues carved out of salt. That afternoon we went to Rzeszów, the home of my aunt and cousins. We had dinner in one of the hotel restaurants with over 50 people in attendance. It was time to get reacquainted with our relatives who some of us had not seen since the war and who some of us had never met. The next day we visited the birthplaces of my parents. We had an opportunity to visit the medieval churches in both my mother's and my father's villages. We also observed the celebration of the octave of Corpus Christi, which is celebrated in Poland eight days after the holiday of Corpus Christi. That evening we returned to Rzeszów and had another dinner with the relatives. We left the next day for Warsaw via the historic city of Kazimierz Wielki. We toured Warsaw the next two days.

The Pope was visiting Poland at the same time that our group was touring the country. The Pope came to Warsaw on Saturday, the same day we arrived in the city. I thought it would be a good idea to ask the Pope to say a mass for us at the end of our trip. The Pope agreed, and being the good-hearted fellow I am, I invited one million other Poles to join us. In all seriousness, we attended the Pope's mass in Piłsudski's Square in Warsaw. It was a very moving experience and the culmination of our trip.

Ewa's graduation gave us a reason to participate in a trip of a lifetime. I do not believe it would be possible to organize another such trip again, where the whole family could spend time together visiting the country of our ancestors and meeting long-lost relatives. The trip was an emotional, educational and memorable experience for all of us.

While we were in Europe, Basia and I had the opportunity to visit Kokkola, Dusseldorf and Paris to say goodbye to many friends and associates. The visit also gave me an opportunity to express my thanks and appreciation for the help and cooperation I have received from them over the many years of our association.

I returned to Cleveland to serve my last month in office. Jim Mooney selected Bud Kissel as my replacement. I have known Bud for over two years as he served as a consultant for OMG, and I was confident that the reins had been passed on to a very qualified and capable individual. I was sure that my associates and friends would have an excellent leader in Bud.

My last official function at OMG was my retirement party. My associate and good friend Kris Stepnowski organized it. It was a grand affair, held at the Lakewood Country Club and attended by members of my family and many associates and friends. The main message of the evening was "friendship." That evening, I realized I had made an impact on a few lives, and making friendship the cornerstone of the relationships with my associates was recognized and appreciated by them. It was a warm feeling that I will cherish forever.

OMG Board of Directors (l to r: Bill LeSeur, Lee Brodeur,
Tom Miklich, me, Jim Mooney, Markku Toivanen, John Mooney), 1996.

Signing Joint Venture Agreement with Dinippon, May 1995.

Visiting Dusseldorf (l to r: Helen and Lee Brodeur, Basia, Inge Zimmermann, Jim and Mary Lee Materna, Joie Scott, me, and Mike Scott), August 1996.

Enjoying a laugh with representatives of Hendri Gras, our agent in Poland, October 1996. (He sure knows how to pick them.)

Dinner with associates and customers in Hong Kong, April 1997.

At Discovery Bay in Hong Kong, May 1998.

With Basia in Paris, June 1997.

Cruising Finnish Archipelago, September 1998.

With Johnny Miller at Pebble Beach, June 1998.

With children at playoff game, Indians vs. Yankees, Oct. 1998.

With Ewa at her graduation from
Medical School, June 5,1999.

Family reunion in Rzeszów after Ewa's graduation, June 1999.

Papal mass in Piłsudski Square in Warsaw, June 13, 1999.

With Basia in front of Jagiellonian University in Kraków, June 1999.

Having a laugh at my retirement party, June 26,1999.

Get together with Kokkola associates before retirement, May 1999.

Family reunion at our home in Polk, PA, August 1999.

Enjoying retirement with grandchildren
(Michael, Meagan, Alexandra), Colorado, July 2000.

Ewa and Dan's wedding, May 12, 2001.

Enjoying golf with Chi Chi Rodriguez, 2001.

EPILOGUE

I hope that by having read this autobiography you have gained a better understanding of the events and influences that have helped to shape my life.

An early simple and peaceful existence was shattered by the storm clouds of war. This led to exile in Siberia, followed by years in numerous refugee camps. The fortuitous immigration to America, the early struggles in this country, and good old-fashioned hard work finally helped me reach a good measure of success.

The difficulties encountered in our early travels are somewhat diminished by modern standards since the world today is so different from the world in the 1940s. The thousands of miles of forced transit from Poland to Siberia, Iran, Pakistan, India, and England are difficult to adequately understand by today's standards. Being forcibly transported by primitive trains and ships, surrounded by armed and hostile soldiers and often unsure of our final destination, was an extremely traumatizing experience. Life in the refugee camps, even though tolerable, was always accompanied by the anxiety of an unknown tomorrow.

It is also important for you to appreciate the concept that Siberia is, to this day, more than just a geographical location to Poles. For generations, patriotic Poles had been deported to the *Nieludzka Ziemia* of Siberia where they endured unthinkable persecutions. From the 18th to the 20th centuries, the limitless steppes of Siberia received many who fought for Poland's freedom or who were simply regarded as threats to the Russians' control of Poland. Now we followed in the footsteps of these national heroes, paying the price for simply being Polish. Siberia, thus, is still the Polish *Golgotha* to Poles everywhere.

This is also why it is so important to me to be Polish. I was raised in Polish culture and traditions and they sustained us in the most difficult times. The cost of being Polish was high, and the suffering which we endured for our nationality drove that precious heritage deep into our psyches.

You may now appreciate the importance I place on having faith in God—it is because I witnessed the miracle of people being rescued from the Siberian hell. Our faith kept us hopeful through the darkest times of our journey. It was always our foundation, and remained so even when the horrible times evolved to good ones.

Another foundation for me is my family. I lost so many relatives early in life without having the benefit of knowing them. That experience gave me a better appreciation of the ones who are still around me. Also, the friends who have surrounded me over the years have much importance to me. They helped me be the recipient of so many positive things in my life. They also helped console my grief and celebrate my achievements.

Finally, I hope you appreciate the importance that America has for me. This country contrasts all of the evil that I have experienced. I came to America not because I rejected my Polish roots. Quite to the contrary, when I came to America, it was the only country where I could continue to be proudly Polish in safety, and at the same time, grow to love my second homeland, the United States. America afforded me the opportunity to receive a good education and succeed in business. It also gave me a place to raise a fine family and have my children grow up in an environment conducive to pursuing careers of their choice. It also allowed me to meet and befriend so many wonderful people.

Now my life journey continues, albeit in a more subdued fashion than in the past. I have set new goals for myself so that I may repay my family, friends and society some of the benefits I have been privileged to receive.

First, I plan to be available to my family, especially my grandchildren, for guidance and support. I plan to be a consultant to my former associates, offering advice and counsel—but only when asked! I hope that my experience may shed a different light on the issues they may be pondering.

Secondly, I would like to help promote Polish culture, customs and traditions to those Poles and Polish–Americans who seek to get in touch with their native roots. For that reason, I have agreed to be the president of the Polish American Cultural Center honoring Pope John Paul II. The organization serves as a conduit to help people re-establish a connection with their heritage.

Thirdly, there are several charitable organizations dealing with children that I might be able to help. These include Laski, the Institute for the Blind, located near Warsaw; Polish Children's Heartline Inc. of Brick, New Jersey; and Charitas, the charitable arm of the Polish Catholic Church, to name a few. I am looking forward to working with these organizations and providing whatever assistance I can.

These goals provide me with more than enough challenges and activities to keep my future busy. In addition, my pursuit of lower golf scores will continue to entertain and frustrate me in my free time. I don't anticipate my activity level to decrease in my retirement.

I would like to close with a sincere thanks to everyone who touched my life. Please accept my apologies if I have omitted your name in the pages of this autobiography. It is difficult, if not impossible, to include everyone who I have come across. Please also accept my apologies if, in the past, I have not been able to express my thanks to you in such a way that fully reflects my feeling towards you.

Bibliography

Anczarski, Ks. Józef . *Kronikarskie zapisy z lat cierpień i grozy w Małopolsce Wschodniej*. Kraków, 1996.

Anders, Władysław. *An Army in Exile*. Nashville, TN: The Battery Press, 1981.

Czartoryski, B. and B. Sulik. *Polacy w Wielkiej Brytanii*. Paris: Instytut Literacki, 1961.

Dadleż, Anna. *Journey from Innocence*. New York: Columbia Press, 1988.

Dobroński, Adam. *Losy Sybiraków*. Warszawa: Zarząd Główny Sybiraków, 1977.

Herling, Gustaw. *A World Apart*. New York: Roy Publishers, 1951.

Królikowski, Lucjan, OFM. *Stolen Childhood*. Buffalo: Franciscan Fathers Minor Conventuals, 1983.

Lapo, Henryk, et al. *Z Kresów Wschodnich RP na Wygnanie*. Hove Sussex: Caldra House Ltd., 1996.

Radzik, Tadeusz. *Szkolnictwo Polskie w Wielkiej Brytanii po Drugiej Wojnie Światowej*. Lublin, 1991.

Szmagier, Krzysztof. *Generał Anders i jego Żołnierze*. Warszawa: Instytut Wydawniczy Pax, 1993.

Szujecki, Andrzej. *Do Rozstajnych Dróg*. Warszawa: Wydawnictwo SGGW, 1999.

Teczarowska, Danuta. *Deportacja w Nieznane*. London: Veritas Foundation, 1981.

Wańkowicz, Melchior. *Monte Cassino*. Warszawa: Instytut Wydawniczy Pax, 1989.

Wróbel, Elzbieta and Janusz Wróbel. *Rosproszeni po Świecie*. Chicago: Panorama Publishing, 1992.

Polak w Indiach, *Polish Weekly*, Bombay India, August/September, December 1944; April, July, December 1946; August 1947.

Archives, Polish Military Museum in America (PAVA), New York.

Archives, Piłsudski Institute of America, New York.

Polacy w Indiach, Koło Polaków z Indii. London: Anthony Rowe Ltd., 2000.

Exiled Children, Archiwum Fotograficzne Tułaczy, Warszawa, 1995.